New Building Today

EUROPEAN ARCHITECTURE OF THE 1990s
EDITED BY ARCHITEKTUR ZENTRUM WIEN

BIRKHÄUSER VERLAG
Basel•Boston•Berlin

1st VIENNA ARCHITECTURE CONGRESS
NOVEMBER 11 - NOVEMBER 14, 1993

AUSTRIA CZECH REPUBLIC GERMANY FRANCE GREAT BRITAIN HUNGARY

ITALY THE NETHERLANDS NORWAY PORTUGAL SLOVENIA SPAIN

New Building Today

Belgium Croatia Denmark Finland Greece

Ireland Romania Sweden Switzerland Slovakia

2 nd | **Vienna Architecture Congress**
November 4 - November 6, 1994

RESULTS OF A "VIENNA CONGRESS".
DIETMAR STEINER.

New Building
in Europe?

1ˢᵗ Vienna Architecture Congress, 1993

t is curiously characteristic of the history of the ideas of modernism that it always believes itself to be in a "state of crisis", vacillating between the claim of saving the world and despair in this self-same world. Euphoria and weakness are closely linked, and architecture as a reflex that is logically tied to the cultural situation has likewise experienced both during the past decade."

This book takes us on a journey through Europe: It is a pictorial and critically reflective tour of current European architecture and a discussion of the most important buildings of the past few years. Nevertheless it is very different from a cursory glance at famous contemporary architecture and represents much more than an overview of the most significant buildings of the late 80s and early 90s in Europe. It is also a report on the First and Second Vienna Architecture Congresses and, conjuring up historical connotations of an earlier "Congress of Vienna", it is a kind of current survey of the terrain of European architecture. To these two Congresses we invited renowned "experts" on the architectural situation in the 22 countries that are represented in this book. Historians of art and architecture, critics, directors and staff members of architectural institutions - all of them offer their own necessarily subjective assessments of what they consider to be the most significant building projects of the past few years in their respective countries. These assessments are, however, linked to content analyses that also inform us about the state of the architectural debate in the various countries. The connection between buildings and the critical reaction they elicit is constitutive of a country's "architectural culture" and thus allows a much more comprehensive

insight than the mere presentation of individual buildings. An annual Architectural Congress has always been an important item on the agenda of the Architektur Zentrum Wien, which was founded in 1992. This institution was initiated by the Austrian Federal Ministry of Education and the Arts and the Municipal Offices of Urban Planning and Culture of the City of Vienna in order to provide a forum for an international debate on architecture through conferences, events, congresses, symposia and publications. Furthering the development of this debate is a relatively simple task. The concept of a "Vienna Architecture Congress" is, however, an ambitious goal. The Vienna Congress, which has taken place in November of each year since 1993, is intended to function both as an antenna-like receiver of the current state of architecture and its future and as a forum for discussion. Its objective is to provide in-depth insights and to look for new horizons, for it makes no sense to either declare the end of architecture or euphorically hail its new role as long as it is not even clear which architecture we are talking about. Our starting point was therefore the acceptance of the basic dichotomy or contradiction of contemporary architectural production which is as follows: Never before in the history of architecture has such a large audience been interested in the cultural achievements of this field. This is certainly an asset. But on the other hand the actual role of the architect, as the autonomy of this profession was defined in our society about 150 years ago, has never been so endangered in its basic existence as it is today. This extreme polarisation of the state of architecture creates in the minds of those who analyse it and follow its course a vague feeling of a necessary and

imminent change. And this change will be far more fundamental than the hectic changes of style and fashion we have witnessed over the past thirty years. We experienced the faith in the unlimited possibilities of a visionary technology during the 60s, the social dimension of urban functions and the retrospective look at the historical roots and principles of architecture in the 70s, the boom of spectacular images in the 80s and the subsequent crisis of the early 90s. Now, as the century draws to a close, we feel that architecture again means something new and different from what it has meant during the past decades.

In every country we witness exciting developments and manifestations, but we also see the tragedy of loss. And we are no longer or not yet able to formulate a simple neo-modern or postmodern manifesto that postulates a new direction and possible new values and would be generally accepted at least within the architectural community.

The future is more uncertain today than it has been for some time. We know that a new century, in fact a new millennium, is approaching and such times have always been times when apocalyptic visions were painted on the horizon of world history, accompanied, however, by the release of strong creative and productive forces.

It was a simple question which I wanted the First and Second Architectural Congresses to answer: Is there a common tendency in European architecture in the 90s and can the developments in the various countries be compared? The answer that has emerged is ambiguous. As one can see from the examples selected, there is a common tendency in contemporary European architecture, a new "direction", in which the contemporary social, technological and urban tasks and issues are discussed productively and new definitions are sought. At the same time, however, it is equally remarkable that even in a United Europe there are no common developments across borders. The national and regional cultures are still so strong - and will probably remain so for a long time to come - that they are clearly recognisable as such. Of course the different underlying conditions for the production of architecture in the various European countries play an important role. The social and cultural agreement on the definition and the necessary qualifications of an "architect" and on the nature of "architecture" still differs very much between one country and the next. We can observe, however, that the protection of architecture as a profession which its representatives constantly demand and which is now threatened by the European Union, and the claim of licensed architects to be the sole representatives of "architectural culture" has no inevitable connection with the quality of the resulting buildings. Spain, where there is a binding obligation to involve architects in any building project, has given rise to an exemplary architectural culture. Similar professional conditions in Belgium, however, have only led to a few isolated instances of high-quality architecture. On the other hand, in countries like Switzerland and the Netherlands the profession of the architect enjoys no protection at all. In these countries anyone may call himself an architect and design buildings. The main reason why these two countries nevertheless have a very high architectural culture is the cultural understanding of a society that knows how to appreciate the achievements of "genuine" architects.

A Journey Through Europe Today

Although we now live in the prophesied "global village", the geographic main stream of the architectural debate is still rooted in the interchange between Europe and North America. Of course in the past few decades Japan has also developed into a focal area in its own right but it has not yet entered into an equal interchange with the main stream. A similar situation exists in Latin America where one can still talk of a colonialist system of reference to the European-American cultural sphere. The hope of arriving at a global architectural culture which would be able to carry on a sound interchange with Asian, African and Latin American cultures does not seem very probable for the near future in view of the existing power of the economic and telecommunication networks. The "global village" has only a few centres and a lot of periphery and is far from covering the entire globe. With a touch of irony we have therefore decided to begin and end our journey through Europe at the geographical points of interface with North America. We start in the Netherlands and finish in Ireland and in between we have tried to establish larger cultural areas and interrelationships. For various organisational reasons Poland, Luxembourg and Bulgaria are not represented here. At the time of the first two Architecture Congresses in the early 90s it was not yet entirely clear where the future cultural eastern border of Europe might be. In the meantime the Baltic states have been reestablished, but the situation in former Yugoslavia is anything but clear. In future the Architektur Zentrum Wien will have to play its role in the clarification of such questions concerning Central Europe.

This book takes us on a journey through Europe.

More than an overview of the most significant buildings: a reflective tour of current European architecture.

Dietmar Steiner

Is there a common tendency in

European architecture in the 90s?

This was the simple question of the congresses in Vienna.

Shane O'Toole, Jöran Lindvall, Marc Dubois

Neven Fuchs-Mikac, Wilfried Wang

Jöran Lindvall. Sweden

Bart Lootsma. The Netherlands

In every country we witness exciting developments,

but we also see the tragedy of loss.

After Modernism and Post-Modernism now the crisis of architecture?

The Netherlands are the decisive bridge-head between the European continent and Great Britain and the United States. There is hardly a young Dutch architect today who has not been either a student or a visiting professor at Columbia or Harvard or at the Architectural Association School in London. English has become the *lingua franca* in Dutch academic circles and according to some critics the interpretation of "space" in the Netherlands is American rather than European for the very reason that a new country without history was created there. And yet the current Dutch architecture would not have achieved its rank without the leading figure of Rem Koolhaas. He has opened up the view from the ossified conventions of modernism to the new cultural and urban realities. For this reason the new architecture has become "fuzzy", it is situational and laconic and with its self-reflective approach has developed a new type of link with society. There are a surprising number of young Dutch architects who have already achieved a certain prominence and who are able to meet every international challenge.

The neighbouring country of Belgium, on the other hand, has only awoken in recent years. Against the backdrop of a generally catastrophic architectural situation, faint indications of a new high-quality archi-tecture have sprung up. The first signs of this were the pavilions designed by Paul Robbrecht and Hilde Daem for documenta 92. There is hope that the young generation of architects born after 1950 will give adequate expression to this small and internally divided country with its European tradition. The Scandinavian countries of Denmark, Norway, Sweden and Finland are con-fronted with a common fundamental problem - they are all countries with a tradition that is both classical and classically modern, a convention of simplicity and a belief in the social role of architecture. These countries have an unbroken tradition of an architecture in agreement with the society which searches quietly and inconspicuously for the right way to build. Only a few individual architects disturb this harmony of the traditional. This quiet and social convention was overlaid by the new force of the economic boom of the 80s. The postmodern sumptuousness shook the foundations of Scandinavian archi-tecture: a fragile sumptuousness that showed its true face during a serious economic crisis in the late 80s and early 90s. The aesthetic canon that was based on the social order had disappeared and laboriously and with small projects architects linked back to the timeless values and to the tradition of serving the society. However, in saying this we should not forget the largely ahistorical character of Scandinavian buildings. In Sweden, for example, 95 per cent of the space used today has been built only in this century. It is no coincidence that in Finland, where during the economic crisis the profession of the architect was marginalised and almost destroyed, the consequence was a certain cynical acceptance of fate, accompanied by bizarre autistic projects and c.v.'s that culminated in the symbolic figure of the "Leningrad Cowboys" Pop group and Kaurismäki's cult films.

Marc Dubois. Belgium

Neven Fuchs-Mikac. Norway

It makes no sense to either declare the end of

architecture or euphorically hail its new role.

Such a large audience has been interested in architecture, but the role of
the architect has never been so endangered as it is today.

Roger Connah. Finland

Kim Dirckinck-Homfeld. Denmark

Vladimir Šlapeta. Czech Republic

Andrej Hrausky. Slovenia

Alexander Laslo. Croatia

Now we feel that architecture again means something new

and different from what is has meant during the past decades.

And this change will be far more fundamental than the hectic changes of style and fashion.

Ákos Moravánszky. Hungary

From Scandinavia we turned back to Central Europe and the architecture of Germany. After the postmodernist era of the International Building Exhibition Berlin 1984, the school of the respected German architects who were by then regarded as the "Old Masters" was striving for a new "appearance of simple greatness" for the reunited Germany which culminated in the so-called Berlin architectural quarrel. In the meantime, however, the German public has been sufficiently sensitised so that the promising younger German architects of the post-IBA era will succeed in creating a new architecture. In any case, at this point German architecture is more varied, exciting and interesting than the hardened fronts of the current "Berlin debate" would make us believe. Quite generally, and this is also a promise for the future, German architecture is better than its current international reputation.
Switzerland, although a small country, has succeeded in maintaining a high-level architectural debate, supported by excellent journals and publishing houses of international renown. While during the 70s the Ticino was the focus of development, today the attention has shifted to the German-speaking part of Switzerland with Basel as its centre. There is already talk of a new "Swiss minimalism", which is spreading internationally. But this would only be a superficial way of looking at the issue. In reality the major Swiss impulse is the architectural concern with the perception of everyday environments and research into the substantive issues of the entire building process - one might call it the sensualisation of the magic of making architecture. This results in a new relationship to reality that regards the field of force of the ever-new situation and the conditions of the specific project as the major architectural task. If the basis of this attitude is attributed to the architectural research laboratories of Diener & Diener or Herzog & de Meuron we must yet critically ask whether in this case the younger generation of architects is not once again turning a situation that has been conquered by their elders into an empty convention.

Far more confusing than the clear-cut situation of Swiss architecture is the situation in equally small and equally heterogeneous Austria. Here we find an irritating simultaneity of several "architectural generations". In addition, the regional architectural cultures of the various provinces exist next to one another, even though in recent years a more open interchange has been going on among the younger generation of architects. Thus Viennese architects are increasingly leaving behind their obsession with details in order to arrive at larger and more generous solutions. Similar developments can be seen in the once so eruptively expressive architectural scene in Graz. On the other hand the architects from Vorarlberg are turning from simple building tasks to more and more complex issues. The fact that this small Austria, which is smaller than Bavaria or Catalonia, is nevertheless able to make a disproportionate contribution to the contemporary architectural culture is due to the political responsibility of its public authorities that accounts for large public investments in housing projects or the building of new schools even in times of crisis.

In the meantime, however, Europe has grown. Eastern Europe has opened up and new countries have formed which now strive to rediscover the significant roots of their own architectural traditions. This is true above all for the Czech Republic and Slovenia. Hungary, Slovakia, Croatia and Romania are still struggling for a basic definition and determination of their architectural identities.

Even in a United Europe there are no common developments across borders.

The national and regional cultures are still so strong and will remain for a long time.

Annette Becker. Germany

Otto Kapfinger. Austria

Henrieta Hammer-Moravčíkova. Slovakia

Although we now live in the "global village", the

geographic main stream of the debate is still

rooted between Europe and North America.

We start in the Netherlands and finish in Ireland, the geographical points of interface
with North America.

Yorgos Simeoforidis. Greece

What is common to all the reform democracies is the fact that housing is a major problem due to the dissolution of the large state authorities and the fact that many flats and houses no longer conform with current standards. Of course Western investors have also discovered these countries and often want to make money quickly through cheap and poor architecture - a kind of colonialisation which in the final analysis also says a lot about the catastrophic state of current architecture, witness the lavishly decorated box-like office buildings and hotel "palaces".

Since the collapse of the Soviet rule, the Czech Republic has now rediscovered its proud modernist tradition. However, in that country, too, the central problem is that of defining the role of architecture somewhere between the banal meeting of the demand for essential building construction and the greedy private ostentatiousness favoured by the new investors. Nevertheless, the future of architecture in the Czech Republic may be viewed positively, since the great cultural tradition need not fear any interynational comparison.

On the other hand, the problem of architectural identity is a very real one for newly created Slovakia, the other half of former Czechoslovakia. At the turn of the century Bohemia and Moravia, which today make up the Czech Republic, were the creative reservoir for the achievements of the often quoted myth of "fin de siècle Vienna". Slovakia was then a "peasant state" with a rich potential of unspoiled and natural folk culture and as such had an inspiring effect on the urban cultures of Budapest and Vienna. For this reason the Slovak architects are now especially eager to develop a new architectural culture. In contrast to the relaxed and open atmosphere in Slovakia, the attempt to formulate a new and national Romantic architectural identity has become a current political issue in neighbouring Hungary. Even before the Iron Curtain was dismantled, an almost traumatically nationalistic and bigoted subculture spread in Hungary with its laissez-faire "goulash communism". This subculture found its fulfilment in old organic forms and is today often taken to be representative of Hungarian architecture. What is criticised in Hungary itself is the lack of a tradition of theoretical discourse. For this reason in the past few years the concern with both the nationalist and communist cultural myths has been of particular importance. Hungary is currently on its way to overcoming this burdensome heritage. Slovenia is a special case among the so-called reform democracies. For decades there has already been an intensive contact with the neighbouring countries. The Italian architectural scene with the Venice School has had its effect as has the constant contact with Styria and Vienna. Therefore in Slovenia all the developments of Western European culture were accompanied by independent architectural achievements. The symposia held regularly at Piran are of international importance, the Ljubljana School exerts a considerable attraction. The core of Slovenia's architectural self-confidence, however, are the achievements of Jože Plečnik and Ivan Vurnik, whose work during the first half of this century resulted in the generally rare situation of an architectural identity of a city and country being created by individual architects.

Due to the lack of comparable leading historical figures, neighbouring Croatia finds the struggle for its new architectural definition more difficult. This is, however, compensated for by a young and fresh architecture. At present it seems that a host of young talented Croatian architects are trying to gather new impressions from all over Europe and the first European successes are already clearly visible.

Architecturally and culturally, Romania is one of the most exciting Balkan countries. In the 20s and 30s Bucharest was one of the most dynamic cities in Europe with an international and culturally open climate and some excellent examples of modern architecture. All of this was destroyed by the Ceaucescu era, but has not been forgotten by intellectuals and artists. With forceful anger the totalitarian era is being left behind and new forms are searched for.

The current situation of Greek architecture may be seen as a very irritating phenomenon. Of course Greece is the cradle of Western civilisation and architecture. Of course there are excellent examples of modernist buildings. Of course the climatic and topographical conditions of the Mediterranean favour

debate which only in recent years has tried to laboriously break through the national ignorance and absolute domination of tourism-related building speculations. Self-critically, the Greek architects are moving on thin ice, trying to follow up the current debate with relevant buildings here and there but without any political support.

A similar situation has led to a standstill of architectural culture in Italy in the wake of the political crisis, while at the beginning of the 80s the Italian architectural debate was perhaps the foremost in Europe and the concept of typology as the constitutive element of a historically based architectural identity was more or less invented in Italy. Today helplessness reigns and the heroes of the 80s live off the glory of their early years and design buildings abroad, in Japan, Germany and Holland.

Marco De Michelis. Italy

Ana Maria Zahariade. Romania

While Italy was the southern European focus of architecture in the 80s - with the actual researches having taken place in the previous decade - Spain is without doubt the discovery of the 90s, with the relevant positions having been developed in the 80s. Of course, before an architectural culture can become influential and significant it needs years of searching and research, of debate and experiment. Spain's cultural flourishing is based on the revolutionary cultural development since the end of the fascist Franco era which has arrived at new and modern positions after a rapid recapitulation of its own history. An important element in this was the political struggle against Franco's centralized state which strengthened the new regional identities - a political regionalist struggle which, however, along with the architectural debate, felt committed to a general international view of the new issues. It was above all the Spanish architects who rejected Kenneth Frampton's theory of "critical regionalism" as the root and stimulus of a new architecture and wanted to see their problems discussed in a wider international context - proof of the fact that the true regional identity of a country can only be realised in conjunction with a consistent international claim.

The Iberian peninsula is almost a continent of its own and only to a certain extent a part of Europe. Evidence of this are the architectural achievements of the Moors as is the issue of whether Latin America should properly be called Ibero-America. A part of this Iberian "continent" is Portugal, which experienced an entirely different political emancipation. As far as the international perception is concerned, a single architect, Alvaro Siza Vieira, succeeded in throwing open the doors to the discovery of an entire national architecture. Only since Alvaro Siza's contribution to contemporary architecture have we been ready to perceive also its roots, to discover Lisbon's modernism, and to rescue the achievements of Siza's predecessors from oblivion.

Crossing the border from the Iberian peninsula back to Europe is just one step but the cultural and emotional implications are enormous. On this side of the Pyrenees we enter one of the chief countries of Europe, France, which after Spain and Portugal seems like a different world. In the 80s nobody talked about French architecture. Instead one heard of the "grands traveaux", the great projects. France seemed sufficiently characterised

by the success of the Centre Pompidou and the disaster of Les Halles. Moreover, the French debate was not particularly interested in an international exchange of ideas. France's political and cultural identity has long had an unbroken relationship with technological progress, but there was no sensorium for the postmodern themes of the 80s. Only when the new modernity made itself felt, when it became clear that in future architecture would have to search for new ways also in terms of technology, did the French architecture of the 90s move into our realm of consciousness. This has certainly been recognized in time by the French architects.

These days the Chunnel connects Great Britain with France but whether this has also created an emotional tie with the continent remains to be seen. The situation in Great Britain is still one of considerable individuality. British architecture is threatened from several sides. In contrast to the situation in France it does not enjoy any political protection or have any political mission to fulfil, but is more likely threatened by those in power (witness Prince Charles). In addition the shift of the public and political interest from architects to investors has led to a disastrous decline of architectural culture in England. A boundless euphoria of privatisation has reduced the public sector and eroded the architect's profession. The architectural role of Great Britain, or more precisely of London, is today above all that of a clearing-house of ideas, a place of training, the site of important architectural offices. As James Stirling said in his most recent interview, "Germany is the best place to build".

As the last stop of our journey we look at Ireland, another small country situated in the west of Europe, across the ocean from America. In the past few years a new architectural self-confidence and a new architectural scene have developed in Dublin. As has also been the case in other historic cities, at first it was the concern with the protection of endangered buildings which in time led to a new creative discourse and new solutions. In this debate Ireland has established ties to Scandinavia, not least in order to distinguish itself more clearly from England.

The Future of European Architecture
At the end of our tour of current architecture in Europe we recognize more clearly the new issues and many new answers. We have asked the participants from the 22 countries for the best buildings of the past few years in their

own country and we could see that the "long wave" of a common cultural development does exist and that it has two end points: the search for new national or regional identities on the one hand and the new concern with the architect's profession and his possibilities as a social force on the other hand. To put it briefly, one could locate this interest somewhere between the former (critical) regionalism and the new realism.

This dialogue of cultures took place at the First and Second Vienna Architecture Congresses. Asynchronous developments as well as close relationships were detected. This book now presents an overview and a confrontation. I want to take this opportunity to thank all those involved, the experts and friends from all over Europe who, with curiosity and enthusiasm, seized this first opportunity to put their analyses of current architecture up for discussion. I would also like to thank those who subsidised our undertaking, in particular Dr. Hannes Swoboda, Councillor of the City of Vienna for Urban Development, Planning and Transportation, Dr. Ursula Pasterk, Councillor for Cultural Affairs, and the Federal Minister Dr. Rudolf Scholten, for bringing about the existence of the Architektur Zentrum Wien and the Vienna Architecture Congress. Furthermore I want to thank the entire team of the Architektur Zentrum Wien for the concept and organisation of these congresses, in particular Birgit Seissl, who made them her own personal concern and without whom the Vienna Architecture Congresses could not have succeeded.

It will be the task of the Third Vienna Architecture Congress to take up where this survey has left off and to deal with the cultural bases of this heterogeneous European architecture. We will no longer have to look for the best buildings in Europe, for these are discussed and documented in this book. The theme of the 1995 Vienna Architecture Congress will be "Common Places/Conventional Thoughts in the Chaos of Europe".

Wilfried Wang. Portugal

Marta Cervelló. Spain

François Chaslin. France

At the end of our tour of current architecture in Europe

we recognize more clearly many new answers.

The search for new national or regional identities and the new concern with the architect's profession are the questions of "New Building Today".

2nd Vienna Architecture Congress, 1994

Richard Burdett. Great Britain

If we leaf through the magazines Holland looks like

a testing ground for architecture where a thousand

countless flowers bloom.

The Netherlands between Modernism and Experiment.

1 | TALKING ABOUT MY GENERATION.
BART LOOTSMA.

The Nether-
lands

Form of State: Parliamentary Monarchy since 1848, **Area:** 41,864 km2, **Inhabitants (1992):** 15,184,000, **Capital:** Amsterdam
Gross National Product 1992, per capita: $ 20,480, **Gross Domestic Product 1992:** $ 320,290 Mio, **Unemployment (Average, 1993):** 8.3%

In 1990 Geert Bekaert and Peter Buchanan were commissioned by SNAM (Stichting Nederlandse Architekten Manifestatie) to give an overall survey of the architectural landscape in the Netherlands. Their inquiry resulted in architectural approaches as represented by Herman Hertzberger, Rem Koolhaas, Moshé Zwarts, Mecanoo, Sjoerd Soeters, Carel Weber and John Körmeling (1).

Four years later, the situation of Dutch architecture has changed a lot, or so it seems. Certainly, the above-mentioned names are still dominant. Some of them, for example Sjoerd Soeters and Carel Weber, still enjoy great influence, whereas others like Moshé Zwarts are not as present any longer. Nevertheless, this classification is unsatisfying.

With this survey, the interest in the specific differences got lost, and - more important - the buildings these architects completed during the last five years are not among the best. The new approaches and deeper insights these architects doubtlessly achieved were realized mainly in the early 80s, in the case of Hertzberger even as early as around 1960. Therefore there must be a new generation which is able to cope with the former and even to surpass it without any problem.

Spontaneously the following buildings come to my mind which are certainly among the best five built in the last five years: the Rotterdam KunstHAL by OMA (1992), the Karbouw Office Building in Amersfoort by Ben van Berkel (1991), a day nursery in Soest by a group of young architects (1992), the library in Zeewolde by Koen van Kelsen (1989) and the Academy of Art and Architecture in Maastricht by Wiel Arets (1993).

Having chosen them raises the question if they have anything in common.

At first I thought they have not, and, strictly speaking, this is true. But the longer one thinks of it, the more obvious it becomes that all these realized projects share common traces, a certain mentality, a provoking withdrawal from the current rigidity of the Dutch architectural practice. A selection like this of course always begs the question of whether the Dutch architecture as a whole. I think they are not, I think they are not even typical of the small number of buildings published in the magazines.

Rem Koolhaas and Ben van Berkel studied at the AA, the Architectural Association in London. Wiel Arets studied from the late 70s to the early 80s at the Technical University of Eindhoven, a new school which was - compared to the Delft University of Technology - not restrained by tradition: the reception of the international debate could take place without any institutional resistance. This influence can be traced in many of Wiel Arets' designs. Wiel Arets, Rem Koolhaas and Ben van Berkel taught at Columbia University and at Cooper Union in New York. All of them have an international frame of reference.

It is, however, hardly possible to give a representative survey of Dutch architecture on the basis of a few buildings. The most fascinating aspect of Dutch architecture is after all its incredible variety, by which architects of the most disparate trends operate alongside each other: Modernists and Postmodernists, Rationalists and Expressionists, High tech enthusiasts and Anthroposophists, Structuralists and Deconstructivists. If we leaf through the magazines Holland looks like a testing ground for architecture where a thousand countless flowers bloom. But honestly speaking, this variety of styles all too often leads to a superficial cacophony. Local councillors in cities like Amersfoort, the Hague and Groningen in particular treated this testing ground as a mailorder catalogue from which, like nouveaux riches, they could pick what pleased their fancy till their money was up. After that they opted for slightly cheaper imitations. The filming quarters in Almere and the estate of Kattenbroek in Amersfoort are splendid examples of the shoddy bazaar quality that can result from an approach of this sort.

The building for the Dutch Architectural Institute designed by Jo Coenen, commissioned by Adri Duivesteijn, former councillor of the Hague and now director of the Institute is the incoherent symbol

Maybe the main problem of Dutch architecture is that it really has no tradition. Of course there were great architects, like Berlage, Cuypers and Dudok, but at least 70% of the Dutch built environment was realized after the Second World War - more than in any other West-European country.

So Modernism seems to be our tradition and even ouP Postmodern architecture, like that of Mecanoo for example, almost always quotes highlights of Modernism. Different to countries like Switzerland, Austria, Italy or Spain there are, strangely enough, almost no monographs on our architectural history by Dutch architects. The only exceptions are Wiel Arets, Wim van den Bergh and Umberto Barbieri (2). Dutch architectural magazines until lately have not paid much attention to topics which had to do with our architectural history. Historical research was mostly left to art history whose interest in history is quite different from that of the architects. Art historians are interested in history as such, whereas the architects are interested in topics which could have an actual meaning.

The roughness of their materials and their detailing emphasizes that architecture is about something else, not about the sheer phenomenon itself.

Bart Lootsma on his selection of the best five buildings in the Netherlands.

New concepts are constantly worked out in order to be at least able to produce architecture in a rapidly changing society in which traditional hierarchies are hardly to be felt.

Architecture as a social programme.

The lack of architects interested in their own tradition led, together with the predominance of Modernism, to a very confusing situation. In the first place because Charles Jencks taught that Modernism was bad (and the Dutch are always prone to accept critical views from Great Britain) and in the second place because it was no longer clear what the ideological contents of our modern Postmodernism or postmodern Modernism really was. This led in 1990 to the famous congress, initiated by Rem Koolhaas: "How modern is Dutch architecture?" At that occasion the critic Hans van Dijk came up with the term "Onderwijzersmodernisme" ("Schoolteacher's modernism"). The result was that from then on every architecture resembling White Modernism was refused as superficial. Strangely enough, the whole debate concentrated more or less on stylistic aspects. Hans van Dijk's lecture had greater impact than the others, because it was held on a separate occasion and was afterwards published in "Archis" (3). The Dutch Architectural Institute seemed extremely happy that this typical Dutch characteristic had

to promote Dutch architecture in a travelling exhibition with the title "Modernism without a dogma" and afterwards they fought it in their exhibition "Stijl" (4), which pretended to rewrite Dutch architectural history on the presumption that Modern architecture played a very marginal role in it, and a bad one too. The funny thing was, however, that only very few architects and critics tried to investigate what modernity (when leaving out the stylistic aspect) really meant at this moment. And this is where I come to the selection of the buildings I have chosen. The five buildings are interesting because I think that in all of them discoveries have been made in the design process about what the preconditions for architecture today really are. They function as investigatory instruments that expose these preconditions, turning them inside out. As in the case of a coat, you can immediately see how they are made. It is tempting to paraphrase Rem Koolhaas here: "If there is a method in this work, it is that of a systematical idealization, a spontaneous overestimation of the existing, a theoretical bombardment, in

and ideological acts even the average is taken into account (5)." The buildings I have chosen function as certain works of conceptual art do, for examples the "Mirror Cubes" of Robert Morris, that only reflect their surroundings, or the "Condensation Cubes" of Hans Haacke, that show climatic changes inside a closed glass cube. But these five projects are not exclusively didactic. Just as wearing a coat turned inside out is subversive, so these buildings are in all senses subversive. And again I am tempted here to quote from an early essay by Koolhaas about "Neue Sachlichkeit" and about the continuation of the Functionalist tradition.

This essay is a plea for programmatic thinking and for the notion that architecture can have a direct influence on the content of contemporary culture which, according to Koolhaas, is based in the first instance on population density, technology and social instability (6). All five projects are sober and not only because of lack of money. The roughness of their materials and their detailing emphasizes that architecture is about something else, not about the sheer phenomenon itself. When asked about the supposed bad detailing of the KunstHAL Koolhaas replied angrily that according to his impression perfection was not what the world really needed at the moment: "There is an obscene relationship between the completely desintegrating chaos of the world and a strange kind of urge of the architects to make as smooth a result as possible (7)." At present Rem Koolhaas' influence in Holland cannot be overstated. This influence can in part be seen immediately - for instance, in the work of former assistants and collaborators who have started working for themselves, such as Dolf Dobbelaar, Hermann de Kovel and Paul de Vroom (DKV), Willem Jan Neutelings, Kees Christiaanse, Winy Maas, Jakob van Rijs and Nathalie de Vries (MVRDV). More interesting however is Koolhaas' invisible influence, especially on an architectural thinking in terms of programmatics and functionality. Interesting as well is his invisible influence at the administrative level. The reorganization of the Dutch prison system can to a large extent be ascribed to him, and he has also contributed to the fact that highrise developments in the Netherlands have ceased to be a

taboo subject. But the most remarkable thing of all is that Koolhaas has stimulated a number of architects to develop in a similar way new strategies by which architecture could resist the continuous attempts of the politicians and the market to encapsulate it and to exploit its image for their own purposes. Wiel Arets, for example, was a founding member of "Wiederhall" and published several books (8). Ben van Berkel and his wife Caroline Bos have already written many texts (9). This interest for the theory of architecture takes into account the developments of contemporary philosophy.

Of all the architects whose buildings I have selected only Koen van Velsen does not write, but all of them are teaching architecture (10). Two of the selected projects, the library by Koen van Velsen and the office building by Ben van Berkel seek for a new formal link to the chaos around and in architecture. Two others, the KunstHAL by OMA and the Academy of Art and Architecture by Wiel Arets do not as much seek for new formal references, but allude to the social conditions. They try to present themselves as a kind of "heterotopia" - a term coined by Michel Foucault signifying places that withdraw themselves from the control of society (11). These buildings serve as social condensers spreading new kinds of thought and behaviour over the city. The day-nursery by a group of young architects led by Ton Venhoeven combines both aspects (12).

The role of Gilles Deleuze's philosophy for most of these architects is significant. Traces of his thinking can be found in Koolhaas' approach: the image of the architect as a surfer; the complex

conceptual link of his projects to the city and to the idea of the folded space. In Wiel Arets' project Deleuze's influence causes a conceptual link to the city, whereas the architects of the Soest day-nursery stress the expressionist aspect - as does Ben van Berkel - and use the rhizome as a new kind of working community. It is probably this influence which distinguishes these architects from the former generation; new concepts are constantly worked out in order to be at least able to produce architecture in a rapidly changing society in which traditional hierarchies are hardly to be felt. It is an architecture which does not confine itself to self-sufficiently referring to its own métier as was the case in the 80s, but an architecture representing society and programmatically being linked to it.

OMA/Rem Koolhaas. KunstHAL, Rotterdam 1987-92 - photos: Hans Werlemann

The shape of the KunstHAL is in fact an antishape:

an aesthetic composition instead of a conceptual one.

Concept dominating aesthetics: the motto of the new Dutch architecture.

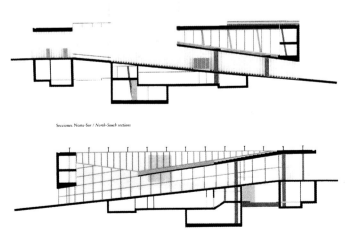

Secciones Norte-Sur / North-South sections

North-south section

With the exception of the Villa dall'Ava in Paris, the Rotterdam KunstHAL is the best work that OMA has produced until now. During the 80's museum buildings became the prestige objects of architecture. As a result, all the most famous architects of this period have at least realized one museum project. Parallel to the trend in art for a comeback of sculpture and easel painting and the reappraisal of art history, museum architecture has recently witnessed the replacing of large rooms and flexible layout possibilities with sequences of self-contained halls and galleries. After the turbulent years of the 50s, 60s and 70s museums are once more becoming havens for a discourse on history. This was expressed in the postmodern architecture of the buildings. Despite its international reputation OMA had never produced a museum. OMA's most interesting contribution to the architectural debate does not lie so much in a historical discourse on the language of architecture as in the staging of series of events and the uncovering of mutual relationships with the aid of architecture. Seen in this light it seems logical that OMA's second building with a cultural function after the Nederlands Dans-theater in the Hague should not be a museum but an Art Hall; a space, in other words, that has no permanent collection and that operates with a minimum of staff and where what is aimed at is a maximum "live" confrontation with art. Koolhaas even prefers to talk about a "palais des festivals" in the spirit of the pavilions in world expositions. Rotterdam, which largely lacks a cultural infrastructure since the German bombardment of 1940, has built up a tradition of cultural festivals in an attempt to fill this lacuna (13). OMA's first design for the KunstHAL in 1987 in particular relates to this tradition of festivals. It consisted roughly of two

raised floors with a "robot" in the middle. This robot was in fact a large crane that would raise and lower sections of floor, thus giving the building a genuine multi-functional character. This design had quite some influence on the programme of the building, because at the time OMA started designing it a director had not yet been appointed.

The KunstHAL is part of the Museum-park, for which OMA produced a city development plan in 1987. This Museum-park is in fact a route, an axis extending from the Architectuurinstituut at one end to the KunstHAL at the other. The park was also designed by OMA, initially in partnership with the French landscape architect Yves Brunier who has since died. OMA's design for the Architectuurinstituut was originally incorporated into the plan. The closed-off black tower of the Architectuurinstituut where the collections of dead architects were to be housed would, with its character of a mausoleum, have provided a contrast with the robot tower that should run the life of the KunstHAL. Unfortunately this was never realized. The choice of Jo Coenen's design brought about a completely different situation and at the same time the appointment of a director brought about some programmatical changes. The point of departure for this new situation that ended up being decisive for the building as it now stands, was the urban envelope as presented in the city development plan. A service road on the lower level parallel to the river embankment where the KunstHAL is situated was to be preserved. The programme required a linking route between the embankment and the Museumpark lower down. Both routes are tunnelled through the design athwart each other. The complex form that is brought about in this way contains, amongst other items, three exhibition halls, an auditorium, a café-

restaurant and office space. The halls have separate entrances but in the case of a large-scale event they can be linked in a continuous routing. A spiral-shaped internal routing winds round the cruciform tunnel structure making the building into a kind of giant transformer. Taking the preconditions literally leads immediately to a quite exceptionally spectacular three-dimensionality. The shape of the KunstHAL is in fact an antishape: an aesthetic composition instead of a conceptual one, like Bruce Nauman's sculpture of 1966, "Platform Made Up Of The Space Between Two Rectilinear Boxes On the Floor". As with Nauman's work the dry-as-dust points of departure themselves set up an indefinable tension. Despite the clear conceptual narrative one does not experience the KunstHAL as a built programme. The layered structure of the plan leads step by step to a complexity with numerous exceptions. These exceptions are deliberately not synthesized; rather their exceptional character is highlighted. Thus the immediate sensuous experience prevails over the conceptual one and the building comes to life. A separate layer is formed by curious surrealist-looking additions like the columns wrapped in hollow treetrunks in the hall on the first floor and the sculpture of a camel by Henk Visch. These additions offer a foretaste of the bizarre scenarios that might unfold in this building.

KunstHAL: "palais des festivals"

Here, the deconstruction of

the box reaches its climax.

The Library in Zeewolde by Koen van Velsen: materialized transparency.

Façade of concrete - photo: Gerhard Jaeger

Koen van Velsen's library in Zeewolde was one of the first public buildings in this new town in the polder. Of course there was a city development plan. The site is located at one end of a prospective building block. It is enclosed by streets on three sides while one of the corners should be visible from the prospective church square. The city planner had provided a continuous arcade along one of the three streets. At the point that Van Velsen began working on his commission, however, nothing was known about what the surrounding architecture would be. This led to a design strategy by which Van Velsen left a verge of five metres free both on the side of the prospective building block and to the rear of his building. He placed a number of loose additions on this strip that made it impossible for any later developments to be stitched on to it. On the verge between the library and the building block, for instance, he put up a detached circular fire escape and a readymade container as storage space. In the verge (which is also five metres wide) on the side by the shopping street where the city plan had only provided for an arcade of two and a half metres, Van Velsen sited a long narrow box on high thin steel legs with glass walls all round. Pronouncedly independent in relation to the actual library building through the fact that it is slightly off-centre vis à vis the ground plan, this box contains the offices and the book depository. At one of the short ends between the glass and the prospective adjacent volume no more than half a metre of space will be left. The main

entrance to the library is sited below the glass box. It is, however, not only on the scale of urban design that Van Velsen elevates this separating and autonomizing of things to an art; he has also pushed it through the whole building as a consistent design strategy far more drastically than he did with previous designs. The perforated concrete façade of the actual library building, for instance, seems to float freely above the ground. The roof in its turn seems to float over the building; it is slightly off-centre to cover the offices as well. Inside the building has two storeys. On the ground floor there is a large open area 4.20 metres high for the library itself. On the upper floor there is a reading room, a staff lunch room and a large partially covered roof garden. The upper storey can be reached by a ramp and two spiral staircases, one of which folds round a services core with toilets and a lift. The reading room is sited inside the upper storey like a kind of free-floating glass house, whereas its roof overtops the library's. The upper storey is supported by a group of three thin concrete columns that splay out at the top like bouquets. The aim of this is not just to emphasize the structural aspect of the building, but rather to prevent the bookcases from being placed against them. The bookcases which are standard Lundia shelves but adapted by Van Velsen are freestanding like all the other items of furniture in the space. In fact the design is very simple and the structure is also clear. The use of materials is equally direct and undisguised. A striking feature in this

respect is the interior wall on the upper storey where the insulating material remains visible behind transparent corrugated sheets. Here, the deconstruction of the box reaches its climax. As in Van Velsen's earlier work there are in this library references to the work of Gordon Matta Clark. The large circle that has been cut out in the façade is - in the way it is placed, in its three-dimensional effect and in its play with light - suggestive of Clark's installation "Day's End" of 1975 where he sawed a semicircular hole in the side façade of a huge shed in the docks of New York. The library contains even more references to the "post-minimal" art tendency Clark is said to belong to. The way in which the outside walls are designed like a free-floating box makes one think of Bruce Nauman's "Floating Room" of 1972, while the curious pattern formed by the twisted columns reminds one of a work as such as "White Breathing" of 1976 by the same artist. Just as with Gordon Matta Clark, so in Bruce Nauman's work one can speak an intriguing tension between an almost unemotional approach on the one hand and a spectacular aspect with an intense psychological impact on the other.

Inside the Library - photo: Gerhard Jaeger

Koen van Velsen. Library, Zeewolde 1989 - photo: Gerhard Jaeger

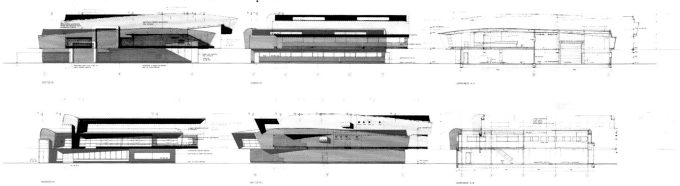

Elevations and sections

Ben van Berkel. Office building Karbouw, Amersfoort 1990-91 - photo: Jan Derwig

Foyer - photo: Jan Derwig

In its completeness and in its perfect

detailing and finishing Karbouw is a

genuine Gesamtkunstwerk.

Ben van Berkel shows that architecture is after all a sensual experience.

Karbouw is the firm of Michel Schoonderbeek, a young property developer. The office Ben van Berkel designed for him serves as a showpiece for the company. The premises are situated on the edge of a new business park in Amersfoort, one of the most rapidly expanding municipalities in Holland. Over the past few years business parks like this have been springing up on the edges of almost all Dutch towns. With their elementary urbanistic layout and their shamelessly shoddy commercial architecture which is often not even designed by architects, they dominate the landscape alongside the freeways. The situation hardly offered Van Berkel much inspiration for a design. Determining factors were the freeway curving round the site and the projected viaduct that will link this freeway up with the business park service routes system. Van Berkel produced a design consisting of two volumes: the upper volume turns, as it were, to face the intersection while the one underneath is in line with the city plan grid. In this way he has not only given the building an unmistakable shape, so that the upper half, like a Brancusi sculpture, has an eye-catching plinth and siting; he has also succeeded in incorporating the programme into it in the clearest possible fashion. The showroom is situated downstairs at the front with the offices jutting out above, overlooking both freeway and intersection like a racecourse grandstand. Behind there is a storeroom occupying the upper part of the building. The twist in the building created at the corner a logical place for the entrance, which is a glass box that looks like having been pressed into the building. From the freeway curve one can look down on the curved aluminium roof. Via a staircase in the glass box of the entrance one arrives at the office reception area. The offices are oriented orthogonally vis à vis the glass front façade. Everywhere there are huge sliding doors at right angles to the glass façade so that one can see the lower front everywhere and an informal circulation area is created. The office has an unprecedented openness as a result. Van Berkel did not only design the building; he did the same for the interior, something that is unfortunately rare in the Netherlands. The dominant materials are light and dark wood, corten steel and smooth white stucco. The ceilings follow the curves of the roof which makes for a spatiality that manages to be elegant as well as lavish. Work tables, desks and a large conference table were designed that with their mixture of roughness and structural stylishness remind one of the famous specimens by Eames, Prouvé and Nelson dating from the 50s. The desk in the reception area is also analogous to the building in that it is made of two angular shapes that are just put together, one of wood and the other of concrete with a radiator in it. This detail shows how much importance Van Berkel attaches to the sensual experiencing of his architecture. In its completeness and in its perfect detailing and finishing Karbouw is a genuine Gesamtkunstwerk.

The day nursery "Het Kasteel" ("The Castle") in Soest was designed by the architects Kirsten van den Berg, Daan Bakker, Mirjam Galjé, Matthijs Bouw and Ton Venhoeven. The latter is the only one who is a graduate of the Technical University of Delft. The others are still students there. Since the contract was given to Matthijs Bouw a different situation came about than is normal for a firm of architects. This situation was in fact taken advantage of to explore a design approach that is more appropriate to the current state of the profession. Architects are no longer the authorities, the master builders, they still were at the beginning of the century. The amount of regulations have increased and, what is more, the knowledge required in the process of construction is often so specialized that they have to consult a large number of advisors. The offices employ quite a few assistants on every individual project. They also have to deal with various subcontractors during the actual work of construction. In the Netherlands, these subcontractors are not so wilfully accepting authority, preferring to solve details in their own way for better or for worse. Last, but by no means least, architects have to deal with clients who often take the form of committees. All these people have an influence on the design in one way or another, even though architects try to make it look otherwise. In building this day-nursery the five designers agreed right from the start that they would operate on a basic of complete equality. Not only should every idea be taken seriously, all suggestions and contributions should leave their mark on the final design. This meant, for instance, that they often worked on each others' drawings. In a way this design approach is similar to that of the Surrealists' "cadavre exquis", with this difference however, that there the individual contribution of the participants was always recognizable, which is not the case here. The design developed like a healthily growing root that constantly produces new joints and branches, like the rhizome that Deleuze and Guattari described in their book "Mille Plateaux" (14). The way the project developed, however, was also a lot like a squatting action. The entire interior structure of the original building - a domestic science school of the 50s in a traditionalist style - was altered and a new interior put in its place. The reason for this was not just that the building was to be given another function; just as important, if not more so, was that the structure of a machine for instilling discipline, - as Michel Foucault has described it (15) and which a domestic science school first of all is - should be largely removed. In its place a structure was introduced that offers the children a small but real world, a world that has to be discovered, where they can explore their own possibilities and impossibilities and that is not completely lacking in danger. For example there are various rooms that are more or less inaccessible for the supervisory staff. According to the designers, Alice in Wonderland is just as much a model for this world as are the street and the jungle. In this sense this day-nursery is the complete opposite of the standard current practice in Holland, where pastel colours and cliché toys constantly remind children of their character as children without ever giving them the chance of developing their own individuality. In addition to Deleuze and Foucault, Witold Gombrowicz' novel "Ferdyduke" (16) was a particularly important source of inspiration for the designers.

Exterior view - photo: René de Wit

Room to play for children between 4 and 6 years
photo: René de Wit

Kirsten van den Berg, Daan Bakker, Mirjam Galjé, Matthijs Bouw and Ton Venhoeven.
Day-nursery "Het Kasteel", Soest 1992 - photo: René de Wit

**The design developed like a healthily growing root that constantly
produces new joints andbranches, like the rhizome that Deleuze
and Guattari described in their book "Mille Plateaux".**

Architecture as philosophy: the day-nursery "Het Kasteel".

Room to play for children to 4 years - photo: René de Wit

Wiel Arets. Akademy for Art and Architecture, Maastricht 1993 - photo: Kim Zwarts

Students are given the possibility of exploring their ideas and concepts in complete freedom.

The autonomous architecture of Wiel Arets' Academy escapes the laws of formal discipline.

Auditorium - photo: Kim Zwarts

Studio building - photo: Kim Zwarts

The renovation and extension of the Academy of Art and Architecture in Maastricht by Wiel Arets is the only building in this selection to be located in the centre of a historic city. All others are situated in a kind of "waste land" - in the polders, in industrial areas and suburbs. The building serves as a gateway to a new square, the "Herdenkingsplein", on what was previously the courtyard of a housing block with newly built houses by Mecanoo and others. At the level of urban morphology Arets' intervention was clearly influenced by Giorgio Grassi. The building is what Grassi calls a "reconstruction" (17). It is admittedly not a literal reconstruction of the historical situation but it renders the historical situation visible through the placing of the building volumes. The building also clearly shows the fissure with the historical situation: it has the appearance of an operation scar in the tissue of the city. In the treatment of his projects Arets is much more of a minimalist than Grassi, whose architecture always has an unintentional air of melancholy due to his historicizing formal idiom and craftsmanlike approach. This is something that is completely lacking in Arets' work. His building for the Academy exposes the historical conditions like a didactic project, like an essay or work of conceptual art. To an important degree this is also the aesthetics of the project: in Arets' words, the scar is like the scars that primitive peoples like the Masai use as adornment.

The new building of the Maastricht academy has the look of an enclave, like a mysteriously enclosed bulwark in the city. In this sense it is related to those buildings by Tadao Ando that are sober meditative enclaves in the midst of the commercialized city. The façades with their blocks of reinforced glass have the aspect of masks. In the first instance it seems as though Arets wanted to achieve a completely autonomous architecture analogous to that of Eisenman or of Terragni in Tafuri's interpretation (19). There is no visible entrance; the actual entrance being located in the old building. The studios and workshops can only be reached via an overhead bridge at the level of the treetops. These are loftlike spaces occupying an entire storey. They are not split up by interior walls. Students can claim their own space by setting up their easels, tables and partitions. Thus a parallel world inside this building is created that escapes the laws of normal discipline, something that looks like what Foucault called a "heterotopia", a

miniature "Walled City". It is a model exceptionally suitable for an art school, giving the students the possibility of exploring their ideas and concepts in complete freedom. Like the group of designers of the day-nursery in Soest, Arets is also influenced by Deleuze and Guattari. In Arets' case, however, that does not have any immediate implications in terms of the design process; it does, however, have an effect on how the building functions in the city. Buildings, in this case the academy, link up with the network of roads, communication lines and "strands of desire" that combine to make up a city. In this way the ideas and concepts explored in this building percolate through to the city as a whole (20). Arets talks about "a virological architecture", about an architecture that, like a virus, produces invisible and unpredictable social changes in the city (21).

Notes:
(1) Geert Bekaert/Peter Buchanan, Rapport van de selectiecommissie, Stromingen en ontwikkelingen in den Nederlandse architectuur, in: Cees Boekraad (ed.), Van Ruimte tot rizoom, Rotterdam 1994
(2) cf. Umberto Barbieri/Cees Boekraad, Kritiek en ontwerp, Proeven van architectuurkritiek, Nijmegen 1982
Wiel Arets/Wim van den Bergh/William P.A.R.S. Graatsma, F.P.J. Peutz 1916-1966, Heerlen 1981
Wiel Arets/Wim van den Bergh, Casa come me: a sublime alienation, AA-Files 18, 1989
Wiel Arets/Wim van den Bergh/Kim Zwarts, Luis Barragan, binnenkort te verschijnen
(3) Hans van Dijk, Het onderwijzersmodernisme, in: Bernard Leupen, Wouter Deen, Christoph Grafe (ed.), Hoe modern is de Nederlandse architectuur?, Rotterdam 1990
(4) cf. Hans Ibelings, Modernisme zonder dogma, Rotterdam 1991
Bernard Colenbrander (ed.), Stijl, Norm en handschrift in de Nederlandse architectuur van de negentiende en twintigste eeuw, Rotterdam 1993
(5) Rem Koolhaas, Die erschreckende Schönheit des 20. Jahrhunderts, in: Jacques Lacan, OMA, Rem Koolhaas, Zürich/München 1991
(6) Rem Koolhaas, Unsere "Neue Sachlichkeit", ibid.
(7) Ed Melet, De perfecte wanorde, Detaillering en constructie KunstHAL, de Architect, 1993/1
(8) cf. Wiel Arets, Architect, Rotterdam 1989
Wiel Arets, An alabaster skin, Rotterdam 1991
Wiel Arets, Maastricht Academy, Rotterdam 1994
(9) cf. Ben van Berkel/Caroline Bos, Ben van Berkel, Architect, Rotterdam 1992
Ben van Berkel/Caroline Bos, Delinquent Visionaries, Rotterdam 1994
Ben van Berkel, Mobile Forces. Mobile Kräfte, Berlin 1994
(10) Janny Rodermond, Koen van Velsen, Architect, Rotterdam 1994
(11) Michel Foucault, Andere Räume, in: Felix Zwoch (ed.), Idee, Prozeß, Ergebnis. Die Reparatur und Rekonstruktion der Stadt, Berlin 1987
(12) cf. arch+ No 117, 1993, Sonderheft Rem Koolhaas "Die Entfaltung der Architektur"
Wiel Arets, Raster en Rhizom, in: Wiel Arets, An alabaster skin, Rotterdam 1991
Gijs Wallis de Vries, Deleuze en de architectuur, ARCHIS 11, 1993
John Biln, Line of Encounter, Flexible realism/Grenzlinien, flexibler Realismus, in: Ben van Berkel, Mobile Forces/ Mobile Kräfte, Berlin 1994
(13) Peter de Winter, Evenementen in Rotterdam, AHOY', E 55, FLORIADE C 70, Rotterdam
(14) Gilles Deleuze/Felix Guattari, Capitalisme et Schizofrenie 2, Mille Plateaux, Paris 1980
(15) Michel Foucault, Überwachen und Strafen. Die Geburt des Gefängnisses, Frankfurt/Main 1977
(16) Witold Gombrowicz, Ferdydurke
(17) Giorgio Grassi, Architettura Lingua Morta, Milano 1986
(18) Wiel Arets, An alabaster skin, Rotterdam 1981
(19) Manfredo Tafuri, The subject and the mask. An introduction to Terragni, Lotus international 20, 1978
(20) Wiel Arets, Raster en Rhizom, Rotterdam 1991
(21) Wiel Arets, A Virological Architecture, A+U 1994: 02

PERSPECTIVES.
MARC DUBOIS.

Belgium

Form of State: Parliamentary Monarchy since 1831, **Area:** 30,528 km2, **Inhabitants (1992):** 10,045,000, **Capital:** Brussel
Gross National Product 1992, per capita: $ 20,880, **Gross Domestic Product 1992:** $ 218,836 Mio, **Unemployment (Average, 1993):** 12.1%

Belgium's most important contribution to 20th century architecture has been mainly restricted to a number of exalted private houses.

No sign of a radical change in Belgium's architectural policy, but a lot of impulses.

Belgium, a creation and a compromise of the 19th century, is first of all a small country located very centrally in Europe between the Netherlands, Germany and France. Within a wider historical perspective, it has always been a transit zone breathing a markedly individual and liberal atmosphere. At the turn of the century, Belgium, or rather Brussels, attained a leading position on Europe's "architectural map". After the Art Nouveau, it again became a void.

In his book about Belgian architecture between 1945 and 1970 Geert Bekaert emphasize the deep-seated, strongly laissez-faire attitude of the government as a factor in the establishment of the architectural environment.

The government regards the stimulation of individualism as one of its principal functions. It looks also as if the Belgian government, since the birth of Modern architecture, has fearfully withheld contracts from architects who were playing a leading role in their own country. Between Belgium and the neighbouring countries there are huge differences, whose origins are to be found in the distant past. Successive occupations have led to an aversion to government as an institution. As far as the status of the architect is concerned, it must be said that both the title and the profession of architect had already received legal protection in 1939, a clear sign that architecture was ranked among the liberal professions. This protection has not, however, provided for broader architectural discussion in Belgium.

In France, for example, competitions are organized for almost all public buildings. In Belgium only in exceptional cases was a competition organized for the granting of an official commission. It is quite understandable that public housing does not really mean much in a country where a mere five percent of all homes are managed by government institutions, compared to more than 30 percent in the Netherlands and France.

Belgium's most important contribution to 20th century architecture has been mainly restricted to a number of exalted private houses. It is a country with a rich tradition, with the Palais Stoclet and the houses by Victor Horta, Louis Herman De Koninck, Gaston Eysselinck. In the post-war era, beautiful houses have been built by Jacques Dupuis, Peter Callebaut, Marc Dessauvage and Charles Vandenhove. For the younger generation, the situation is the same.

Following the presentation in Venice Architecture Biennale of 1991, an international interest was awakened for Belgium, and especially for the architectural scene in Flanders, the Dutch-speaking part of Belgium. In 1993, for the first time, the Italian publishing house "Electa" published a book offering an overview of the Belgian architecture from 1970 to 1992. In April 1994, the French review "L' Architecture d'Aujourd'hui" dedicated more than 40 pages to recent production in Flanders. This year, the Italian review "Domus" published five realized projects in Flanders! In October the German review "Baumeister" released a special issue about Stéphane Beel.

Never before there was a greater interest for the building activities in Belgium. Anyone studying the Belgian situation will soon reach the conclusion that very little has changed fundamentally here. A young generation has emerged, however, which presents a strong profile and is given more opportunities to publish its work in foreign journals.

There is no sign of a radical change in architectural policy. There are, nevertheless, signs that the government is gradually coming to accept architecture's cultural dimension. It was on the initiative of the Minister of Culture that a first Architectural Yearbook was published in 1994. It is a perilous undertaking to choose five architectural works. The danger is inevitable that this selection is seen as a "top five", so that all other interesting buildings are relegated to the second division. Because this is not the intention, but rather to present a number of new steps, it is essential to mention the exciting work done by other architects such as Marie-José Van Hee, Christian Kieckens, Xaveer De Geyter, Eugene Liebaut, Jo Crepain, Luc Deleu and Philippe Samyn.

In my selection I present work of the architects Stéphane Beel, Paul Robbrecht & Hilde Daem, Bruno Albert, Georges Baines and Bob Van Reeth.

Georges Baines makes reference to the Modernist tradition

and its quest for a subtle purism with a controlled spatiality.

The sensitive restoration and extension of Maison Guiette.

Georges Baines. Annex to the Maison Guiette, Antwerp 1992-94 - photo: Lautwein & Ritzenhoff

Georges Baines (born in 1925) first realized works, private homes built in the late 50s and the 60s, were heavily influenced by Scandinavian architecture. His early interest in the work of the avant-garde architects and artists was stimulated by personal contacts with Georges Van Tongerloo and the Zurich architect Alfred Roth. It was partially due to Baines' efforts that Le Corbusier's only Belgian work, the Maison Guiette, was saved from demolition.

The Antwerp painter René Guiette commissioned Le Corbusier to design a house and studio for him at the end of 1925. For Le Corbusier it was the first opportunity one year before the Weissenhofsiedlung in Stuttgart (1927) to put his investigations concerning the "Citrohan" type into concrete form. Le Corbusier wrote in his "Oeuvre Complète" (1929) about this house: "An entirely specific solution, imposed by Belgian land division, characterized by a 6-metre façade and a very great depth."

It is particularly the continuous staircase and the studio on the top floor that give this home an exceptional command of space. Le Corbusier devoted much attention to polychromy in the interior. The plot to the left of the house remained undeveloped for more than half a century. After Guiette's death, plans arose to build on this fallow ground a documentation centre for Modern architecture, into which the house would be integrated while retaining its own identity. The architect Baines drew up a design, as did several students from the ETH in Zurich. In the end the house was sold to a young couple who commissioned Baines not only to do the restoration work, but also to augment Le Corbusier's work with a fashion design studio and a photographic studio on the top floor. The exceptionally careful restoration, especially of the details, was a result of the "Le Corbusier Year 1987". The second phase was the addition. Because the entrance hall was set further

back, the house's original bar-like form could be retained. The large angled window in the façade allows sufficient north light into the studios. The two are linked only on the second floor so that the spatial character of the 1926 building is kept completely intact.

In the Ronny Van De Velde art gallery in Antwerp, built at roughly the same time, Baines also makes reference to the Modernist tradition and its quest for a subtle purism with a controlled spatiality.

Façade from the back and annex to Maison Guiette - photo: Lautwein & Ritzenhoff

Connecting wing - photo: Lautwein & Ritzenhoff

The most important architect in Wallony is undoubtedly Charles Vandenhove (born in 1927). His opus magnum is the University Hospital on the Sart Tilman Campus near the city of Liège. Considerable international interest was awakened primarily by the conversion of the Hotel Torrentius and the Hors-Château residential area in Liège's historical centre. Vandenhove received a tremendous number of commissions in the Netherlands after his retrospective in the IFA in Paris and a presentation in Amsterdam. He hardly received any new commissions in Belgium and certainly not in Liège. The second important architect from Liège, Bruno Albert (born in 1941), has also received important commissions in the Netherlands. Albert carried out a large-scale housing project on the KNSM island in Amsterdam, within an urban planning scheme by Jo Coenen. Almost all works by Vandenhove, Albert and other architects from Liège were produced in cooperation with the engineer René Greisch. This gifted bridge designer certainly contributed to the creation of a great spatial quality in these buildings, within often rigid financial limits. A good example of this is the new "Hautes Etudes Commerciales de Liège" business school, in the centre of Liège, designed by Albert with Greisch as engineer. It integrates itself into the existing urban fabric almost naturally. All the functions open onto a central indoor street with zenithal light from above. The main entrance lies on the axis of a transverse street. This large, glazed entry also links the garden at the rear to the school's car park, and is also accentuated by a round stairtower. The large auditorium is clearly distinguishable within the whole composition. A classified 17th century building situated at the back, part of an old monastery, was thoroughly restored and functions as an administrative wing for the school.

As in his other work, Albert here also seeks to insert the whole in the most natural way possible into its surroundings without spectacular formal additions.

Bruno Albert. "Hautes Etudes Commerciales de Liège", 1991-93 - photo: Marc Dubois

Bruno Albert seeks to insert the whole in the most natural way possible into its surroundings without spectacular formal additions.

The "Hautes Etudes Commerciales de Liège", a design marked by urban points of view.

Model

Zenithal light from above - photo: Marc Dubois

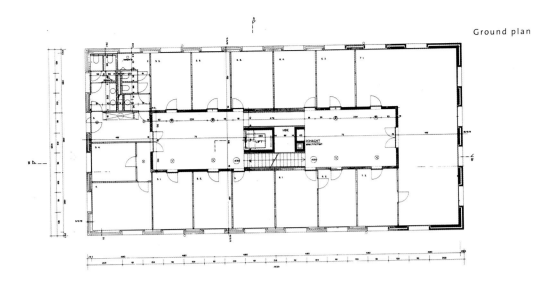

Bob Van Reeth. Office building for the Averbode publishers, Averbode 1992-93 - photo: Marc Dubois

Like memory, architecture is always new and current but its content is an eternal dream whose reality is greater than anything which has ever existed.

Insight into the complexity: Bob Van Reeth's architecture.

Immediately after completing his studies in 1968, Bob Van Reeth (born in 1943) affirmed himself as a non-conformist, talented designer with a number of exciting designs. Among these was the readaption of one of the houses in the Beguinage at Mechelen, which is now his own living quarters.

According to Geert Bekaert, Van Reeth's work has been sustained from the beginning by "an insight into the complex relationship between un-premeditated actions and the need for an ordered structure".

Architecture, as far as Bob Van Reeth is concerned, is the memory of something that has never existed. Like memory, architecture is always new and current but its content is an eternal dream whose reality is greater than anything which has ever existed. Two of his most well-known and publicized productions from the second half of the 80s are the Van Roosmalen house and the "Zuiderterras" café and restaurant. Both are located on the Scheldt quayside in Antwerp. It is therefore not coincidential that Van Reeth makes use of "maritime" formal elements in these buildings, even making reference to Otto Wagner. In his most recent work, Van Reeth is looking more and more for the most elementary architectonic form. For the "Antwerp, European Cultural Capital 1993" event, Van Reeth designed a floating theatre called "The Ark". The volume has clear associations with the historical image of the Ark, an image that Massimo Scolari has already included in his work "The Ark" (1982). The new office building for the Averbode publishers fits particularly becomingly into the monastery's hierarchical layout. It was conceived as a straightforward rectangular building, typologically related to the farmhouses of the Kemps region,

and it forms a new link in the series of service buildings extending along the slope at the foot of the monastery complex. Built in dark-brown brick, it appears as a sober, introspective volume that hardly contrasts with the back-ground of the surrounding woods. The concept was prompted by the economy inherent to the elementary and the durable. The number of materials, selected on the basis of quality and employed with a consistent logic, was kept to a minimum. The brickwork does not contain any concrete beams, for instance, the window openings being spanned by upright brick courses reinforced with stainless steel rods. The relationship between architecture and art is central to the work of Paul Robbrecht (born in 1950) & Hilde Daem (born in 1950). Therefore, much of their work has involved a close cooperation with artists such as Munoz, Vercruysse, Genzken and Iglesias. Among their most interesting works are the Mariën-Meert and the Hufkens art galleries, both in Brussels. Their most vivantly discussed controversial building up to now has been the Aue Pavilions, a temporary exhibition space for documenta IX in Kassel in 1992. They evoked the image of shunting train wagons and of displacement. This power-ful project, with the connotations of arriving and departing art, were, at the end of 1994, re-erected in the borough of Almere, near Amsterdam. The architects received several com-missions from the BACOB Bank, which alone chose to invite various talented architects to design small branch offices. The exteriors of these buildings are, emphatically, not characterized by uniformity but precisely by uniqueness. The bank in Kerksken (1988-1989) is situated on a main road running through

the village. Virtually the entire length of the road is lined by characterless ribbon development. In volumetric terms, the building is in the form of a beam, cut at an angle and projected onto the parallelogram-shaped building plot. The interior space is enclosed - something which has been dictated by the function of the bank itself - by a two-storey-high gallery, whose irregularly high pillars reverse the normal sense of perspective. On the street frontage, the gallery serves as a covered bus stop. The building contains vague reminders of the large simple sheds found in both agriculture and industry, to lend it an almost marketlike character. Inside, besides standard banking activity, the high reception hall also serves as an informal meeting place for local people. The rigidity of the building's exterior contrasts greatly with the unrestrained expressiveness of the interior where a curving partition separates public areas from internal working areas.

The rigidity of the building's exterior contrasts greatly

with the unrestrained expressiveness of the interior.

Functional architecture: the bank branch in Kerksken by Paul Robbrecht and Hilde Daem.

Paul Robbrecht and Hilde Daem. Bank building in Kerksken, 1987-89 - photo: Kristien Daem

Stéphane Beel. KULAK University, Kortrijk 1991-94 - photos: Lautwein & Ritzenhoff

Given its minimalism, the masterly restraint

of the form is awesome indeed.

Geert Bekaert about Stéphane Beel's reduced architecture.

Among the architects who have emerged strongly since the second half of the 80s, Stéphane Beel (born in 1955) is undoubtedly the most fascinating figure. Geert Bekaert has described his work as "irritating logic" and a struggle to create space around walls. In this architecture there is no place for a concept such as interior, unless it is descibed as being the proximity of the wall.

Beel's first great work is the renovation of the Spaarkrediet, a bank with adjoining offices and exhibition halls in the historic centre of Bruges. Here, Beel has shown, in a stunning way, how a space can be scenographically created around a long newly-built wall. The interior is reached through an "architectural promenade", and there one discovers the poetical strength of the light pouring into the upper central space within. The space and the control of the light cannot but evoke an image of Victor Horta's houses. Other interesting realized projects are: BACOB Banks in Ostend and Bruges, a terraced house in Mortsel and the 60-metre-long villa near Bruges. For the latter, he received a mention in the Mies van der Rohe architectural awards in 1992. In 1991, the Catholic University of Leuven organized a limited competition

for the expansion of its campus in Kortrijk (KULAK). The KULAK had been built in the late 60s in anticipation of future growth, which left a number of buildings unconnected in an open landscape. The expected growth failed to materialize, the campus never really was used as intended. One year before, the Italian architect Bernardo Secchi had won the competition for a new urban plan for Upper Kortrijk, where the campus is situated. The proposal that Beel submitted in 1991 takes up Secchi's concept. As if by force of habit, Beel has taken as his point of departure the existing situation and endeavours in the most economical way to bring to the fore its latent lines of force.

For Bekaert "Beel not only provides insight into the existing state, but completes it in such a natural and fluent manner that it seems as if there were no other solutions". The volumes of the two primary blocks, two faculties, are made to interrelate with a "spine". Beel introduced the main pedestrian circulation axis within the complex: On the ground floor, this is a sheltered walkway, on the upper floor an enclosed corridor. Even the intermediate space loses its negative character.

In continuing the scheme's development, Beel has managed to keep the competition's basic concept intact. With the new Faculty of Applied Economy, Beel has demonstrated how he himself conceives of this elaboration. On the ground floor, the landscape continues beneath the building. For Bekaert: "The means employed are extremely limited, but their potential is exploited to the full with a whimsical airiness. Given its minimalism, the masterly restraint of the form is awesome indeed."

The values handed down through

generations were threatened.

At the beginning of the 80s the crisis in ideology has reached Denmark and its architecture.

3 | "Optimism Reigns Again in Denmark - at Long Last." Kim Dirckinck-Homfeld.

Denmark

Form of State: Parliamentary Monarchy since 1953, **Aera:** 43,094 km2, **Inhabitants (1993):** 5,180,600, **Capital:** Copenhagen
Gross National Product 1992, per capita: $ 26,000, **Gross Domestic Product 1992:** $ 123,546 Mio, **Unemployment (Average, 1993):** 12.1%

f anyone had asked me two years ago to make a speech on the state of Danish architecture, I would never have used this title. At that time, Denmark was in the middle of a deep financial crisis of almost biblical timing - it lasted seven years, from the beginning of 1987 up until this year. The absolute low came in 1992-93, when building activity practically came to a standstill. This was a situation which in many ways was even worse than the previous low point in 1949.

The economical crisis revealed certain fundamental problems for Danish architects. These problems not only were based on structure and power, but also had an ideological character. These conditions were independent of the changes in market trends, and were thus of a more serious character. Today there is a high rate of unemployment among architects and only about 30 percent of the architects are employed in the building trade. It is their problem that would like to discuss. I'll start with the structural crisis. As in so many other countries, the restructuring of the building trade from traditional craftsmanship to industrial production created a number of problems for architects. Previously, Danish architects controlled the building process from the birth of the concept to the mounting of the door handles. However, with the increases in complexity of the building trade, they lost influence and control. In brief, the following circumstances arose: The building process became increasingly technocratic and segregated, and the architect's role as a coordinator was greatly reduced. A number of work areas were removed in part, or wholly, from their jurisdiction. This included programming, site supervision, work scheduling, client advising, budget control, and so on. A general contractor replaced the individual contractors. The client and the building's users grew ever more anonymous. Large capital concentrations among the contractors and others weakened the architect's position and influenced the commercial structure of the profession. There was an increasing tendency toward fewer and larger offices. Architects lost influence in central administration and building research. The reorganization of the building process in favour of non-skilled workers meant a loss of knowledge and skills among construction workers. Building technology deteriorated. The project period was reduced and price competition amongst architectural offices increased. Architects were blamed for all this misery. They soon developed a bad image, almost as bad as that of lawyers and politicians. I could go on naming other developments, but the tendency is obvious. This is a serious problem for a profession in which development and learning is based on quality craftsmanship. There was also an ideological crisis. At the same time, the profession found itself in an existential crisis. The values handed down through generations were threatened. This crisis escalated during the 80s and was influential in weakening the architects' professional preparedness, and thereby also their resistance to the invasions of others. Two main elements in the Danish architects' self-conception were subject to enormous strain: their social responsibility, and the system of aesthetical values, which could be called the professional ethic of Danish architects. The awareness of architecture's social mission goes back to the middle of the last century, but its basis was seriously established at the beginning of this century, at first, by socially indignant pioneers, and later, by the weight of the entire profession. This movement had its parallel all over Europe. In Denmark, however, it continued throughout this century. The purpose of architecture was seen in serving society. Peder Vilhelm Jensen Klint, architect of Grundtvig Church in Copenhagen, said in 1908: "This whole effort is based on the fact that we demand today that everything around us should be subject to this culture of beauty." That claim had generally been accepted until about 1985. The same sympathetic orientation involved architects in the industrialization process and in large-scale building projects. But it was also architects who were open to environmental problems. They reacted with the neoromanticism of the cluster housing movement. They believed in architecture as a revolutionary tool for a participatory democracy which could exist in symbiosis with nature and the cosmos. We again had something to be proud of: The cluster housing movement, the collectives and housing cooperatives during the 70s and early 80s; the ecological experiments; and the cozy security, created in harmony with images existing in folk culture. Vandkunsten Architects were the sovereign interpreters here.

The works and theories of Robert Venturi, Charles Jencks and

more recently Derrida and Peter Eisenman and so many others

are nothing less than a frontal attack on this tradition.

Architectural contradictions, inconsistencies and informative figurations with double-coded architecture.

n the 80s these ideals lost their appeal. The dizzying economy of the Yuppie years, the growing egotism and the Postmodernist rejection of values threatened the great social project, which was no longer modern. And for better or worse, we, the architects, had built the welfare state. So there we were, with no social project, as cold winds began to blow in from the right wing. However, the most crushing blow came when we discovered that even our aesthetical values had become obsolete. Some architectural theorists feel that Danish architects act on the basis of a more or less fixed set of values. Although formal languages develop superficially, the deeper lying norms are maintained, and in this lies the gravity of tradition. The fundamental principle is harmony, but parallel with this are values such as: honesty, simplicity, clarity, character and homogeneity, structural logic and a precisely controlled play of textures. Tradition tempers that which comes from

outside sources, changes occur, although not radically, not disruptively. Basically, the Danish tradition aims to return to the classical principles of order, or in any case toward a formal monism that requires one, and only one, formal principle of order and one visual code. With some major exceptions, this is also expressed in Danish Modernism, both in terms of Arne Jacobsen's subdued Modernism and Kaj Fisker's Functional tradition. Even Jørn Utzon must be included here. In later years, these principles of unity have still been maintained, though in more complex forms. Thus the works and theories of Robert Venturi, Charles Jencks and more recently Derrida and Peter Eisenman and so many others are nothing less than a frontal attack on this tradition. Suddenly we must live with architectural contradictions, inconsistencies, informative figuration and with Postmodernism's quotation-filled assemblages. With double-coded architecture; yes, even with architectural

conflict theories. But this doesn't really sit well with the Danes. Therefore we have only had a few Postmodern projects, and they appeared very late in the movement. C. F. Møller's office was the first to venture into this area in 1982 with their disciplined administration building in Lem. The youthful office of Nielsen, Nielsen & Nielsen employed Post-modernism almost as a manifesto from their very start, but with a sober reference to the Danish tradition, which in a postmodern context was ingeniously achieved. This resulted in several "inclusive" one-family houses and culminated in 1990 with a large, overloaded and quote-filled academic Congress Hall in Holsterbro. Vandkunsten Architects attempted their own double-coding in the Garvergården housing project from the 80s.

The fundamental principle is harmony, but parallel with this are values such as: honesty, simplicity, clarity, character and homogeneity, structural logic and a precisely controlled play of textures.

Danish tradition referring back to the classical principles of order.

Tradition seems to resist.

Recollections of the past as a way out of the crisis?

They rebuilt an old shoe factory, and had, as can be seen, a difficult time doing it. The results are irresolute and seem to be an intermezzo on their way to a new formal expression. On the other hand, Aldo Rossi's, and to a lesser extent, the Krier brothers' Neorationalism seems to be better suited to the Danish school of thought. Its influence appeared earlier, and more frequently and typically as a sort of Neoclassicism. The first project in this direction was Claus Bonderup and Jacob Blegvad's winning proposal in the 1977 new town competition in Høje Taastrup. It bears a striking resemblance to Leon Krier's La Villette project, but as opposed to Krier's, their project was realized, although unfortunately in a flat, industrialized classicism. Bonderup, Thorup, Waade and Birch won the competition for the Arctic center in Rovaniemi, Finland, which was reduced to a particular symbolism: a glowing line in the snow. Poul Ingemann displayed a somewhat characterized classicism at the

housing exposition, Blangstedgaard, in 1988. This was followed up several years later with an addition to the Johannes Larsen Museum in Kerteminde, though in a more subtle version. Henning Larsen employed the classicist idiom in his proposal for the Kammergericht in Berlin, which unfortunately was never built. However, his winning proposal for the foreign ministry in Riyadh was realized. It reveals an architect who was able to rapidly shift from Structuralism's process-oriented architecture, such as his university projects for Trondhjem and the FU Berlin, to Classicism's closed and formal solutions. He transplanted the Danish/Islamic symbiosis from sunny Riyadh to windblown Copenhagen with his business college and housing scheme from 1990, a project that appears extremely rigid in its symmetry. Danish Deconstructivism can also be traced in more or less fragmented versions in projects like the Køge Bugt Art Museum competition won by architecture student

Søren Lund in the 80s. It is now under construction and seems to have a clear Rem Koolhaas inspiration. Others interpret Mario Botta. A few originals, like Carsten Hoff and Susan Ussing, seem to be totally unaware of which way the wind is blowing in their praiseworthy common house in Toftlund.

A re-evaluation of the Modernistic heritage has come to the rescue.

For Kim Dirckinck-Homfeld there are good reasons for optimism.

The many theories are absorbed by the elite at the architecture schools. Abstractions and theorizations fly through the air in a way never seen before. However, the "ism's" seep into the professional offices as an extension of their formal repertoire. Traditions everywhere: "It's amusing to discover that the deconstruction theories result in an arched roof", says Nils-Ole Lund. Tradition seems to resist. But it is not very amusing to be old-fashioned, to fall behind and feel rootless. One tries to keep pace. One plunges into architectural magazines. Some architects succeed and others end up with unintegrated borrowed images. It's just this schism between a tradition-oriented architecture and the conflict-oriented new directions that gives a sense of dissolution. There is evidently no help to be found in these theories. They seem to become increasingly abstract and nebulous as the distance between the schools and the profession increases. But there is a reason for optimism. A re-evaluation of the Modernistic heritage has come to the rescue. The study of Functionalism's classics has been revived. The Australian Glenn Murcutt's regional Functionalism is inspiring. The young Spanish architects display a brilliant command of architecture's elementary effects: rhythm, light, structure, texture and colour. The young are rediscovering the heroes of Nordic Functionalism: Asplund, Aalto, Jacobsen and Lassen. They practice concentration and contemplation: to draw and to redraw again. Architecture

has again become a media in itself, and not just a semantic purveyor of messages or purely transcribed linguistic theories. Projects now lean toward the same degree of simplification as they did in the early 50s, and toward almost symbolic effects, as is evident in KHR's Danish pavilion at the 1992 World's Fair in Seville. A younger office, Schmidt, Hammer, and Lassen, made their debut with refined simplification and powerful design in their first prize proposal for the Culture Center in Nuuk, Greenland, in 1992, and their pierced black monolith-like proposal for the addition to the Royal Library in Copenhagen, an international competition that they won in 1993, which will presumably be completed in 1997. Nielsen, Nielsen & Nielsen have painlessly replaced their postmodernist ideals with a refined Neomodernism as can be seen here in their Vingsted Center. Quite naturally, Henning Larsen also masters this discipline as can be seen in his excellent in-fill project for the recently completed Berlingske Tidende newspaper building in Copenhagen. Niels Sigsgaard and Flemming Nøhr's wonderful swimming hall in Kolding was completed this year. And the architects from Vandkunsten have again regained their balance with the poetic scheme of Diana's Have in Hørsholm from 1993. There is also the question of architectural politics. Generally speaking, the Danish architectural arena seems to be glowing with optimism at the moment. Not only has the ideological dilemma seem to have dispelled, but architecture received

much needed aid from the government's proposal for a new architectural policy, which was likely to be passed in the 1993 parliamentary session. Furthermore, the much feared EU public service directive has had the unexpected effect, that once again architects seem to be playing first violin in the building trade. This is due to the fact that all public building projects with professional fees exceeding a certain amount must be open to the tenders among architects. And finally, the architects' organizations have agreed to build a new headquarters on the Copenhagen water front. A competition was recently completed with Nielsen, Nielsen & Nielsen as winners.

Nielsen, Nielsen & Nielsen. Courthouse in Holsterbro, 1992

Elements ranging from Functionalism to Deconstruction are combined, all bound by the tense form in a dynamic balance.

The courthouse building by Nielsen, Nielsen & Nielsen.

Court room

The assembled cube represents the

building's basic conceptual idea

The heating power plant in Horsens by Lene Tranberg und Boje Lundgaard.

Lene Tranberg and Boje Lundgaard. Power Plant in Horsens, 1989

I would like to review five recent projects which I feel represent the reason for this growing optimism. The first is the new Courthouse in Holsterbro by Kim Herforth Nielsen and Lars Frank Nielsen.

Their office was established in the 80s, immediately after their graduation from architecture school. They started with a strong theoretical attitude, which in their early projects had a somewhat demonstrative character. But their courthouse, completed in 1992, represents a change in direction, one that has moved them into the upper echelons of the profession. The comparatively small building is situated just north of Holsterbro, in an older villa neighbourhood, whose villas and ordinary building-lined streets are respected by the courthouse in both volume and scale. It stands slightly back from the street to create a plaza and entrance drive. The administrative offices occupy a long, two-storey wing. Toward the villa area, the building is split into smaller units which correspond to the scale of the surroundings. The entrance façade toward the north has a somewhat classicistic countenance, suggested by the three propeller-shaped columns next to the main entrance. The glass wall behind is penetrated by the courtroom's massive concrete monoliths. All this is covered by a floating aluminium roof, shaped like an airplane wing. One finds here an artful rendition of the classic

repertoire, interrupted by shifts in motif exemplified by the courtroom skylight. Elements ranging from Functionalism to Deconstruction are combined, all bound by the tense form in a dynamic balance. There is a certain symbolism at play here. The seriousness and claim on infallibility of the judicial system are expressed in the weightiness of the concrete mass and in the sophisticated and superb detailing: the open society is expressed in the building's transparency. In my opinion, it is the Judicial Service that seems to be given priority here. A local farmer will probably feel discomfort in this perfectionistic judicial machine regardless of its accessibility.

The next project is the Skærbæk Power Plant in Horsens by architects Lene Tranberg and Boje Lundgaard. Boje Lundgaard, in collaboration with Bente Aude, made his debut on the architectural scene with the Sjølund cluster housing scheme in 1978. With Aude as his partner, he also won the Trapholt Museum competition in 1988, which is among the finest works of Danish architecture in recent years. I might have included it in this review, were it more recent. In past years, he has established a new partnership with Lene Tranberg. They have been extremely productive and have also worked with ecological problems as well in their Nørre Alslev scheme as in the urban renewal project for the Vesterbro quarter of

Copenhagen. They were the main contributors to the grand Blangstedgaard building exposition in 1988 and were responsible for its general planning as well as for a number of housing schemes and projects. Their work here demonstrated a remarkable range of formal expression. Their major work so far is the district heating power plant in Horsens, Skærbækværket, the result of a 1989 design competition. The concept was based on a Danish wooden cube toy by Kay Bojesen, which is a difficult puzzle to solve when disassembled. The assembled cube represents the building's basic conceptual idea.

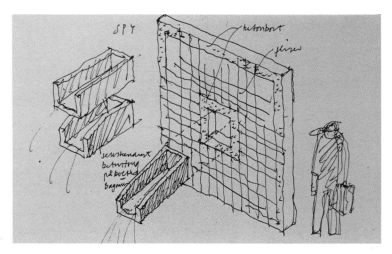

The cube is partially submerged in a moat that surrounds the entire complex. The inner workshop court divides the cube in two parts, one soiled and the other clean. The incinerator is on one side, and the turbines and workshops on the other. But where does the architectural poetry arise? Is it in the rhythmic juxtaposition of volumes? In the tension between the square and the circle? Is it in the fragile, delicate skin of reddish-yellow glazed tile, which takes its colour from the natural surroundings: the sky and the sea? Or is it in the constant shift of the glass block walls from transparency to opaqueness? Or is it in the awareness of the complicated, inner confusion of pipes, turbines, valves? The vital arteries of our society are wrapped in a gentle building form, while all the life-giving heat and electricity are transported along hidden paths. Technology's fineness and purity are light-years from the 30s fascination with machines, chimney smoke, thunder and dynamics. Only the chimneys betray this building's function.

The Bornholm Art Museum was designed by architects Fogh and Følner. They refer to Kaj Fisker and the Danish brick architecture tradition as part of their architectural baggage, and to Mogens Lassen. It is quite clear that their sources of inspiration are purely Danish, although I feel that architects like Kåre Klint and Carl Petersen have a great influence here, and even Vilhelm Wohlert and Jørgen Bo. A look at the main room at Egedal Church from 1990 proves this point. The ceiling bespeaks its traditionally Danish character. Fogh and Følner had their breakthrough in 1982 with their first prize winning project in the Nordic competition for a museum for the dry-docked Royal ship, Wasa, in Stockholm. Unfortunately they were not allowed to build it. A second prize in the 1988 competition for the museum at Køge Bugt did not bring them much luck either. But finally they succeeded with their winning proposal for the 1991 Bornholm Museum competition. This scheme was completed in 1993 and lies on a sensitive natural area near the Sacred Cliffs. It aroused a great deal of local criticism: 15,000 of Bornholm's 40,000 residents protested. Sentiment was so strong that they buried their protest document and signatures at the laying of the cornerstone to tell future generations that this building was a mistake. Thankfully, the county mayor refused to succumb. The building is organized around an inner museum street that follows the sloping terrain. The sacred spring emanates at the upper end of the entrance hall and runs down through the glass-roofed street in a granite channel. The elongated building is organized along a street-like space, which traverses several levels. This central space ties the different halls together, which toward the East appear as separate volumes, and toward the West as shifted wings. The materials are rich and varied. The walls are primarily mortar-brushed brick with glazed brick bands. The paving in the street space is tile, whereas the exhibition halls have wooden floors. The exhibition areas in the western area of the scheme have alcoves as at Carl Petersen's Fåborg Museum from 1921. One of the skylit spaces has effects similar to Trapholt. It is a building with many areas of experience, colours, and variety. As a sequel to this story, the museum has become so popular with the local citizens that they dug up their protest papers to express regret with their resistance. This represents a rare victory for architectural quality.

Bornholm Art Museum, foyer

A rare victory for architectural quality.

In the meantime the museum has become popular with the local citizens.

The materials are rich and varied.

The Museum in Bornholm by Fogh and Følner.

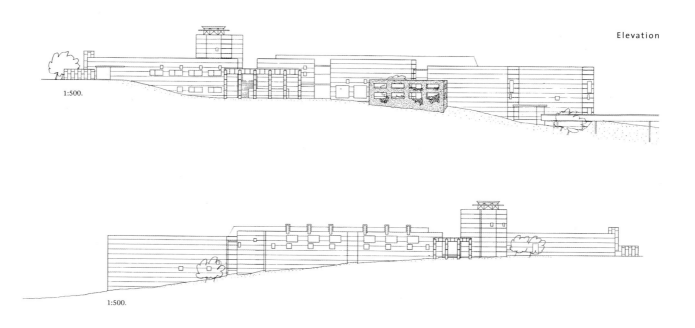

Elevation

1:500.

1:500.

Fogh & Følner. Bornholm Art Museum, 1993 - northfaçade

The "Pihl og søn" building by KHR-architects with Jan Søndergaard is composed on a right angle consisting of two three-storey office wings separated by a continuous skylit gallery. As an irregular component, the staff restaurant is built as a two-storey appendage to the main body. The office wings are precise in form, defined with great accuracy with glass and masonry in exactly the same proportion which creates a delicacy in texture and counterpoints between mural and transparency. The gallery space takes on an almost lyrical quality as the sun and the clouds play off the interior surfaces. The entrances are constructed as three-storey high towers with solid walls along the office wings and a full-height glass wall marking the entrances at the end of the galleries. The galleries are of full-height steel frames into which various building elements are integrated, i.e. stairs, railings, skylight system, reception desk, etc. In the inner angle is an exhibition space, whose glass façade fronts the reflecting pool and opens to the gallery. The spatial experience is almost Miesean.

The gallery space takes on an almost lyrical quality.

The building by KHR- architects and Jan Søndergaard.

KHR-Architects. Danish Pavilion, EXPO Sevilla, 1992

KHR-Architects and Jan Søndergaard.
Building "Phil og søn", 1993

Building "Phil og søn", 1993

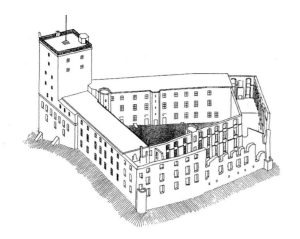

Johannes and Inger Exner. Reconstruction work of Koldinghus castle, 1972-92

to be clearly expressed. "Narrative value" is what the Exners' call the traces that bear witness to the building's previous life, and allow its accumulated history to be maintained for posterity. In Christian IV's ruined church hall, three delicate chandeliers symbolize the former stellar of the past" is the Exners' haunting question. This building is a narrative, a drama, which can be read by those who can and will see. The original project for the hall consisted of a light, steel structure - rustic and straightforward, complying with the existing structure.

The existing portions of the building are retained

and the renovated areas are clearly marked.

No attempt at restoration: the reconstruction of Koldinghus castle.

Experimenting with new constructions and building

elements created an ordinary and dignified

architecture of great structural clarity.

Architecture as a reference to daily life, this is the essence of the norwegian architecture.

4 | WORKING WITH THE LIMITS.
NEVEN FUCHS-MIKAC.

Norway

Form of State: Parliamentary Monarchy since 1905, **Area:** 323,877 km2, **Inhabitants (1992):** 4,287,000, **Capital:** Oslo
Gross National Product 1992, per capita: $ 25,820, **Gross Domestic Product 1992:** $ 112,906 Mio, **Unemployment (Average, 1993):** 6 %

Norwegian architecture is, even more than the architecture of other Nordic countries, strongly influenced by its particular cultural geography. Its position on the northernmost "periphery" of Europe enabled it to emphasize two experiences: openness toward the "centre", but also the freedom and solitude of distance: inside and outside at the same time. Following a confusion of styles, the effort to revitalize architecture in the 20s brought together classical order and vernacular freedom, pointing out their common roots. It was a movement back to "beginnings", a search for the "fundamental" principles. The messages of the functionalism of the 30s, committed to creating the Scandinavian welfare state and social equality, generated open and friendly spaces, purposefully simple and sensitively related to the landscape. The International Style became human and mature in the north, avoiding ideological orthodoxy and affectation. The standardized industrial production of architecture was challenged by the experiences of traditional local crafts. Experimenting with new constructions and building elements, the sensitive approach to materials, particularly the use of wood and the feeling for spatial economy, created an ordinary and dignified architecture of great structural clarity, full of references to daily life and common origins. It was architecture of proximity, unpretentious atmosphere and great emotional resonance, and its intention was to produce quality of life not works of art. There was a constant effort to both confirm and transform the strands of existing culture as well as to give expression to its new social contents. Both aspects provoked Nordic architecture into being quietly polemical, an attitude which constantly undermined everything that purported to be a total explanation of the world. Seriously questioning the ruling ideologies of architecture, the formal languages and the accepted definitions, it developed its own practices of translation to make cultural codes understandable and

recognizable, liberating, in this way, its own approach. Mediating between different, often opposite, ideas and values, it tended to cultivate the spaces of harmony, continuity and meaning. Dedicated to bringing architecture closer to life and the country, it developed spatial sensitivity for related and differentiated orders and enriched the practices of composition. Man-made geometry was conveyed by the geometry of nature, which integrated the irregularities and rhythms of landscape or fractured them where location and programme demanded. The feeling for tranquility and contemplation was laden with expressive tensions, the safeness of enclosed spaces with the feeling for openness. From this location, where close contact with nature is everywhere and the limitations imposed by climate, topography, and light are felt so strongly, it was possible to claim a universal cultural heritage. Architecture was brought close to the forgotten strata of dormant awareness of "timeless" values and the "primitive", as an expression of what is honest, genuine, true and real: fundamental and self-evident architecture - its constructional precision was created in resistance to the forces of nature and its beauty was not dependent on time. Architecture was to be human by being "unimportant" in its expression, following the natural lines and rhythms and the silent indications of movements. Its cultural task was to search for the "eternal" qualities in things and places and for the "fundamental" experiences inherent in the rhythm of man and landscape, the path of sun, snow and rain. At the beginning of the 80s, the cultural homogeneity of Nordic architecture was undoubtedly threatened by "baroque" architecture, supported by money and the free market. The simple was replaced by the complex, the pure by the manifold, the meaningful by the liberated world of choices, associations and images. The globalisation forces of today make the situation even more unstable and uncertain. The processes no longer represent a simple bipolar picture

of "centre and periphery". Rather, they form a mosaic of different points with manifold categories of meanings. How Norwegian architecture will react to these new conditions is not yet clear. I have chosen six buildings that I would like to present, instead of five: a glacier museum, an olympic ski-jumping arena, an art gallery, a university building, a truck garage and, in addition, a little "summer hut", a modest building that I felt was suitable for summarizing the ideas and images which I wanted to convey. The buildings represent quite different architectonic positions, they are the work of individuals who, on the basis of their feelings and convictions, mediate between the broken tradition and the new natural, social and physical realities, trying to find possibilities for today's architecture and what it can still contribute to place and everyday life. These attitudes are made physically present by the way the buildings are constructed and their space is organized and used, in the manner of their structure, in their relationship to the ground and the way that they create a dwelling, and by the way they use materials. But it is not their physical presence alone which gives life to these attitudes. It is the inner, architectonic dialogue they try to establish with the limitations of climate, topography and light, searching for new codes of adopting both natural and cultural information - this dialogue enables these buildings to be seen in specific ways, so that they can be experienced, reflected on and used.

The great museum is the globe itself, the lost objects preserved on its surface. The sea and the sand are the great masters of preservation: they make the journey into eternity so slow that we can find the key to the birth of our culture in this pattern", wrote architect Sverre Fehn at the time when he was working on the archaeological museum in Hammar, a museum suspended over the excavation site of the seat of the old bishopric. "Every single thing stolen from the depths of the earth is part of the magic of history." The contemporary museum becomes a place for "the dance of 'dead things' in which the artefact and its relation to human movement is what is important [...]. The objects may be born again and find space for an existence 'beyond the horizon' in their new context." So that the objects could regain their new identity, many subtle inventions of iron, metal, marble, wood and concrete were created to hold them in a new, clearly defined museum space, where they appear in a previously unknown light.

In 1991, Sverre Fehn built the Norwegian Glacier Museum in Fjærland in Western Norway. The object to be "exhibited" is a magnificent piece of Norwegian landscape, the Jostedal Glacier, which is the largest in Europe. How to approach this problem in spatial terms, in a leisure-orientated society in which nature is subjected to our choices and judgements, reduced to an object of visual beauty?

The concept of a glacier as a physical element was very much present during the planning of the museum. This enormous mass of ice and snow lies around vast expanses of land like a bandage. Concealed in this mass are secrets of the past, captured by the transparent opaqueness of the glacier. The glacier has something animal in its essence, in its slow gliding movement, which leaves great imprints on the crust of the earth and in the water masses as they run towards the sea..."

"The museum is located on the last projection of the Jostedal Glacier - a delta which runs out of Fjærland fjord, a part of the Sognefjord complex. The whole of Fjærland and its fjord ressembles a huge floor in a natural space, with the mountainsides forming gigantic walls. In this space with the plain as a plinth, the museum rises like an instrument, in which the visitor becomes the focal point in a total panorama, providing him with the tranquility in which to experience his own dimension."

"A traditional museum seeks to show lost objects. Today we feel it necessary for museums to make visible the invisible, to create a link. The atmosphere we have breathed through centuries hides its data in the Alpine mountains of ice, which, if there were to be a minimal increase in temperature, would flood the fertile plains of the earth..."

Let us take a look at the building's section, for a while. Architecture is, of course, never just a section. But if we look, we find a simple and direct gesture that acts like a focus for human movement and light, giving their physics architectonic expression. Its precise construction enables us to find the old and beautiful dream of creating a space without objects, just with our own presence. "As the ferry slowly moves along Fjærland fjord, you look behind and see the Glacier Museum lying on the lush bright plain like a huge pale-gray stone. I always wondered where the giant moss-covered stones which are to be found in the Nordic landscape come from."

Sverre Fehn. Norwegian Glacier Museum in Fjærland, 1991

Model

We find a simple and direct gesture that acts like a focus for human

movement and light, giving their physics architectonic expression.

The experience of the space: the Glacier museum in Fjærland.

ØKAW Architects. Olympic Ski-jumping Arena in

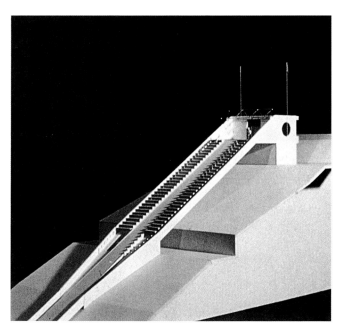

Model of the Ski-jumping Arena

We have been used to imagining ski jumping arenas as extremely fascinating constructions that spectacularly dominate the Alpine hillscapes. The ski-jumping arena, with its 120 and 90 m jumps, built for the Lillehammer Winter Olympics in 1994 by ØKAW Architects, followed the opposite strategy.

Here, the main concern was to adapt the required jumping-profile to the existing hillscape configuration, by merging the natural and man-made elements of the construction. However, there was no intention of imitating nature. Rather, the individual parts, the earthworks, the concrete and the stone structure were approached with a clarity which took their individual architectonic functions into consideration, in order for them to complement each other and perform their functional roles within the new spatial whole.

Modern ski-jumps are built according to an international standard that defines their size and vertical profile. For the safety of the jumpers, the position and the shape of all the parts of the jump have to be designed in order to provide as much protection as possible from the wind. Ideally suitable slopes, which do not require any major alterations to the existing terrain, are difficult to find. Conditions in Lillehammer meant that it was basically possible to use the existing profile of the terrain as a flying-hill. However, the slope below the jump was too steep to create a horizontal run-off and had to be artificially heightened by using local rubble to create a 17-meter-high, semi-circular mound. As a contrast, the towers which form the upper part of the hillside with the start, in-runs and the cantilevered jumps, were constructed in raw concrete dyed with bluish iron-oxide, thus creating a counterbalance to the landscape. The spectators area with 40,000 seats is firmly anchored to the ground, providing a solemn, low-profile focus for competitions and ceremonies, to counterpoint the sweep of the jumps.

The individual parts, the earthw

stone structure were approached

their individual architectonic fun

Merging nature and construction:the Oly

The new building of the Art Gallery represents

a distinctive, almost unique, expressive statement.

The new Art Gallery in Lillehammer, a strategically conveiced building.

Entrance

The Lillehammer Art Gallery extension was built by the Snøhetta Office for Architecture and Landscaping as the main contribution to the cultural activities during the 1994 Winter Olympics. The new building represents a distinctive, almost unique, expressive statement. However, under the surface of its original, formal gesture, it seems to be a very strategically conceived building. Traces of the same approach are also to be found in some of Snøhetta's other projects, particularly in the project for the New Alexandrian Library, now under construction.

The production of architecture today is confronted at various levels with an ever growing complexity of conditions which are, as a rule, unstable. Therefore, architecture is expected to provide an open structure which is not fixed in a ny way, to retain a high degree of spatial freedom and to accommodate the complexities of life. At the same time, it is increasingly expected to be singular and distinctive, to react precisely to the given requirements and to be an expression of the genius loci. To conceive these two layers in such a way that they could relate organically to each other according to an overall spatial idea is considered by Snøhetta to be a central issue.

The simplicity of the building programme for the new building, including the areas for temporary exibitions, offices and technical services, was challenged on two points: the difficult conditions which accompanied the extension to the existing gallery space and the indeterminate, somehow fluid character of its urban setting - Lillehammer's Town Square, a place underlined by the strong presence of the regular urban layout, but without clear spatial boundaries and surrounded by a messy assembly of

heterogeneous buildings. In fact, the new art gallery acts as a large extension to the gallery spaces on the upper floor of the existing Town Museum, a brutalist concrete structure from the 60s. Its ground floor was given the separate function of housing the town's cinema, making a new entrance from the square necessary. The new building has been clearly detached from the old part of the gallery and the intervening space has been made into an articulated sculpture garden. The exhibition rooms of both buildings are conceived in the form of an extended, sinuous telescope. The dramatically cantilevered protrusion of the new building colonizes the Town Square, giving the new building a striking presence in the town's centre.

The surface of the square is continued through the glazed vestibule underneath the prow up to the granite steps leading to the gallery plateau, and passes under the covered bridge overlooking the garden on the way to the exhibition areas in the old building. The spatial idea is based on the theme of a large plateau configuration and on the generous, unbroken spatial movement which can easily accommodate the complexities of the programme with a great degree of freedom. This passage through the building is carefully organized and articulated into rhythmical spatial sequences and complemented by the incidence of natural light. Enveloping or containing structures are another theme. They are easily able to react to individual formal intentions, spatial needs and light and communicate these qualities to the outside world. They are like huge spatial vessels, usually devoid of traditional openings and roofscapes which allow natural light to fall from above. The undulating, hovering hulk of the gallery,

clad in the pale larch-wood, seems like a piece of furniture when seen from the square. Its tranquil monumentality underlines the autonomous character of the new object and questions the scale of the surrounding buildings. Inside, it seems like a special device to store the works of art and to give them space and light; it precisely measures the effect of the mysterious messages of its inner life on the public urban space.

The configurations of extensive plateaus and enveloping structures have been conceived relatively independently of each other. Organized and constructed in relation to the nature of the given architectonic problem, these two configurations permit various architectonic interpretations. The architecture becomes an "artificial mountain", more an "organism" than just a building in which the different movements of its inner life are turned into outer expression.

Façade

The new building for lectures and classes, which was designed by Blå Strek Architects, is envisaged as the first phase of major extensions to the University of Tromsø in Northern Norway. The project is located in the central area of the university complex: it was built according to an open-plan Sixties scheme in a leftover, undefined spatial void, between anonymous clumps of buildings of the different faculties. The tacit movements of the sloping terrain that connect this space to the distant North-Atlantic coast are the only visible reminder of what is local and specific to the site. Urban voids, fragmented and disintegrated environments, are becoming the most natural sites for architecture today. These are places without any immediately re-cognizable qualities, without anything predetermined that architects could relate to and use to legitimate their decisions - nevertheless, these places have a certain vague identity. In what way can such places create a context that is culturally relevant and supportive

of the architecture of the future? In the case of the central area of Tromsø University, the sloping, empty site is planned as a public green space with regular rows of trees. The dense perspective of the rows of trees gives it the character of an undulating park landscape. The trees fill the void extending to the walls of the old buildings and allow the existing undefined spatial area to be experienced as a new shape. This new shape, the homogeneous green mass of trees, the mediating space of a gradually emerging new landscape will be the new context - in both conceptual and real terms - of the project. The extensive public green space is seen as an integral part of the architectonic proposal and as the objective of its design. The new architecture is intended to be placed in the park as a cluster of added and sculpturally individualized simple structures arranged in a collage-like composition. The variations of their formal and material properties are a reference to the simple functional units

of the building programme: the triangular auditorium is clad with black stone, the semicircular row of small rooms with metal sheets, the linking gallery structure is constructed of wood. They will determine the spatial qualities of the new landscape by defining its boundaries anew, organizing new spatial sequences and new local landmarks, linking and separating areas. They will, in this way, allow local qualities which were previously hidden to appear again as a part of the new spatial constellation and transform them into specific places.

The variations of their formal and material properies are a reference

to the simple functional units of the building programme...

A new landscape: the new building for classes and lectures at the university of Tromsø.

Detail of the construction

Ground plan

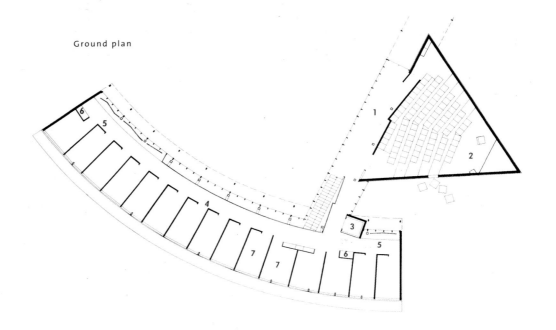

Blå Strek Architects. Annex to the University in Tromsø, 1994

Interior View, construction detail

Jan Olav Jensen. Truck-Garage, goods terminal Rølvsøy, 1990

The essence and meaning of the architectonic design are to be found

in its constructional logic and its inventive pragmatic approach.

A constructional clarity and the honest use of materials: the Garage in Rølvsøy.

52 | 53

Ground plan and section

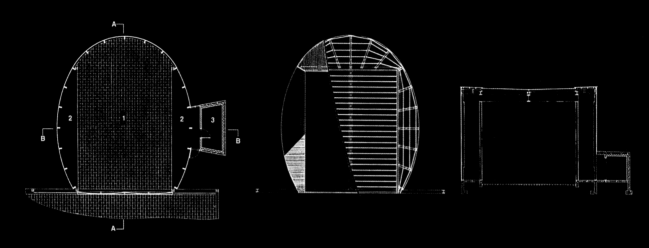

The ideas of constructional clarity and the "honest" use of building materials are an integral part of Nordic architectural thinking. Their conceptual roots are integrated in the cultural values of society and trace their distant origins back to the ethics of traditional crafts. Precise articulation of bearing and borne structural parts is openly stated and, therefore, easily readable. Load-bearing elements are experienced and understood as bearing loads, cladding elements as elements which clad, meeting the ground as a dramatic moment of building that is to be revealed as such. Materials and their structural properties are to reveal themselves directly.

By articulating the structural elements, different openings and incidences of light appear, allowing in Nordic light in its wealth of varieties. Where structure and light meet, the world of shadows emerges, which, in turn, makes the experience of light and space possible. The concept of architecture is centred around the "timeless" values of construction and material and the "basic" principles of making. Confrontation with a real building programme requires absolute precision. Seen in this way, architecture could once again become the

"natural" and inevitable answer to the needs of everyday life. The garage to house and service a huge 42-ton gaff-truck for loading and unloading containers was built by Jan Olav Jensen in 1990 on a faceless, flat site inside the goods terminal in Rølvsøy, which is located on the industrial periphery of Oslo: a simple and functional building - a shed which does not stand in isolation - of straightforward clarity and precision and experienceable as such. But let us use the architect's own words: "The stabilizing main steel construction, rectangular in its ground plan, is encircled by the secondary construction, oval-shaped and made of wood. The oval-shaped outer wall is interrupted by a double sliding-gate. The roof surface between the steel construction and the outer wall is covered with the translucent plastic sheets which provide the area used for maintenance of the truck with light. The frame of the outer wall is constructed of laminated wooden posts, held in place by steel shoes in the lower part of the stable steel construction and anchored to its upper part by double wooden rafters ... The axial distance between the laminated wooden posts is over two metres. The fact that the outer

wall is curved makes this possible, without creating any instability in the panels." This description is like a little manifesto. The "essence" and meaning of the architectonic design are to be found in its constructional logic and its inventive pragmatic approach to building, in allowing its constructional reality to become clearly visible. It is in the manner of instructions for "do-it-yourself" assembly, as if it is expected that the building process will be repeated often.

Small houses, huts and cabins are fascinating structures. Born out of the confrontation with life and natural elements, they express a preference for anonymous architecture, either vernacular or modern. They are, owing to their modesty and tranquillity, seldom topics of architectural exhibitions. If architecture is about how people live and use things, how they come and go, then these innocent buildings are perfect examples of how this is accomplished: they are forms where human life and the life of a place come together in a most intimate way. The place becomes the inside, identified with the familiar movements, with whoever dwells there for a while. This is due to the private, almost personal nature of identification with the human body. They represent an architecture of the interior an this is what makes all the blinds, shutters and locking devices so important. Small and well-constructed, usually in wood, they are frameworks of the minimal dimensions of life. They do not have a definite façade; rather, it changes its expression during the course of the day and night and as the seasons progress and change. Basically, they deal with the unfinished as they belong to the processes of growth and change. In Norway people call them generation-huts because they reflect the progress of families. They grow when new members are added to the family by adding new units under the same, common roof. The Hagem summer hut was built in Melbyfjorden on the southern coast of Norway in 1990 by the Lund Hagem

Office of Architects. It is a simple building with a wooden framework construction, which follows the coastline and sensitively relates to the rocky granite landscape. It is placed in such a way that it follows the natural course of the terrain, through which a path passes. The outside areas are an important part of the ground plan, an external gallery, a passage, an open kitchen and a terrace; they connect the life of the individual units and provide ventilation in the warm summer months. The row of identical, small rooms ends in the family living room which is located on the west side and lets the evening sun in through the smooth surface of huge window-panes - beyond this is the reflection in the water of the rugged surface of the granite rocks. The floor of the summer hut closely follows the lines of the landscape; the protruding, flat roof is a reference to the horizon and to the open sea. The hut is a simple but intricate human structure, where the "greatness" of its architecture lies in its simplicity. This is architecture which is capable of eluding our conscious perception.

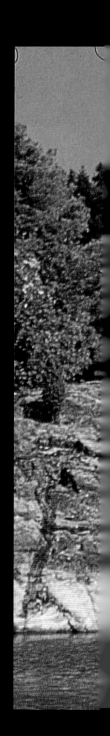

The hut is simple but intricate human structure, where the greatness of this architecture lies in its simplicity.

A reference to the horizon and the sea: the sommer hut Hagem.

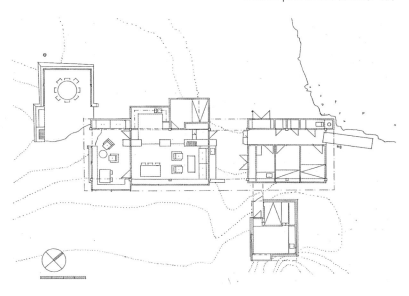

Lund Hagem. Sommer hut in Melbyfjorden

A modest simplicity is traditionally the character

and the beauty of Swedish architecture.

Jöran Lindvall on the fundamental principle of Swedish architecture.

Sweden

Form of State: Parliamentary Monarchy since 1909, **Area:** 449,964 km2, **Inhabitants (1992):** 8,712,000, **Capital:** Stockholm
Gross National Product, 1992 per capita: $ 27,010, **Gross Domestic Product 1992:** $ 220,834 Mio , **Unemployment (Average, 1993):** 9.6%

t is not only a rhetorical phrase to say that poverty has been very important for the development of Swedish architecture's specific character. It is the absolute truth. This may seem hard to believe as Sweden today is such a wealthy country, but here are some facts. 25% of our population left the country for America by the end of the 19th century because they were starving. Only Ireland lost more of its population. At the turn of the century the average life expectancy was only 52 years and in the early part of the 20th century, Sweden was still a rural country with miserable living conditions for its population. Stockholm was known to be one of the most horrible cities in Europe. The turning point came with a massive exploitation of the forests and other natural resources towards the end of the 19th century and the establishment of several successful industries at the turn of the century. But it was only in 1955 that half of the population had moved into towns, much later than in most other European countries. This late migration process also explains why almost the entire stock of buildings in Sweden today is comparatively young. Almost 95% of the built space which we use today have been built in the 20th century, 75% of all dwellings have been built after 1945, and 50% after 1960.

A modest simplicity is traditionally the character and the beauty of Swedish architecture. By the end of the 18th century, the new Neo-Classicism came to Sweden and in short time became a widely accepted and beloved style for buildings, furnitures and many everyday objects. That Neo-Classicism was characterized by a sophisticated simplicity which quite easily could be adopted to the limited resources of our relatively poor country aristocracy and the equally poor population in our cities. That classicism, "married" to vernacular building techniques and craftsmanship, evolved into a specific Swedish and Nordic building tradition which has then, with some few interruptions, remained the dominating character of our architecture. This building tradition is very rational and well adapted to our functional demands. Its decorative elements are rather few but painstakingly elaborated and adopted to the regional style. Wood often replaces stone. Painted walls imitate textiles. Furniture has a somewhat clumsy elegance. The first two decades of our century were strongly dominated by these Neo-Classical traditions but with new, even more simplified variations which outside

our country became known as Swedish Grace. Parallels appeared all over the Nordic countries and this have later been named Nordic classicism. Most of this architecture expresses again a functional rationalism within limited resources. Particularly in housing, the classical elements were very reduced to simplified decorations within elegantly controlled proportions. Modernism came to Sweden in the late 20s and made a tremendous breakthrough at the Stockholm Exhibition 1930. The other Nordic countries also rapidly adopted these new ideas which in our countries were called Functionalism. The architects of that time recognized the new style as a radical change in their work and their architecture. There is no doubt that they experienced a new ideology which opposed Classicism and gave them a new freedom in designing their buildings. Today, based on our new understanding about the roots and the regional variations of Modernism, we can see that Nordic Functionalism, in many aspects, also can be described as only a further step in the development and simplification of our Nordic Classicism. The rational character of that Classicism and its already reduced ornaments and decorations is the key for understanding this development. Both Neo-Classicism and early Functionalism were created within quite limited resources. That is also true for the period from the late 1940s to the late 1960s, today considered a golden age in Swedish architecture. That is when the modern welfare society was consolidated within harmonious housing areas and a large number of well designed public buildings characterized by a strong stoicism. In the late 1960s a process of great change started in our society. We developed from a situation of quite limited resources into a society where much greater economical possibilities existed and an obvious affluence was established. That has strongly effected our entire society including its architecture. Both private and public investors started to commission buildings of more sophisticated ambitions, buildings meant to be impressive, buildings that should announce the power and creative development of their owners. All kinds of new styles were introduced and many buildings were made to look as if they stood in one of the great metropolises of the world. New materials and new techniques were introduced without reasonable control of their consequences. Today we have a large stock of buildings

in various, often extravagant styles, but these are buildings which are already deteriorating badly, which are severely detrimental to the health of their inhabitants and users. Some of these building might be perceived as interesting architecture but what does that matter if our children develop lifelong allergies from living in them. The essentially unsatisfactory condition of contemporary architecture in Sweden as in many other countries has developed from the general situation in contemporary society: large and quickly earned profits seem to mean more than long-term ambitions and responsibility. Too much money has been available and far too many of those involved in the modern building process have not accepted their responsibility. Harsher critizism has been earned by all those clients and investors who have not more carefully examined what they have received for their investments. On the other hand, I must make clear that we also have a considerable number of serious and talented clients, architects and builders who have worked with great responsibility and created solid and healthy buildings of architectural quality. Our hope for the future must remain with those who can carry on and further develop the traditions of modest simplicity in our architecture. We can see that a number of different styles are in parallel use, that many architects look back to national and Nordic traditions in order to find solid ideals for future developments and that they try to explore a new simplicity combined with very contemporary influences.

During recent years I have had several reasons to study museum buildings, both in Sweden and abroad. For a long time we could read about all these European new museum buildings. And I must admit that we were rather envious. We felt that we had been left behind and that we had no buildings of this new and impressive character. I then started to visit these new museums, where I met directors and museum people who were rather disappointed with what they had received. Their new museums did not fulfill their requisites. Their museums were sophisticated architecure rather than functional museum buildings. There had been severe shortcomings in the dialogue between the architects and their clients. Sometimes I had the impression that the new museums were mainly manifestations of local or national politicians. Later I also had reason to study all museums which had been built in Sweden over the last ten years. To my pleasant surprise, I found many more new museums than I had known. Most of them rather small but very important for their enviroments. And I found a number of satisfied museum people. They have achieved what they wanted with their new museums or annexes.

These buildings are not particularly spectacular but they fulfill, within their circumstances, their purpose better than many of the great new museums in Europe, which makes me happy and proud. I also learned that all these museums had been built within very limited resources. The clients had been forced to act cleverly in order to achieve what they wanted. They had been able to establish a good dialogue with their architects, who in turn had listened to museum people in a serious way.

Most of this architecture expresses a functional rationalism within limited resources.

Classical elements, simplified decorations and elegantly controlled proportions were characterizing most of the housing projects in Sweden.

Carl Nyrén. Housing in Starrbäcksängen, Stockholm 1989-92
photo: Åke Lindman

Housing in Starrbäcksängen, detail of the façade - photo: Åke Lindman

This architecture is a good representative of

the Swedish building traditions on the

borderline between Classicism and Modernism.

The aesthetic principle of Johan Celsing's housing block.

Johan Celsing. Housing block Princen,
Motala 1994 - photo: Fabio Galli

Housing block Princen - photo: Fabio Galli

One of these museums is the extension
of the County Museum in Jönköping by
architect Carl Nyrén. For a long time the
museum had required more space but
the local politicians had not found it
possible to invest in a new museum
building. Finally it became necessary
to build new storage space for the
growing collection of the museum.
The old exhibition premises were
converted into storage space in 1991.
The new museum, realized in simple
but elegant materials, has been
considered among the best architecture
of recent years. It therefore introduces
my list of good new Swedish architecture
I have chosen from some different
tendencies which I find interesting
and representative for the best of what
we build.

The new museum, realized in simple but elegant materials, has

been considered among the best architecture of recent years.

The County Museum in Jönköping by Carl Nyrén.

Carl Nyrén. County Museum in Jönköping, 1991
photos: Max Plunger

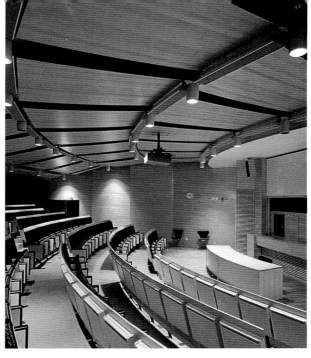

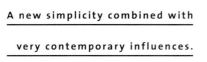

A new simplicity combined with

very contemporary influences.

Skandinavian tradition as a model for future development.

Lecture hall of the Enskilda Banken - photo: Kjell A. Larsson

Rosenberg Architects. Skandinaviska Enskilda Banken, Rissne 1992 - photo: Kjell A. Larsson

The Graphics Centre has been conceived in a style which is slightly unusual for Sweden. It is however well used in a very functional and modest way.

The building's performance fulfils the expectations.

Stintzing Architects. Graphics Centre in Tumba, 1991 - photo: Bertil Bylin

The Graphics Center in Tumba south of Stockholm by Stintzing Architects (1991) has been conceived in a style which is slightly unusual for Sweden. It is however well used in a very functional and modest way.
The Office for Skandinaviska Enskilda Banken, Rissne, in the northwest surburbs of Stockholm by Rosenberg Architects (1992): In its east-west-dimension, the very large building adapts to a regional highway on its northern side. The large northern façade is simplified but very strong in its design. The building's interior has, despite its size, a graceful elegance based upon the modest simplification of many details.

The Housing area Starrbäcksängen in Stockholm by the bureau of Carl Nyrén (1989-92) has taken great inspiration from the Stockholm Exhibition 1930 and represents distinctly that new Functionalism which, in its proportions, was greatly influenced by the Nordic Neo-Classicism of the 1920s. The circular city plan was designed by Alexander Wolodarsky of the Stockholm City planning office. The buildings in the centre have light colours which become somewhat darker on the periphery.

Similar the Housing block Princen in the centre of Motala by Johan Celsing (1994): This architecture is a good representative of the Swedish building traditions on the borderline between Classicism and Modernism.

Is architecture in Finland likely to

remain merely a religious substitute?

Roger Connah on clarity as an architectural dogma in Finnish architecture.

6 | FIVES. FIN DE SIÈCLE TRACES IN FINNISH
ARCHITECTURE. ROGER CONNAH.

Finland

Form of State: Republic since 1919, **Area:** 338,139 km2, **Inhabitants (End of 1993):** 5,080,000 **Capital:** Helsinki
Gross National Product 1992, per capita: $ 21.970, **Gross Domestic Product 1992:** $ 93,869 Mio, **Unemployment (Average, 1993):** 18.2%

Five. The sum of four plus one. The hour five. Five o'clock tea. The five supposed mental faculties. Sign. Touch. Smell. Taste. Hearing. A five-finger exercise. A five-finger architectural exercise. List the best five buildings during the last five years. In your country. In anyone's country! Don't you just hate catalogues? Finnish architecture! Brilliantly competent, aesthetics of the unadorned? Admirably humane, deliciously restrained? Or, Nordic nononsense, circumstance without pomp? Listing five buildings with traces of the fin de siècle is a hard task in any country. But in Finland, we need to throw away the safety net. For too long, Finnish architecture has appeared homogeneous. We even speak of Finnish architecture and not architecture from Finland. The nationalistic urge to define space and place offers itself a little too readily. We think, especially as foreigners, that we know what type of buildings, what type of environments will be produced in such a society. We occupy a model of architecture in our brains. We scan the buildings to suit that model. At least I know I do. We expect - and invariably are not disappointed - buildings of sound construction, immaculate detailing and finishing, climatic ingenuity and Finnish endurance. "Sisu" is the word used to explain Winter War endurance and Rally Driving success. We would get architecture with a heavy right foot, if it were not for that other mythology, clarity. A quest long past its sell-by date: is architecture in Finland likley to remain merely a religious substitute? Clarity is a seductive promotional quality. Clarity might also just be one of those attractive errors that modernism thought it had got away with. Clarity is like the perfect murder until someone decides to make a TV series out of it. We can sypathise with the words of the architect from Finland, Kai Wartiainen who sees Le Corbusier as a "socially disturbed person" longing for the simple, lonesome cloister life. If this produces a monastic vision of modernism, then Finnish architecture collides so well with this vision. Clarity became ineffable and unchallenged. Clarity ruled. Yet clarity, like restraint, always threatens its own myth. Finland is a strong Lutheran society with a desperate Soviet hangover. It is also a society hung on self-righteous tradition. The architects - let us at present speak of them collectively - have become comfortable with what is a grounded, even essentialist, vision of architecture. Finland was politically correct before

the term was invented. The dialectic stubbornness of the 1960s and 1970s produced a period of amputation that is only now seeing its fall out researched. What we can call Marxist panic removed the tradition that Finnish architecture was founded on. In the 1980s, that confusing decade of pluralism, architecture opened itself to the simplistic if not naive thrill. Everyone was seduced. It takes talent to pluralize, to carnivalise. We must remember; there is no Paul Feyerabend in Finland. An older generation of architects now find themselves in political and cultural power, yet the status of architecture as problem solver, as organiser of a social life, is at its professional lowest. In architecture, no risk becomes the best risk. A doomed strategy. Realisation of this loss of status for architecture has produced a new essentialism. The profession has closed up rather than opened to the contemporary tension. Architects are found trying to re-instate the very tradition their virtuous amputation cut off. It is no surprise that whilst the lectures on phenemonology and animalism, Heidegger and Bachelard, the young refuse to drink beer and turn their own architecture into a performance art. They speak of taste, architectural metaphor and material eclecticism. The stakes in Finnish architecture are high because the winnings seem so poor. This is crucial for the present. In a society where it was once fashionable not to debate architecture but do, it is now criminal to do without debating. The critical discourse is painfully absent. There is an immense reluctance to attempt any analytic view of the immediate moment. Architects are playing - to use Rafael Moneo - the "noble savage". A rather privileged savage in Finland. Moneo is right; to reflect on architecture is an imperative mandate. If we applaud the Finnish scene for not getting too involved in architecture as text, and other philosophical scaffolding, we should know also what it has lost by not encountering this discourse. Paradoxically the time is radically out of joint. It means this. Some architects are now carring out projects that should have been done ten or twenty years ago. Lost zones of an architectural modernism are dicovered as if they are a new cultural birthright for late ideologues. Candela, Otto, Tange, Archigram, The Metabolists, Chernikhov, Finsterlin, Scharoun etc. - not to mention Haring, Mendelsohn, Taut - are rediscovered by a generation of teachers that wilfully left them out of the modernist

agenda. I said we should throw away the safety net. Whatever the claims for an architecture that is admirable, restrained, even a brilliant swerve within an orthodox modernism, we must begin with the obvious. Finnish architecture has survived for a period in extreme self-righteousness.
In the 1950s the architect was God. In the 1960s the architect was dialectic. In the 1970s the architect was demolition man. In the 1980s the architect was every man. In the 1990s the architect - with exception - is a spinning "noble savage". It is time for architecture to come out. I propose to introduce five exceptions which will help us analyse the decentralised and decentralising tendencies in architecture this far north. We must attempt, however impossible, a mapping of the best contemporary traces in the architecture. To explore and map the heuristic values of these projects I will tie them to the five senses and five recent statements made about Finnish architecture. The five projects selected here for this purpose are as follows:
Feeling Mantyniemi. We look at Reima Pietilä's final project, The Official Residence of the President of Finland in Helsinki. Courage, paradox and ideological nature.
Touching Tasa. In Jyrki Tasa's Library in Kuhmo, Central Finland we explore not mediated minimalism but the minimal carnival.
Smelling Lusto. Ilmari Lahdelma and Rainer Mahlermaki's Forestry Information Centre is called Lusto. It is in Punkaharju near Savonlinna. We try back up the hearse and sniff the future not the past of architecture
Tasting Wartiainen's. Understanding taste, fashion and architectural production in Kai Wartiainen's Factory 2000, Santasalo.
Hearing Saarijarvi. We visit the young architect, Matti Sanaksenaho's little chapel, The Empty Space in the deep forest in Saarijarvi, Central Finland. We listen to the silence the professors only talk about.
Each of these projects stands, in their own way, in the shadow of others. We will have little time to explore this but it needs stating; they develop in and across the work of others.

To balance some of the gloomier statements made earlier about the current state of the profession and discipline, it must be recalled that the actual architectural development and debate in Finland is often privileged as a built debate. Arguments rage in silence across restaurants and bars but the real forum for the essentially mute majority in the Finnish culture is within the built architecture. We should look for the positive traces and signs, the intellectual alertness and relocated interest that indicate future moves within architecture and its role in society. Architecture might not be as privileged as it imagined itself to be some five years ago.

Feeling Mantyniemi

"The building is of the past and I'm only interested in the future." The Official Residence of The President of Finland as a building has become identified through its place name: Mantyniemi. Literally this means "pine-point". Recently a member of the lost generation in the Finnish architecture, one of the many armchair Marxist-Leninists, responded with the comment: "The building is of the past and I'm only interested in the future." Coming from a collective mind that had systematically excluded whole zones of architecture from the agenda in the 1960s and 1970s this statement is revealing. Does going back in time intellectually imply a less sharp focus on contemporary architecture? Mantyniemi with its clear literal symbolism, its obvious phenomenological resonance, prompts the society to ask the obvious. How and why does it exit the forest and cultivate its own existence? Has colour, form and modernism masked the noble savage? Does the noble savage merely want cultivated images and experiences of what is "out there" in the wilderness? The consistency with which Pietilä's civil courage and critical bravery have been ignored, along with his architecture, long demonstrated the thinness of critical debate in Finland. We must identify this architectural courage. Mantyniemi is pivotal in the Finnish society's discourse with identity, symbolism and the ideology of nature itself within the culture. Pietilä was too good an architect not to know that nature is but one alibi for the architectural sequence and form. His alertness to mythology and metaphors made him reassuringly playful before someone else could get there. Mantyniemi both entertains the innocence of such architecture and interrogates it. Mantyniemi may be incomprehensible to many for its own monologue and its isolation from critical interlocutation. But Pietilä was the voice in Finnish architecture that for so long at least kept the conversation going. In a country that can be silent in three languages, Finnish, Swedish and Tourism, this cannot be underestimated. Let's be clear about this. Few Finnish architects have had the ability and nerve to interrogate their own strategies. Critical energy is always outwards, beyond the analytic, tending torwards the journalistic. Few architects have opted for the temptation that the arbitrary point of departure for architecture can be hunted, tracked down and then moulded into an architecture all one's own. Mantyniemi is the result of the flaw. Tireless in this respect, Pietilä thought whilst he spoke, wrote whilst he drew. Pietilä can be said to design also the flaws in the architectural event, errors in the sequence, the twist in the forest, where not quite everything comes out as we think. Before it becomes fashionable to speak of the postanalytic, Pietilä always attempted an architecture on the move. Of course, an architect of confidence can invite the attraction of error into his or her work. An architect of essentialist drama will find this difficult. Pietilä was never far from acknowledging that the essentialist drama in contemporary Finnish architecture used modernism as contingent, arbitrary conventions from which to construct a clarity. For Pietilä, without the reassurance of architectural stealth, some wonderfully wilful mythology and wit, these conventions could never become deep-rooted myths. They could then never become local, in the cultural sense. Instead, acknowledging the fragility of myth itself, Pietilä made no pretence of working within an ambiguous cultural resonance. Mantyniemi demonstrates better than most what this ambiguity between nature and culture is in built form. In a country where nature is read as culture so relentlessly, many other architects prefer to remain detached critically from this task. This is an acceptable stance. But it is not the literal symbolism up there on record for us to follow, it is Pietilä's approach to architecture. It is the process by which he turns a trace into built form. The way Pietilä and Mantyniemi fold everything back into itself and produce the reverse of architecture, will always remain relevant. As analytic diagrams, theoretical errors and cultural logic, the heuristic value of a project like Mantyniemi should be clear. It will, though, take some years before the largely pessimistic commentary and approach to Pietilä in his own country reach some balance. Analytically slippery, Pietilä's integrity remains a painful reminder of what is being left out of contemporary architecture.

Touching Tasa

One often hears the statement. "The Finns are good at doing what they do so well." The tautology is interesting. It is tacit works that should worry the Finns themselves. We also often hear that the Finns do not kitsch or irony so well. In fact, the claims for this grand counter strategy, even an adventurous lightness, against pernicious internationalism, is too often confused with innocence. To put the next building, Kuhmo Library by the architect Jyrki Tasa in context, we might liken it to how Alan J. Plattus uses Rorty's concept of the philosopher as "liberal ironist". "The parallel model of philosophy as a sort of ongoing and even inconclusive conversation, rather than a rigorous analytic exercise or a definitive ontological grounding of things beyond time and space, is an attractive characterization of relationships developed in a project like the Kuhmo Library with its difficult context and circumstances". (Plattus, "Toward a Post-Analytic Architecture.")

Mantyniemi is pivotal in the Finnish society's discourse with identity, symbolism and the ideology of nature.

Reflecting the mythology: the Residence of the Finnish President.

Mantyniemi, interior view

Raili & Reima Pietilä. Mantyniemi, The Official Residence of the President of Finland, Helsiniki 1993
photos: Raili Pietilä, Voitto Niemelä

Nurmela, Raimoranta & Tasa. Library in Kuhmo, 1989
photo: Jyrki Tasa

By going for more lightness and fantasy, more carnival,

Kuhmo indicates a trace of things that come.

A step further in debate on architecture: the library in Kuhmo.

Library in Kuhmo
photo: Anthi Luutonen

I have hijacked the comment of Plattus for our own purpose. But it stands. Much inferior architectures in Finland can have the gleaming spirit of packaged biscuit tins, yet one step into the interiors will demonstrate weak functional movement, a loose treatment of space and ungenerous architectural thinking. Architectural formalism and tacit vocabulary games distort the critical discomfort and should worry us. An international tokenism begins to suggest that architecture in Finland could become satisfied with neither the materiality and dynamism nor the uncompromising purism and architectural production of earlier grander examples. We have to listen to the diaspora of the postmodern debate here. Few do the Post-Modern well, it is also said. Like all who can enter the vocabulary and see the spectacle within the space itself, Jyrki Tasa is a rare Finnish architect. For me it is Tasa's ability to introduce a controlled fantasy into a smuggled form that must be seen as another indication of what can be achieved when a strong ability to interrogate architecture negotiates the unpalatable. The profession is often underhand with such a talent. It can dismiss the work of one architect for the inadequacies of other architecture. It also dismisses it for not conforming to a normative discourse. This is erroneous. Intellectually such an attack assumes the monstrous carnival errors of others naturally follow in Tasa's work. Tasa is too good an architect to fall for this.

His range of sculptural and eclectic comment in Finnish architecture illustrates a wider gamble. He is the "liberal ironist" par excellence. His work has done more to keep the architectural conversation going than many a lecture and theoretical exposé of the phenomenological language and pessimism in contemporary culture. By so doing, by so tilting the balance of simple achievement and going for more lightness and fantasy, more carnival, Kuhmo indicates a trace of things to come. We should search the evidence of the architecture for the talent that lies beyond its own careful and reassuringly playful form. Kuhmo is a spectacular step further in the rather quiet evolution of the Nordic library. Long has been the model of Alvar Aalto's top-lit, elegantly restrained interiors. These are supposed to resonate like a forest clearing. Often it is a Lutheran clearing of stubborn individual study and quietness. In Finland it is a retreat to knowledge so often linked with winter nights and days. A matter of survival, perhaps, this is the necessary twentieth century collision between Le Corbusier's cloistered modernism and the climatic Nordic resistance. Pietilä's Main Library in Tampere, uncomfortably and courageously formed from such arbitrary Celtic points of departure as a dead sheep (finally a capercaille!) gave the library in Finland a new twist. In long winter months, the library as cultural haven, as community centre has long been crucial to smaller Finnish towns.

Like Pietilä, Tasa has always been interested in the dynamic relationship between mass and form. Space is not left to complement the vivid and lucid exterior, it continues the journey that architecture itself can offer. Inside the library, the boulevard, the walkway, interiorises the event. With knowledge we are, always, controlled by its movement. The library is not static, not cloistered, not secluded. Knowledge is adventurous, spectacular even. Knowledge is certainly the carnival. One could speak of a narrative in Tasa's work without being held back by theories of architectural correctness or literary props. We see a fantasy architecture of quiet specific material, locality and space. Tasa's work is divergent not convergent, sculptural not effacing. The dignity is not an applied geometric decor, use of material underscores the careful dynamics. Colour and spaciousness come from a subtle interplay of light, height and colour. Where the neo-modernists opt for enriching a basically grounded minimalism, Tasa identifies the austere and goes for the kill. Taking all the generous qualities attributed to the "correct" architecture, the light-filled central axis, quality of detailing, contact with the landscape, he pumps up the volume with more than the occasional casual gesture. But there is nothing casual about his interplay between the crystalline and organic, between the labyrinth and flame.

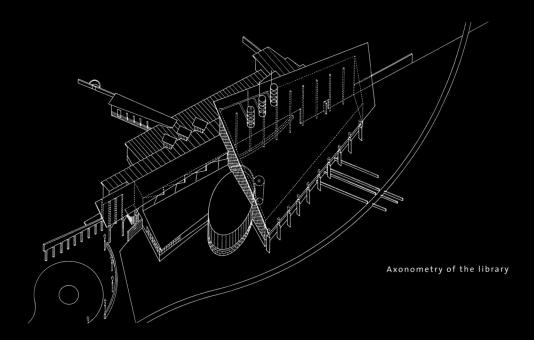

Axonometry of the library

Echo, accentuation and counterpoint make

Lusto a more sophisticated achievement.

Architecture without being cramped or misleading: Lusto the Finnish Forestry Information Centre.

Tasa doesn't so much as intervene in a highly ordered part, he crashes through with renewed vigour. The building can be read as the pages of the children's book there on the shelves. Kuhmo also continues the detachment from the essentialist model of modernism in Finland; the sculptural element is pointed up within an apparent stricter geometry. Tasa quietly gets on with the dismantling and re-assemblage of architectural form itself. Kuhmo begs not for the minimalist appeal to the randow. Instead Kuhmo furthers this sculptural in and breaks with orthodox modernism. Unafraid of introducing the element of fun, we get the suggestion even of magic spaces. Star spangled skies, the oval children's room, the light columns and mushroom forms make a total work. Detail is not so much a reinforcement of the general elegance of the solution, but an assurance of surprise. Taken near the edge of playfulness, Tasa seems to have that ability of knowing how far is too far to go. The Finns are good at doing what they do so well. When, of course, they do it so well.

And Tasa does.

Smelling Lusto

"We don't have the best buildings in the world, but we have fewer of the worst." The statement is an odd one. What begins as a hint of the inferiority complex often met in the Finnish society, can turn quickly into stubbornness. It speaks of the middle ground, the control of excess and extremity. If there is not a stubbornness about international privilege then we can hear the hint of defence. The apologia hints at the uncanny feeling that the

architectural profession has stood still. Whilst splendid versions of a polished late Moderns continue to fill the pages of the magazines, the freshness of architectural debate and detail is far more difficult to identify. Lusto, the Finnish Forestry Information Centre, is a building to be celebrated without the need of an apology of mere competence. Lusto is the work of Rainer Mahlermaki and Ilmari Lahdelma. These are two members of an already established practice from the 1980s called 8 Studio. The group deserves mention for an incredible command of architectural vocabulary and the achievement of winning competition after competition in that decade. Without as yet any full recognition the group, though splintered now into three separate offices, continues to produce work of significant quality and diversity. Lusto is Finnish for the growth ring of a tree and completed in 1993. Bravely, its symbolic point of departure not only sets out the dynamic programme for the architectural thrill and function, it suggests an architecture that can resonate within the natural and cultural. Movement, control and counterpoint make Lusto a memorable achievement. Concrete and wood are set in a continuous dialogue around two main forms; the wood-clad cylinder and the offset rectangle. These house the exhibition facilities and the workshop, office facilities. Lusto is however a building to smell. Concrete is left unadorned, a brilliant surprise when so much of this material has been cosmeticised over the last decade. Exterior walls are slatted and covered

with the local wood, tamarack, impregnated with the mixture of tar and flaxoil. This old shipbuilding method provides echo and olfactory resonance. A resonance continued as the pine and tamarack floorings are impregnated with natural oil, and the internal pine walls slighty bleached and treated with beeswax. Lusto smells; and it smells well. We do not need to reach for Hugo Boss deodorant.

Echo, accentuation and counterpoint make Lusto a more sophisticated achievement than many more recognisable buildings in contemporary Finland. It takes risk with echo whilst providing a thrilling experience of movement in and through the building. The visitor enters top level and through ramps and spatial overlaps, over bridges and a switchback ramp one is always returned to the centre of the drum. It is difficult to see how trace and re-trace differ this movement from Pietilä's more literal symbolic recreation of the forest space. Lusto overlaps space. Without such a subtle density and control, such architecture would be cramped and misleading. Instead the tight curve, the progression of exhibition entry and spatial level, the ramps, switchback and circulation combine to create a complexity infinitely more subtle than say, Heureka Science centre, a building praised for its complexity in the mid 80s. Complexity too has been a favoured dynamic or discourse in architecture in Finland.

Ilmari Lahdelma & Rainer Mahlermaki. Lusto Forestry Information Centre, Punkaharju 1993
photo: Valokuvaamo Jussi Titainen

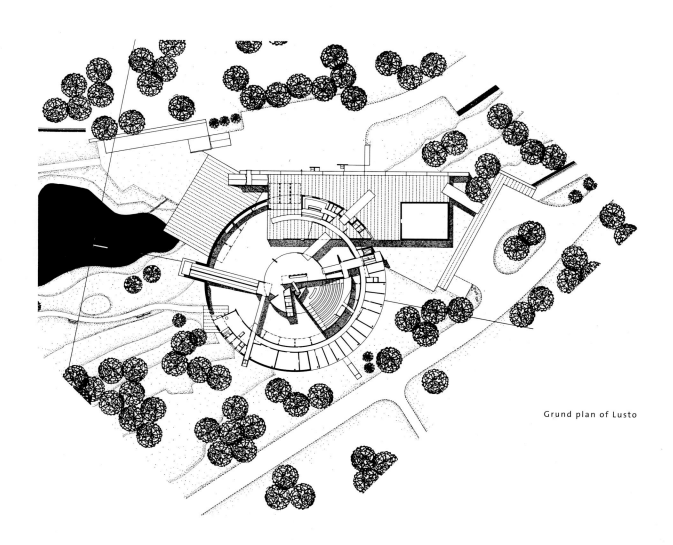

Grund plan of Lusto

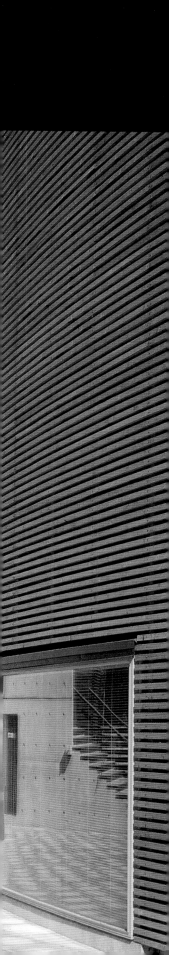

The Santasalo Factory building suggests a parallel enquiry

into the aesthetics and ethics of function, re-use and material.

A real conceptional energy: the Factory 2000.

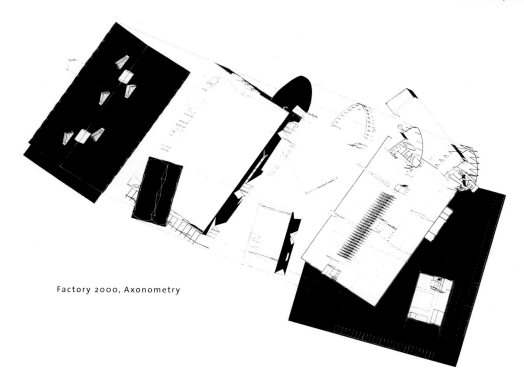

Factory 2000, Axonometry

Matti Sanaksenaho. Chapel Saarijarvi, 1993 - photo: Seppo Sarkkinen

Wartiainen demonstrates an ability to ride these restrictions, whilst seemingly expanding the normal. Not an easy achievement in a risk-free culture. Attempting a landscape through forms and materials, the agenda is clear. In Santasalo the modest, cheap material can, if informed with current ecological awareness, create an architecture that could again reconcile its position in the social structures of normal life. It is an agenda many European architects are engaging; significant for us here is its rarity in critical discourse. Thus for me, Santasalo acknowledges the celebrated joy in smuggling in architecture amidst a restricted discourse. "If Finnish architecture is organic", Wartiainen says, "Swedish architecture is cultivated". Wartiainen takes on the complacency of Finnish architecture with a temperament and swagger much closer to Alvar Aato. But with an iconoclastic talent much closer to Reima Pietilä. Often the establishment's scapegoat, Wartiainen thinks through his architecture. I repeat: he remains one of the few seriously engaged in the cultural and structural logic and production of architecture. In Santasalo, juxtaposition and randomness is used to upset the known artificially cultivated order. Prepared to opt for chance, Wartiainen is - of course - always careful. Reading his buildings indicates why the nuance is not merely in the cultivated detail. The shock of his strategies invites more than a comparison to Gehry. I would agree with Moneo when he says that "the presence of Gehry's architecture has relocated the interests of a younger generation all over the country with amazing vigour." Moneo means America, but the same goes for Europe and Finland. We mentioned the surrealist temperament. Wartiainen not only shares

the civil courage of an architect like Pietilä, he shares that surrealist temperament. Santasalo demonstrates the edge of the surrealist venture; the closeness to a naive gesture determines the expression. A disciplined delinquency served Pietilä well. It will do the same for Wartiainen. In the concrete factory, a project built in 1992, parts of the building were given metaphorical keys. The concrete base of the factory was an anvil. The sand containers was an aerosol can, a graffity spray can. The cement containers were penholders.
The personnel section was a candy bar. The silver paper of the bar was opened on the southern side of the building to form an entrance roof and to shade the control room. The surrealist temperament must engage the innocent, the brave and the nonsensical. Yet the contemporary architectural delinquent also has its own discursive logic. Wartiainen remains faithful to such logic and proceeds to build in a way that continually interrogates his site, space and use of materials. The production of architecture is uppermost. His buildings are generally cheaper than most. This is an innovation that could prove the most promising for tighter urban contexts. If Wartiainen outpaces his own distraction to some predictable rhetorical imagery, he is the architect likely to create a building that others would pilgrimage to. That it hasn't happened yet, does not make it unlikely. Wartiainen irritates and does it well. Taste is arbitrary and his solutions tempt an intelligence that clearly does not comfort the society's demand for the known, the achieved and the accepted. This type of architecture does not underestimate the user. It defrocks the architect-priest. And chancing upon random modesty and monumentality augurs well for Finnish architecture in the

next millennium. Wartiainen demands nothing less from architecture. The small society should do the same.
Hearing Saarijarvi
"Everything done in Finland is done better somewhere else today." This is a statement heard in various versions by architects and students. Symptomatic of the general loss in ideology, with corporate clichés rampant, this comment ignores the very real amount of housing and building that is produced in Finland. Yet much of this building is still heavily polished. The debate on healthy buildings and ecological planning struggles. The legacy of the elite profession seems to resist the radical innovative strategies for cheap but effective architecture. The building industry has, of course, been in a deep crises and shows only belated signs of getting out of what now looks like becoming a decade recession. But the logic is wrong. So often one hears that the architects must wait until the time when they can build again. Instead of hijacking the building production with innovation and the use of cheaper solutions, the architects have handed this role to any and every builder prepared to step in. This flawed moratorium is why the project called The Empty Space is significant. It was begun in Harry's Bar in Venice with nothing more than the urge and will to achieve something in such pessimistic times. Something from nothing. The Empty Space has sheer architectural nerve and, dare we say, architectural balls!
The Empty Space is a small chapel in the middle of a forest in Saarijarvi, central Finland. 400 metres away from the Empty Space there is a sign scrawled out on a piece of timber. This piece of timber is attached to a stake which has been driven into the ground. The sign is located at an obvious place: at the corner of a

One must listen, one must hear the forest

to know this space, this chapel.

The silence of The Empty Space: the chapel by Matti Sanaksenaho.

ork in the forest, where the road leads off from a dust track onto a sand track. This was the place where the tractors had difficulty in negotiating the route with the heavy glued elements of timber prepared separately near Helsinki. From this point onwards, the deep forest proper begins. The sign reads: empty space 400 ms. An arrow shows the direction. The project, as I said, began in Venice in 1992. Precisely, in Harry's Bar. Less precisely, over Bellini cocktails. The rest is determination, vision and stubbornness. A documentary film-maker would call this wonderful and necessary wilful energy, "drive". Architecture in Finland could do with more of it.

The Empty Space is an architectural expression that acknowledges the convention of nothingness and the ritual of space and protection. It also acknowledges the misunderstanding around silence in architecture in order to create another silence. This time, an active silence. One must listen, one must hear the forest to know this space, this architecture, this chapel. But such phenomenological uplift is not as easy as we think. The Empty Space possesses not the passive silence. Not that silence we have seen constructed in so much recent architecture that produces historicism and protectionism. This passive silence seeks distance, detailed brilliancy reaches the calmness of the cloister and is to yoga what jazz music is to aerobics. But such passive silence in architecture cannot be heard. It is deaf to its own architectural poem. Instead, The Empty Space is active, even interactive, in the sense that it forces one to question the very soul of a space itself. One hears architecture as much as on touches the darkness inside this forest tomb-chapel. From the trace of light along the crack, the sensation hints at very sould of building and its production itself. Why? Probably because in such darkness, as if stepping into a canvas in the forest, it is the spaces in between those we conventionally see as silent spaces that "fill" this emptiness. In this way The Empty Space is merely a shard of Sanaksenaho's own developing thinking; a thinking thrust forward and altered at speed with this participation as one of the five young architecture students of the Finnish Pavilion in Seville, EXPO 1992. The claims of that pavilion as a pivotal project in Finnish architecture have been legion. The courage of the

project has been sidetracked into its lucidity. The Seville Pavilion became a confirmation of its "Finnish" signature; the clarity of two forms. The high-tech extended cube and the softer pine keel-like form were felt to be the expression of almost collective will. This argument misses the point of the radical approach the group had and continues to have towards architecture. The Finnish Pavilion's attempt to redefine sculpture within architecture was special. As was the possibility of a romance within the rational. The architects calling themselves Monark expressed the desire to explore material ecology and decorativism in quite a new way from the more conventionally restrained materiality of Finnish architecture. That they were not quite allowed to achieve this, within and without the building, means we have much more exciting work to come from this generation. Sanaksenaho has been heard to say that he is more interested in the spaces between joints, in the details that are - apparently - no details in the conventional sense. I believe him.
He doesn't speak of silence and I suggest it more useful to try and manage without the word. To sense the soul of a space, we might increase ourselves instead by putting to use emptiness. This is close to, if not quite the unquestionable achievement of, Sanaksenaho's Empty Space. For the other side of the canvas in the Finnish forest, we would have to go to Padova and stand in front of Donatello's crafted wooden horse. There's just a chance that there's more to this than meets the eye and René Magritte. Sanaksenaho's proposal as The Empty Space for his diploma project was a brave step. He was carrying out a project that many of his professors would have longed to do but have up until laced the architectural nerve. Calling the project The Empty Space, the architect played off ritual and romance, expectation and architectural traditionalism. If the professors saw a return to the unadorned birthright, to the purity of the undecorative shed, they were and have I feel missed the point of Sanaksenaho's wit and panache.
The general climate in the architectural debate in Finland, the loss of confidence and direction in architectural ideology and the profession, the plethora of theory and the distance it takes from practice, suggest that architecture is approached like a sordino; a device used to reduce

resonance and produce a muffled tone. This is an architectural deafness that should worry us. It looks like remaining attractive in its calm achievement of the competent and restrained. But it is a deafness that even the users have begun to wonder about. Buildings can kill. Buildings can be unhealthy. Buildings can be oppressive.
The work of these architects, the exceptional and different approaches and achievements in these five buildings, to me, are traces of things to come, in a society where architecture does not keep the conversation going but tends to muffle debate, these buildings feel, touch, smell, taste and hear architecture. No less is demanded in the future. It has often been repeated that we must lose ourselves continuously in order to find ourselves. No less is this a current task for Finnish architecture. These five projects stand as departures torwards such a task. But Finland once expressed its difference with mundane trends in world architecture, especially during the 1950s and 1960s. It could do so again, if these approaches are any trace of things to come.

It has often been repeated that we must

lose ourselves in order to find ourselves.

Losing and finding - this should be the way of Finnish architecture at the end of the 20th century.

Chapel Saarijarvi
photo: Seppo Sarkkinen

"When, at night, I think of Germany,

I am robbed of my sleep." (Heinrich Heine)

On the condition of architecture in Germany.

7 | **THE LAWS OF REASON.**
        ANNETTE BECKER.

Germany

Form of State: Parliamentary-Democratic Federal Republic since 1949, **Area:** 356,853 km2, **Inhabitants (1993):** 81,338,100, **capital:** Berlin
Gross National Product 1992, per capita: $ 23,030, **Gross Domestic Product 1992:** DM 3,007.3 milliards, **Unemployment (Average, 1993):** 8.9%

n trying to present an overview of archi-tecture in Germany, the first two lines of Heine's nightly thoughts spontaneously spring to my mind. There he writes: "When, at night, I think of Germany, I am robbed of my sleep." So there is a capital city waiting to be built: Berlin. With the sad exception of the countries of former Yugoslavia, Germany is the only European country which happens to be building a capital city and has thus been compelled to reconsider its national self-image. Indeed, Berlin is, at present, one huge building site, with one spectacular competition after another and with architects joining in and withdrawing again, like Oswald Mathias Ungers at Potsdamer Platz. In ten years' time it might be possible to draw a balanced picture. There are also the new Federal Länder which, owing to objective historical conditions, currently present us with the task of providing the architectural living space of 16 million people with new quality standards. The impression one gains from travelling through Germany is unforgettable: the picture of uniform urban settlements is the exception here too. The chaotic spread of low quality architecture is the rule. The report "Zukunft Stadt 2000" (Future City 2000) of the Federal Ministry for Regional Planning, Building and Urban Development even refers to the situation as the most devastating instance of urban sprawl in the history of Germany. To this must be added the continued and noticeable uncertainty in dealing with the architecture dating from the Third Reich. Here I should merely like to mention the German exhibition pavilion on the Biennial Festival site in Venice as a representative example. Although it fulfils its function as an exhibition pavilion in an exemplary fashion, forming a clover-leaf-like motif together with the French and British pavilions at the upper end of a slightly inclined avenue, and,

furthermore, constitutes an element in a century of architectural history that this Biennial Festival site narrates in such an exciting and vivid manner, people talk of its demolition instead of adopting a refined, enlightened and calm though not harmless attitude to deal with this work of architecture. These are but a few brief comments on the situation of architecture in Germany. In my opinion, the question of the best five buildings of the past five years in Germany includes the search for an architecture which characterises the region, for a regionalism in its reduced form, as it has survived in our contemporary "multi-cultural", "post-industrial" culture (1), without becoming provincial or chauvinistic in the process. My search has led me to five architects, 50 to 69 years old, who - admittedly - are certainly not young talents or new discoveries, but to my mind currently represent the prime contenders for a place in the architectural history of Germany in the 20th century. Making a selection is an empirical procedure; one collects and, in the end, one makes a choice - sub specie aeternitatis - and only then does one formulate the criteria one has applied. Architecture, as a part of cultural history, evolves in fashions which are subsequently called styles. Metabolism, Deconstructivism, Post-Modernism and now it is - to use a term which a Düsseldorf advertising agency claims to have coined - the "New Modesty" in which we are living. We are all protagonists of different styles, but I also claim not to have succumbed to the Zeitgeist and not use slogans right now in order to "administer, in times of economic difficulties, the shortcoming with rhetorical gestures" (2). However, it would be an illusion to imagine oneself to be completely free from this Zeitgeist of modesty that is finding expression in so many places. In fact, however, my criteria for judging works of architecture

are very old and have been applied for many centuries now. One can read them in the works of Alberti dating from the 15th century and (although he disputes the assertion that he took them from Vitruvius) that much-cited trias of firmitas, utilitas and venustas. In the 3rd chapter of his first book, Vitruvius describes how people conceived these during the first century before Christ: "However, the construction of these buildings must take into account stability, expedience and beauty. Stability will have been taken into account when the foundations have been lowered until they reach a firm subgrade and the building materials, no matter what their nature, have been painstakingly selected without any meanness; expedience, when the arrangement of the rooms is perfect and does not hinder use in any way, and the location of each single room - depending on its use - is both aligned in accordance with the points of the compass and functional; beauty is taken into account, however, when the building has a pleasant and pleasing appearance and the symmetry of the parts demon-strates the correct calculation of the symmetries." (3)
Even though these demands possess general validity and simplicity, their application has remained a criterion for good architecture right up to the present. And if an architect declines to work on a building project because he is supposed to construct dwellings which are to face north only and would suffer from sufficient sunlight or even a view, since they would be located in a narrow street among high buildings, it becomes apparent that the test of these criteria still remains the new-old task of architecture.

The first example of the buildings I have selected was designed by Heinz Bienefeld. It is the "Haus Kühnen" in Kevelaer, located between the Lower Rhine and the Dutch border, where the "Lange" and "Esters" houses by Mies van der Rohe are also situated. Bienefeld's "Haus Kühnen" was completed in 1988. Proceeding from a residential house with a doctor's surgery dating from the mid-30s, the building task basically consisted in the conception of a living space and the clarification of the entrance area. He marks the entrance with an atrium in its original meaning as a centre providing access to the house and one that is also open to all areas. In the north, a garden hall has been attached as a living room above a narrow, glass connecting element, whilst a library has been located in front in the west. The atrium has been designed for use in the summer and the winter; in the summer, the glazing between the concrete columns to the impluvium can be removed. Nevertheless, the covered part provides enough space to be used in the winter too. Here, those elements become apparent which go to make up the true quality of the building. Firstly, for all the introverted nature of the building, the generous use of glass creates a transparency which, in turn, gives the house a generous character. Secondly, it is also transparent in the metaphorical sense of the word with respect to the employment of materials. Bricks have been combined with natural stone, concrete columns and rafters, which bear the bricks; every element retains its material properties and continues to be recognisable in its function for the building. The paradigms change in the garden hall, although this change is only apparent. The garden hall is a large, longitudinal hall covered with a saddleback roof. Divided by only one concha on its long eastern side and furnished with a stone bench and a permanently installed round table, a uniformly white colour - which has been applied to all materials, structures and details without any ideological timidity - underlines this pure form. Furthermore, the hall is a perfect place for observing nature, starting in the morning with the play of shadows of the columns, which divide the strip windows at the head of the concha; the spectacle continues in the blue glass pane - an allusion to the starry sky - in the southern gable wall before ultimately attaining its crowning glory in the glass wall to the garden. There it is delicately divided by the most slender of profiles on the one hand, and - plastically

- by powerful round pillars, assigned to the interior room, on the other. The library unit once again takes up the notion of the atrium, although here we do not find skylights surrounded by columns but a sealed roof without columns. Here, too, the experience of pure materials - the haptic aspect as it has been called ever since the objects created by Meret Oppenheim - is fascinating. The wall holds the promise that it makes optically. It is solid, without the tinny hollow sound of cladding, without the oppressive lowness of a suspended ceiling. Although it has a filigree profile, its surface nevertheless recalls wrought iron; its floor has the character of a woven textile pattern and, finally, there are in-built, poured concrete shelves through which, over and above all respect for its aesthetic qualities, the mind becomes compellingly aware of its enviable practicability.
All of the basic elements of Heinz Bienefeld's architecture are united in this library: the well-considered use of materials and their treatment, which even include the precise determination of their surfaces; the return to simple structures and, finally, the expert manner in which he uses the possibilities offered by different types of rooms.

Garden hall with a glass connection element - photo: Klaus Kinold

The well-considered use of materials, the return to simple

structures and, finally, the expert manner in which he uses

the possibilities offered by different types of rooms constitute

the basic elements in Heinz Bienefeld's architecture.

The real quality of construction in the architecture of Heinz Bienefeld.

Heinz Bienefeld. "Haus Kühnen" in Kevelaer, library, 1988 - photo: Klaus Kinold

Court of the Dead - photo: Francesca Giovanelli

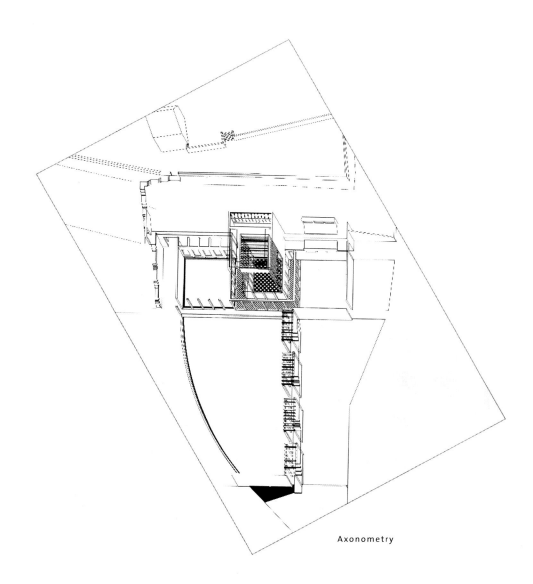

Axonometry

The second project is the cemetery chapel, designed by Günter Pfeifer, of the parish of Maulberg situated in the southernmost part of the Black Forest a few kilometres from Basle. The new cemetery had to replace a small, old mountain cemetery with a chapel. The old cemetery was laid out like a terrace by a slope. Although it contains no direct references, taken as a whole the new cemetery complex calls to mind an archaic sanctuary, the strict procession route of a temple district. The grounds are surrounded by high walls, whilst the old cemetery was separated from the parish by its natural location. The new grounds of the cemetery are to be separated too; this time, however, the separation is to be achieved by architectural means. And the cemetery is to be divided into distinct sections, just as the antique precursors of the cemetery were divided into various districts. The visitor reaches the buildings themselves via gently rising steps divided by landings. The steps ascend the slope along the west side of the anonymous graveyard. At the top of the ascent there is a special courtyard for mourning congregations, the so-called "Court of the Living". It is not only screened by the shadows of its two high walls, but also by four plane trees ensuring that it will

remain quite dark. To the left there is a cube, the chapel proper, which is on the ground floor borne by three pillars linked by a large glass area. A second row of supports has been situated in front of these pillars. Being linked to the pergola it creates a kind of portico, a cloister. The cube, which has been designed to create clarity and to appear closed off from the outside, constitutes a high, bright lunette on the inside. To this end, the interior has been divided by a row of pillars. These pillars and roof ribs also bear the inner roof which supports the glass areas of the surrounding walls. Symmetrical to the "Court of the Living", the "Court of the Dead" is linked to the chapel in the East. It has been laid out with rough, broken stone with the only sculptural decoration being provided by three rough stones broken out of the rock. This violent treatment of the stone can be grasped as a symbolic realisation of the violence of death. The yard is conceived as a place for meditation. One is not supposed to enter it but to walk around its edge. Nevertheless, the units described thus far are not isolated. The "Court of the Dead" contains a spring supplying the drainage duct also in the court. The duct flows round the yard; it passes along the curved wall of the large anonymous graveyard up to the entrance of the cemetery and

forms a watery surface below the enclosing wall. The wall seems to float above the water's surface. The cube of the chapel also draws some of its light quality from the low-level glass. Here, too, a feeling openness is created vis-à-vis the adjoining units. In his use of materials, Günter Pfeifer falls back on earthly substances: ore, clay, stone and concrete. Wood has been simply jointed, avoiding the use of nails or screws. The large cross in the cemetery chapel has been burnt out of a 2.5-cm- thick steel plate, the remaining four plates have been fitted into the floor in front of it. When the sun shines, one is directed by the strict procession route into the light, as funeral processions, which generally take place in the afternoon, proceed from east to west. Both the erected cross and the path towards the sun can be understood as Christian symbols.

Günter Pfeifer. Cemetery of Maulberg
Court of the Living - photo: Francesca Giovanelli

The cemetery by Günter Pfeifer recalls

an archaic sanctuary, the strict

procession route of a temple district.

An architectural formulation of this world and the beyond.

Karljosef Schattner. Rebuilding Schloß Hirschberg, annex, 1992

Eating room

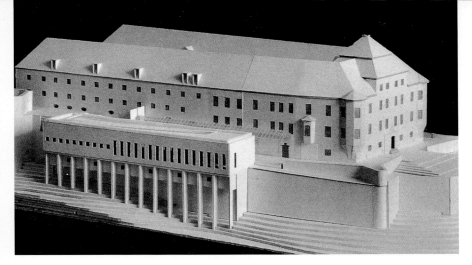

Model

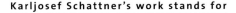

Karljosef Schattner's work stands for

the subtle treatment of materials.

The fascination of craft quality.

Karljosef Schattner's task, when re-building and reconstructing Schloß Hirschberg, was completely different. He did not have to design a total architectural unit, but designs within existing buildings. Schloß Hirschberg is situated on a steep col, to the west of Beilngries in the Franconian Jura. Originally the seat of the Count of Hirschberg in the 12th century, it was rebuilt again as a late Baroque hunting lodge by Gabriel de Gabrieli in the early 18th century as it had been damaged by fire in 1636. The result was

building, of laying out interior rooms in accordance with the needs of today's users and, as this was not possible in the old castle, adding a dining hall with adjacent rooms. This extension is now located as a parallelepiped slab in front of the southern slope of the castle grounds. It is a pre-cast concrete building supported by concrete pillars. The dado of this building contains the ventilation and waste-water installations; the store-rooms are located above these and have a curtain wall made of corrugated aluminium sheet. The kitchen and the

lower half is made of light concrete. The upper part is of dark-grey steel, solidly supported at the bottom, whilst it has an open hanging, positive and negative section at the top (5), linked by a simple handrail. When it is viewed from above, it animates the viewer to fold up the stairway by means of tensile force, thus resolving the tension between the two elements, which are turned 180 degrees. If, like Schattner, one builds for one client at one place and for such a long time, a number of special features are produced. One of these is the superb

From this necessarily determined architecture to a completely different example - one comparable with l'art pour l'art - to Oswald Mathias Ungers' own residential weekend house in the Southern Eiffel, that part of the Rhenish Slate Mountains between the Mosel and the Kölner Bucht. Remote from all civilisation, the house is situated in a small valley and can only be reached via a narrow country path. It is surrounded by meadows and woods, and stands at the foot of a mountain slope covered with trees. The wooden building of a former glassworks dating from the 17th century once stood on the site before it was replaced by a simple stone building. The glassworks was shut down in the 18th century and the building, which now only existed as a ruin, was used for agricultural purposes. Today, the ensemble consists of a main building, the former small chapel, a cross-shaped garden inside the foundation masonry walls of the historical house and a studio building in the place of the old apiary which together with ponds, a spring, old trees and the slightly undulating topography lend it a bucolic character. With the exception of the gables bearing the flat copper roof, the main house has four absolutely equal and identical best sides. It seems to reject nature, an impression which stems, on the one hand, from its location (as compared with the house by Bienefeld) and, on the other hand, from their divergent conceptions of architecture. In terms of architectural typology it is in the villa tradition - especially as cultivated by Palladio, and concretely reminds one of his rotunda (1566/67) near Vicenza. The fact that this recourse to the Renaissance is firmly rooted in the consciousness of the architect is revealed by a draft sketch for the ground plan of the house. This sketch divides a square into three equal right-angles and arranges two squares and a circle in the central field thus arising. These are games with space, of the kind one can see in the many instances of exemplary plans for lordly mansions in Francesco di Giorgio Martini's Codex Magliabechiano II.I.141 (ca. 1489-1492) in Florence (7). Ungers retains this model for his modern ground plans in which a mighty stairwell constitutes the central focal point of his house. The entire staircase has been given the form of a huge cube. Like all the elements in this house, its measurements are calculated from a single module, which becomes particularly conspicuous in the large units of the balustrade of the gallery,

the podium-seats, the shelves of the locked bookshelves and the corresponding, equally large doors. One can also envisage this module as an invisible, regular lattice-work "which assigns each edge and each aperture" - down to the positioning of the furniture - "its place" (8). Apart from taking its orientation from geometry, a second qualitative moment becomes visible, one which is to be found in other examples, i.e. that of the material. The house has been erected from a light-coloured limestone brought from a quarry to the south of Nancy. It has not been clad, but actually made out of solid natural stone. This is fascinating down to the exact execution of the finish, in the precision of the measures and the settlement of the jointing. Here we find that same attention to detail which Ungers also devotes to the wooden elements or the metal fittings.

In the work of Oswald Mathias Ungers

one can see perfect order, which assigns

even the smallest part its place and

allows it to become a part of the whole.

On the focal point of Oswald Mathias Ungers' architecture.

Colour study

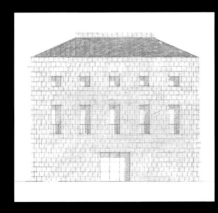

Oswald Mathias Ungers. Residential Building - photo: Wulf Brackrock

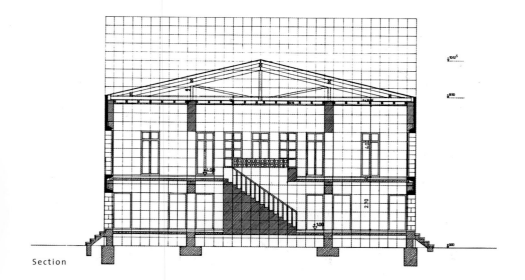

Section

The fact that this recourse to the Renaissance is firmly rooted

in the consciousness of Oswald Mathias Ungers is revealed by

a draft sketch for the ground plan of the house.

Oswald Mathias Ungers and the villa tradition cultivated by Palladio.

The last example of this selection departs from the other works in a number of respects, even though it does represent a continuation of the emphasis on architectural quality. The building, or rather buildings, are to be erected in Berlin in a prominent location, namely alongside the Brandenburg Gate. They will bear the numbers "Pariser Platz 1" and "Pariser Platz 7". It was here that the painter Max Liebermann lived until his death in 1935.

The architect of these buildings is Josef Paul Kleihues. One cannot design a project for such a site without knowing its history. The Brandenburg Gate was erected between 1788 and 1791 after a design by Carl Gotthard Langhans the Elder and crowned by a quadriga and Victory by Johann Gottfried Schadow in 1794. Badly damaged during the Second World War, it was rebuilt between 1956 and 1958 and its sculptural decoration partly renewed. The Brandenburg Gate divides the street "Unter den Linden" in the east from the Tiergarten park. The wing-buildings flanking it were linked with the buildings on the boundary of Pariser Platz and left standing freely after the square had been destroyed during the war. Kleihues' design can be regarded as an initial project. The intention here is, among other things, to recreate the spatial structure of Pariser Platz.

The French Embassy once stood in the northeast corner of the square, whilst the Akademie der Künste stood in the south alongside the famous Hotel Adlon. Although Kleihues is familiar with these historical requirements, he is under no compulsion to disregard them, but is able to present, in a composed manner, his own interpretation of the historical structure of the square. For the vertical order of his buildings he has adopted the cornice height of the buildings at the wings and of the Gate. He responded to the former, unsatisfactory solution of linking the adjacent buildings to the wings of the Gate with a striking separation of the adjacent buildings and the Gate buildings, thus giving emphasis to the autonomy of each in the process. The ground plan conception of the houses is strictly modular and thus avoids firmly laying down their possible uses. The façade is to consist of light, finely cut Elbe sandstone, which is to be variable here too, leaving all possibilities open.

Josef Paul Kleihues. Project for the Pariser Platz, Berlin 1992

Josef Paul Kleihues shows us how one can deal

with, and respect, historical requirements and,

at the same time, develop them further.

Architecture also means the correct treatment of historical buildings: Pariser Platz, for example.

It is worth taking such

architecture seriously.

"More being than appearance": this is the approach of the selected buildings.

Office and commercial building, modell - photo: Heinrich Helfenstein

Hans Kollhoff. Office and commercial building, Berlin 1994 - photo: Stefan Müller

I shall now summarise the arguments for the presentation of these particular five buildings in a few points. In the case of Heinz Bienefeld it is the peacefulness he creates, a peacefulness radiating from his simple rooms, which seem archaic in their use of materials. In Günter Pfeifer's work, the architectonic idea of the dialectic of rooms, which are linked to one another in diverse ways, comes to the fore. He formulates an interior and an exterior, in metaphysical terms: a 'this world' and a beyond - as antitheses - and simultaneously questions this separation. Karljosef Schattner stands for the subtle treatment of materials, consciously aware of their respective unique properties and providing a perfect craft finish. In the work of Oswald Mathias Ungers one can see perfect order, which assigns even the smallest part its place and allows it to become a part of the whole. Finally, in the latest project, Josef Paul Kleihues shows us how one can deal with, and respect, historical requirements and, at the same time, develop them further.

The buildings tend to follow the laws of reason rather than presenting a sensation, they do not define themselves by means of a design concocted during a laborious process of philosophising. There are many other examples to choose from, such as those by Hans Kollhoff, Christoph Mäckler and others. However, I believe that these examples suffice to underscore principles which have been recognised as desirable. These principles are more important than stylistic diversity. At issue here is the search for buildings which are convincing due to their truthfulness and quality. To put it differently: one could also say that behind their attitude lies "more being than appearance" and not vice versa. Everyone can decide for himself whether he would like to have this in filigree high-tech, glass and steel or in traditional materials such as bricks and wood. If these principles can once again be given more weight in the considerations of architects, even if this occurs via fashion, one can view future developments in the architectural environment with a lighter heart. In those cases, at least, in which architects succeed in doing this it is worth taking such architecture seriously.

Notes:
(1) Alan Colquhoun, Kritik am Regionalismus, in: Werk, Bauen + Wohnen No. 3 (1993), p. 45
(2) Fabian Wurm, in: Frankfurter Rundschau, November 11, 1993
(3) Vitruvius, Zehn Bücher über Architektur, ed. Curt Fensterbuch, Darmstadt 1981, p. 45
(4) Gerhard Matzig, Neues im Altmühltal, Karljosef Schattners "Weiterbauen" auf Schloß Hirschberg, in: Bauwelt 16 (1992), p. 886
(5) Manfred Sack, in: Vittorio Magnago Lampugnani, Architektur Jahrbuch 1993, p. 134
(6) Gerhard Matzig, op. cit.
(7) Francesco di Giorgio Martini, Trattati di Architectura, Ingegneria e Arte Militaria, ed. Corrado Maltese, Milan 1967
(8) Ulrich Maximilian Schumann, in: Vittorio Magnago Lampugnani, p. 145, op. cit.
Willmuth Arenhövel and Rolf Bothe (Ed.), Das Brandenburger Tor, Berlin 1991
Vittorio Magnago Lampugnani and Annette Becker (Deutsches Architekturmuseum), Architektur Jahrbuch 1993, Munich 1993
Wolfgang Pehnt, Karljosef Schattner. Ein Architekt aus Eichstätt, Stuttgart 1988
Manfred Speidel and Sebastian Legge, Heinz Bienefeld. Bauten und Projekte, Cologne 1991
Oswald Mathias Ungers, Architektur 1951-1990, Stuttgart 1991
Ulrich Weisner, Neue Architektur im Detail. Heinz Bienefeld, Gottfried Böhm, Karljosef Schattner, Bielefeld 1989

At issue here is the search for buildings which are convincing due to their truthfulness and quality.

Criteria for selecting the five best buildings.

In any case, the above-mentioned examples only constitute

a fraction of constructed reality in Switzerland; the

constructed reality between Rorschach and Geneva,

between Basle and Chiasso still looks different even today.

Architecture as an avant-garde project?

8 | ON THE REALITY OF A SQUARE.
    ULRIKE JEHLE-SCHULTE STRATHAUS.

Switzer-
land

Form of State: Parliamentary Federal Republic since 1848, **Area:** 41,284 km2, **Inhabitants (1992):** 6,968,600, **Capital:** Bern
Gross National Product 1992, per capita: $ 36,080, **Gross Domestic Product 1992:** $ 241,406 Mio, **Unemployment (Average, 1993):** 4.5%

Switzerland's best buildings are well-known, they have been discussed, publicised and have received prizes. They have appeared in architectural journals and even been presented in a book bearing the title "Construction, Intention, Detail". In his introductory essay "The presence of objects - comments on the new architecture in German-speaking Switzerland" Martin Steinmann writes: "One can [...] see the recherche architectural pursued by the architects, who appear here as representatives of an architecture in the German-speaking part of Switzerland, as a search for a degree zero, at which architecture would attain a new presence." The architects mentioned are Burkhalter & Sumi, Diener & Diener,

Herzog & de Meuron, Melli & Peter and Peter Zumthor. It should by no means be understood as chauvinism when I claim that the radical designs which deal with reduction, with the pictorial nature of materials and the significance of symbols, as well as with the tectonics of a work, are currently coming from the northern part of Switzerland. Together with Swiss television, the journal "Hochparterre" has already replied to the question of the top five. In the customary casual tone, they did not only award prizes to the best buildings, however, but also to other products of daily design such as underwear and packaging. The result was not markedly different, at least in the sector of architecture. Peter Zumthor came first, Michael Alder was placed

second and Herzog & de Meuron came third. My presentation of Switzerland will choose a different path. I shall take the liberty to talk of a square in the city of Basle around which some significant buildings have been erected in the past few years. They have not always been the best, yet they can be seen together with the art with which they have been endowed or which the architects themselves have chosen.

The names of those involved are Diener & Diener, Luciano Fabro, Mario Botta, Jonathan Borofsky, Herzog & de Meuron, Adrian Schiess, and Thomas Rueff.

The stone slabs, to which the architects refer as "fabric",

envelop - together with the cornice slabs, which also go

round the entire building - the detailed volumes.

A totality consisting of parts - the design by Diener & Diener.

The first building I shall discuss is the administration building of the Balôise insurance company at Picassoplatz. Until recently Picassoplatz had not really been a square, but a place whose character was determined by the rear side of the art museum (dating from 1936) designed by Bonatz and Christ and by commercial premises characteristic of the 60s, between which the wonderful First Church of Christ Scientists by Salvisberg is hidden, a building that also originated in the 30s. It is intersected by the busy Dufour-Strasse. It is thanks to Diener & Diener's design that a square has been created through the unequivocal location of the graduated block located on its Southern edge. Due to the arrangement of the graduated buildings, which (with the exception of the top floors) are linked to one another, the complex establishes a relationship to the tract (dating from the 50s) located behind it and in its façade articulation to the art museum opposite. The green stone cladding covering the entire Balôise building recalls the stone cladding of the museum, yet with a completely different significance. Whereas stone from all Swiss cantons was used to clad the museum during the 30s - entirely in keeping with the "Country or Local Style" of the time, the administration building is isolated from its surroundings by the slab cladding. And whereas the choice of stone was legitimated by Switzerland's political isolation, at a time when it faced the external threat of Fascism, there are now intrinsic architectural reasons for using stone cladding at this place today. Now the stone slabs, with their joints of various thickness, cover the entire complex and thus hold the diverse volumes together. The stone slabs, which the architects refer to as "fabric", envelop - together with the cornice slabs, which also go round the entire building - the detailed volumes. An impression of uniformity is created, of a whole created

of parts, without the totality disintegrating in the process. The granite slabs of the cladding create an impression of "gravity", although they are in front of the inner, supporting layer made of concrete. This "second skin" in front of the supporting structure presents an ambivalent picture: on the one hand, the plasticity of the heavy slabs and, on the other hand, the membrane which envelops the building on the outside and characterises the building as a totality. On the interior, the exterior figure is reflected inasmuch as the surrounding circle of offices repeats the exterior form in the arrangement of the access points. Luciano Fabro, the Italian artist, was invited by the insurance company to design the surroundings without the assistance of the architects. He reacted to the specific situation in his own manner with his Giardino all'Italiana. The original area, as an element of the extension of the city in the 19th century, was laid out with park-like gardens, i.e. with trees worth preserving. Fabro took up the motif of the trees and isolated them. At those places where trees were already standing or had been newly planted he broke up the slabs, so that it appears as if the forces of nature have torn asunder the urban development of the earth. Inside the slabs he distributed lights which, at night, evoke the impression of a starry sky and call to mind the Milky Way. In between he mounted stelas in a strictly orthogonal grid that masks the incidental location of the trees and the infinity of the starry sky with a basic geometrical order, thus alluding to the orthogonal geometry of the architecture. The stelas recall the stone supports of the pergolas in Tessin. The many levels of Fabro's work met with general disapproval in Basle. I was unable to share this negative judgement. This work of the artist, even though it was realised without any contact to the architects, comes very close to the intentions of the latter.

Diener & Diener. Bâloise Building, Basle 1990-93

A cosmic vision.

The Italian artist Luciano Fabro alludes to the geometry of
the architecture with a masked basic geometrical order.

Luciano Fabro. Giardino all'Italiana - photo: Barbara Graf

Burckhardt & Partner. Façade, Schweizerische Bankverein

The radical designs which deal with reduction, with the

pictorial nature of materials and the significance of

symbols, as well as with the tectonics of a work, are

currently coming from the northern part of Switzerland.

Taking the example of Basle, Ulrike Jehle-Schulte Strathaus demonstrates the search
by Swiss architects for a new presence.

Even now, nobody knows how the Schweizerische Bankgesellschaft imagines the aesthetic surroundings of its company seat. The "Hammering Man" by Jonathan Borofsky stands close by, in front of the offices of the central executive board of the Schweizerische Bankverein. The bank commissioned Borofsky to erect a two-piece work which shows the Hammering Man three stories high in front of the façade of Burkhardt & Partner, with his pulsating heart in the entrance hall.

The large companies in Basle, as can be seen from the development of Aeschenplatz, are profiting from the great names, whether they belong to the world of art or architecture. However, stars are no guarantee of solutions related to a

specific location. The stars apparently develop their solutions, which reveal their signatures, independently of the location on which they are working. A few steps further on - and this is to be the last example taken from the area around Aeschenplatz in Basle - one finds the SUVA building by Herzog & de Meuron. They were confronted with a very special task here: the preservation and renovation of the existing building dating from the early 50s and its extension to include apartments. Herzog & de Meuron decided to leave the old building standing in principle and to clad it with a new, "intelligent", glass façade. The glass exterior wall, which was constructed in three parts for each storey, had to fulfil various

functions. In the top level, shutter windows, which can be raised towards the outside, ensure protection from the sun and divert light into the interior of the building. The lower strip, on the other hand, moves in relationship to the exterior climatic conditions. It closes in winter in order to gain or save energy and opens in the summer.

The neighbouring neo-Baroque building is used as Shopping Mall

Mario Botta. Schweizerische Bankgesellschaft, Basle 1995 - photo: Pino Musi

Mario Botta confronts the square with a building which in a certain way negates the extreme urban situation.

A building which rests within itself and from which the traffic at the square seems to drop down like a liquid.

Herzog & de Meuron.
The new glass façade of the SUVA-
Building, Basle 1994

Herzog & de Meuron decided to leave the old

building standing in principle and to clad it

with a new, "intelligent", glass façade.

Not façade architecture, but an architecture which emphasises the function.

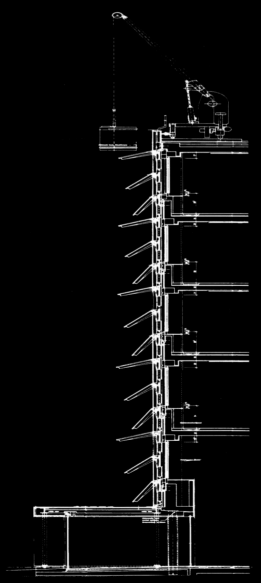

Section of the facade

The name of the firm has been screen-printed on certain sections. The middle layer has been left to the needs of the users, and can be freely opened and closed. This glass sheath over and in front of a stone building dating from the 50s ensures that the building is changed in the course of the day and the season. The architects are fond of drawing a comparison with the analogy of a plant - and the building is secretely driven by 900 motors.

Arthur Rüegg wrote in this connection: "The glass sheath of the SUVA house opens up various possibilities of perceiving the form of the building. However, in its material properties it also represents a contrast to the stone house of 1950. At first sight one suspects that the old and the new are to be related to one another in a dialectical manner, whereby the glass is assigned the part of the "modern". Indeed, it seems as if the architects were just as interested in veiling the stone as they were in revealing the contrast between the materials." In a confusing play of reflection, mirroring, veiling and transparency, the architects offer a number of possible ways of interpreting their building, each of which can appear implausible at any time. They have taken the work with the artists a long way here. Adrian Schiess hung one of his reflecting car-paint surfaces - which cannot be reduced any further - in the entrance hall. Thomas Rueff hung a photograph from his series of stars. The old stone SUVA building included the figure of a falling Icarus created by the Basle artist Willi Hege in 1950. With this symbol the insurance company probably wanted to point out that the self-confident rise of modern man can, at any time, be followed by a fall, which can, however, be made less painful with the assistance of this very company.

The architects have now taken up this subject in the café, in a part of the building in which the levels of the old and the new building are experienced in a particularly acute manner, i.e. as separated by the interstice. Like in the old cafés of the 60s, they have reproduced the well-known paintings by Breughel the Elder in coarse print patterns on the walls and furniture and, as an unequivocal symbol, a complete reproduction of the famous painting in the museum in Brussels too. In Breughel's painting, the fall of Icarus is a secondary affair taking place relatively inconspicuously on the left side of the picture. Here in Basle, right below the relief by Hege, the

evocation of Icarus appears to be quite direct. The demarcation line between the SUVA building and the street takes a motif from landscape design: fine box-tree bushes mark the transition to the public street area. In the case of Herzog & de Meuron this occurs in a linear fashion, whereas in the case of the trust company it is achieved on the basis of an abstract order principle, which seems to be almost Japanese with its staggered, graduated, parallel rows of finely cut hedges. My journey round Aeschenplatz in Basle caused me to believe that the great names are also represented in Basle. It is a commonplace that they are by no means a guarantee of great works.

Basle permitting a debate of the kind described above, in which companies are showing a willingness to place unconventional orders. This obviously does not mean that the best buildings are always constructed. In any case, the above-mentioned examples only constitute a fraction of constructed reality in Switzerland; the constructed reality between Rorschach and Geneva, between Basle and Chiasso still looks different even today.

Herzog & de Meuron. SUVA-Building, model

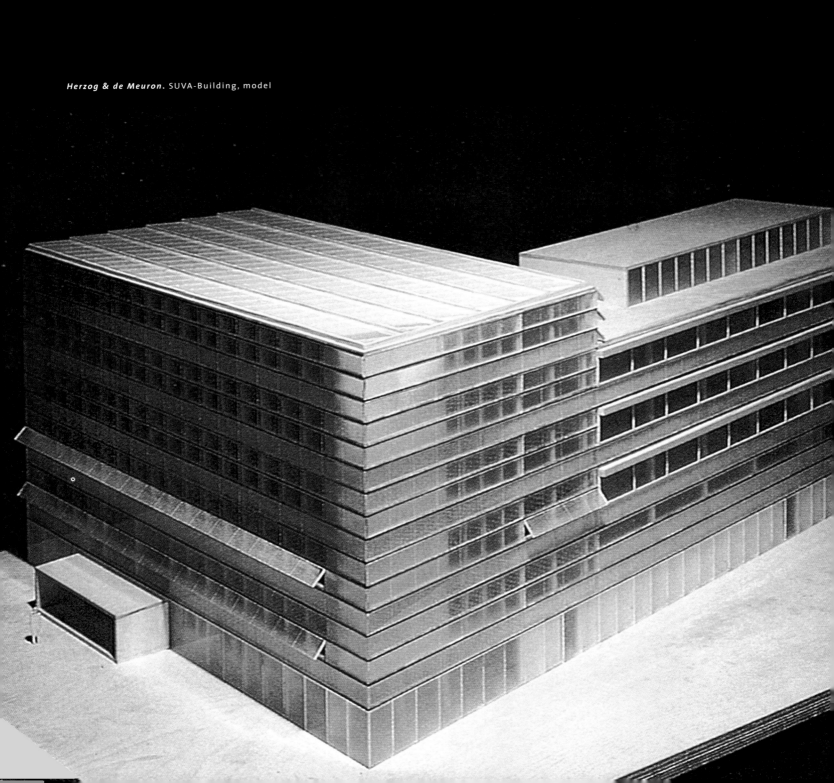

Entrance hall of the SUVA-Building

Café Ikarus

In a confusing play of reflection, mirroring, veiling and transparency, the architects offer a number of possible ways of interpreting their building.

Herzog & de Meuron's building represents the dialogue between old and new.

Inside the Café Ikarus

The Modernist canon has become obsolete.

There are no longer any hierarchies of values.

The weekly list of the Top Ten as a new system of values ?

9 | EXAMPLES RATHER THAN THE TOP TEN.
OTTO KAPFINGER.

Austria

Form of State: Parliamentary-Democratic Federal Republic since 1955, **Area:** 83,858 km2, **Inhabitants (1993):** 7,991,500, **Capital:** Vienna
Gross National Product 1992, per capita: $ 22,380, **Gross Domestic Product 1992:** $ 185,235 Mio, **Unemployment (Average, 1993):** 4.8%

If one wanted to formulate the difference between Modernism and Post-Modernism in an unorthodox way one might put it like this - in Modernism there were no Top Ten. Modernism in architecture attempted to set uniform new value standards, it wanted to found a new and universal tradition. The result was the so-called International Style - an inherent paradox. Post-Modernism - as a general mood of our time - has abandoned such claims. The Modernist canon has become obsolete. There are no longer any hierarchies of values. Seemingly arbitrarily anything can coexist with anything else. Largely unnoticed, however, this new freedom has been subjected to a no less dictatorial new system of values - namely the weekly list of the Top Ten. Modernism was ruled by ideas, or they were at least meant to dominate. Post-Modernism is ruled by economic considerations, the free market of wishes that can be manipulated, and this is true even of our architectural journals. I do not want to pursue this aspect any further here. I can only see the overall theme of this Congress as a provocation. I am by no means able to name the five best buildings in Austria since 1988. It would be a purely popularistic or academic undertaking. An alternative that suggests itself would be naming the five worst buildings, but I do not want to do this neither. Instead I would simply like to present to you 13 buildings since 1988 that for certain subjective reasons seem interesting to me personally. 1988 is therefore implicitly open to discussion as a caesura, a possibly important date for the development of architecture in Europe - comparable to 1989 in the political sphere. I doubt, however, that 1988 represents a comparable caesura for architecture. When leafing through my old texts from 1988 I came across one that puts my view of the architectural scene during that year into a nutshell. The text was entitled "New Severity - Architecture and Design after Post-Modernism" and it discussed a competition decision that attracted much attention at the time and that I want to present to you as my first example.

Post-Modernism is ruled

by economic considerations.

The new freedom, the arbitrary of the Top Ten-list?

Form and content explain each other. Such laconic

matter-of-factness looks for symbolic qualities

beyond historicist and individualistic gestures.

New severity: Local Building Authority in Graz, designed by "ARTEC".

Site plan

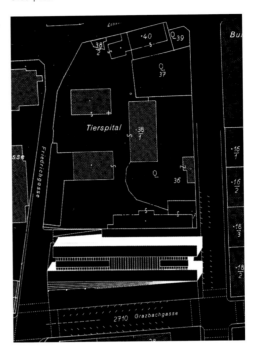

ARTEC. Local Building Authority in Graz, project 1988

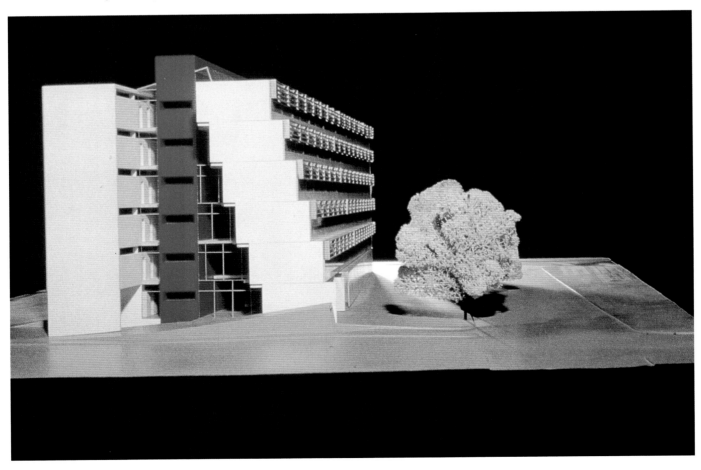

Local Building Authority in Graz, designed by "ARTEC" (Bettina Götz, Ed Hoke, Theo Lang, Richard Mahnahl) competition entry in 1988: The fact that for some years now a new abstraction has become evident as a reaction to a Post-Modernism overloaded with symbols and historical references, that a revaluation of the architecture of the 50s and 60s has set in, that a new severity in details, a new clarity of the building masses and a new way of dealing with industrial materials can be observed, that steel, glass blocks, corrugated metal, exposed concrete, asbestos-cement sheeting, sheet zink, form board, plywood etc. are becoming fashionable - all this indicates the return to a sensitivity that is related to certain positions of Modernism without, however, sharing its positivism. Against this backdrop current movements in Austrian architecture are thrown into higher relief. A competition result like this design for the local building authority in Graz that was judged in summer 1988 would not have been possible five years earlier. Of all the competition entries the design of the victorious ARTEC team was certainly the "most severe" but at the same time also the most adequate solution of the task in hand. Embedded in the Zeitgeist directed towards cool Minimalism and ragged Neo-Constructivism, this design found a jury that was already susceptible to abstraction and stark simplicity.

The 250 identical offices each with its desk and filing cabinet were packed into two slender six-storey disks which - in sandwich fashion - inclose two smaller and higher prisms for the elevators and core areas and an effectively solved system of circulation. The storeys of the south-facing office disk were pushed towards the outside in a stepwise fashion like a chest of drawers in order to widen on the lower storeys the continuous stair hall which receives daylight from above and from the ends. The façades are very simple and repetitive; the walls and ceilings will be done in exposed concrete and the interior core disks will be plastered and varnished red.

People in Austria often refer to such official buildings as "ink castles" or "civil servant silos". In any case this building, which will be put up in the near future, will not present an empty, showily impressive façade, but instead offer those who visit it a spatially pleasing stair hall flooded with light - while all the officials working there will find evenly and well lit workplaces overlooking trees and grass outside. The building will not present bureaucracy as more harmless than it is. Form and content explain each other. Such laconic matter-of-factness looks for symbolic qualities beyond historicist and individualistic gestures - for moods that have to do directly with the reality of the materials, the presence of light, the raw poetics of our metropolises and with industrial buildings freed from the burden of ideologies, without any references to absent historical objects or an ideal realm of forms.

The building will not present bureaucracy as more harmless than it is.

Embedded in the Zeitgeist of cool Neo-Minimalism and ragged Neo-Constructivism.

In the same year 1988 the Kix-Bar in Vienna was designed by Oskar Putz. Martin Steinmann has called it the most beautiful colour space he knows. In the Vienna of the 80s with its numerous highly sophisticated spatial miniatures this is certainly the most radical small space, and it was not designed by an architect, but by a painter. Why do I find this fact interesting? The 80s were generally characterized by the effort to replace purely functional space by a many-layered visual space. All the architectural efforts of overlaying and multiple encoding on the entire scale from type to collage, from Pop Art to Biedermeier, from history to everyday life, strove to give architectural space a new formal density and emotionality. Analogous to this was a multiplication of the range of materials used, a heightened attention and refinement of details. The space created by Oskar Putz represents a high point of such efforts - while at the same time being the exact opposite of what the architects were trying to do. In this space there is no

longer any architectural detail - in the sense of the architecture of the early 80s that was so keen on eloquent or discrete detail. The existing spatial shell of the old building was stripped down to its zero line. The new floor is a silver-coloured button plate; a minimal bar block, a few tables, chairs by Terragni. Walls and ceilings are covered by a new polychrome surface composition. It is the thinnest and most abstract medium of all, the application of colour, that gives this space its extraordinary emotionality and dynamics. Here colour and the light that shines upon it are the simplest and strongest aesthetic and spatial energy. In an aggressive dialogue colour maintains its autonomy vis-à-vis space. On the one hand the architectural conditions of the spatial shell are emphasized by colour, as when loadbearing and non-loadbearing elements in the passageways are differentiated by colour. On the other hand colour surfaces extend beyond the edges of the room, and their nuances create rhythms of their own and a virtual tectonics of its own. In this way a rich

three-dimensional scintillating and attention-getting quality is created which cannot be pinned down materially. What is decisive here in my opinion is the fact that a genuine aesthetics of early Modernism is powerfully recreated. Colour in space has no shape - it activates the spatial feeling through the sense of vision: what is essential here is not any new material form, not any propaganda of a tangible shape, but instead the act of seeing as such, the dynamics of vision, the complexity of our perception.

The application of colour gives this space

its extraordinary emotionality and dynamics.

Colour has no shape: the Kix-Bar in Vienna by Otto Putz.

Otto Putz. Kix-Bar Vienna, 1988

Wolkenstein Cultural Centre at Stainach; architects Florian Riegler and Roger Riewe. This is an alteration, the adaption of a former cinema situated directly across from the railroad station of a small town known chiefly as a railroad junction. If you go there today you will see hardly any architecture, but this hardly anything is immediately palpable in its rural surroundings. It is a hall that is being used for various events by an initiative that is much appreciated in the European network of avant-garde jazz and has since expanded its programme to other cultural areas such as literature, and exhibitions. What is so special about this? In 1990 this small project - with building costs of c. 6 million Austrian Schillings - received the Architectural Award of the Province of Styria despite the competition of twenty other entries, considerably larger buildings that were architecturally at least equally ambitious. The jury one of whose members was Dietmar Steiner justified their decision as follows: "It is not as though those other proud and sumptious solutions were bad, or the pain and effort which made them possible were not appreciated. But today a certain anachronism inherent in them cannot be denied any longer. The media hype which catapulted architecture right into the centre of the laws of utilization of a cultural industry, has to give way to reason, to an inventory of actual achievements. The adequate relationship between task, programme, content and architectural solution is increasingly placed into the foreground. The debate has to make way wherever actual space is being created. And this has happened in the Wolkenstein Cultural Centre in a congenial, honest and committed manner. The economic restrictions and hence the economical way of dealing with the resources has resulted in a solution that is adequate in every way, because it shows commitment." Well, I can only agree with this statement. This building does not provide any aesthetic sensation, but it communicates a very precise, sensitive, future-oriented attitude: the old building was stripped without sentimentality, a lobby was added with a polished and sealed concrete floor, grey stuccowork on the walls, a red parapet disk as a signal by the entrance, wire fences in the stairwell, a bar made of concrete with stainless steel counter, a few folding chairs and folding tables, a visual slot into the hall extending over the entire width of the room, behind it a red curtain, the interior almost all black, galleries inset on three sides, ventilation, illumination, Jacobsen chairs; the sanitary facilities are arranged in the remaining space underneath, the escape stairways on the sides encased in Profilit glass in steel frames. That's it. Neither too much of anything nor too little: the art of minimal intervention.

The Housing project in Vienna, Brunnerstrasse by Helmut Richter, (completed in 1991) seems important to me because it was the first to introduce or rather reintroduce Modernism into housing projects in Vienna, in conjunction with a new approach of industrial building technology for this branch of architecture. It is not a case where an island of massive isolation is cut out from the desolate surroundings of an industrial suburban situation. Instead Richter reacts to the atmosphere of the periphery by exaggerating its potential. On the narrow north-south oriented lot next to an extremely busy thoroughfare Richter used concrete in a skeleton construction for the load-bearing structure. High-tech glazing in zinc-plated steel frames acts as a sound barrier on the side facing the street. At the top tarpaulins serve as roofs for the stairwells, metal "containers" on the ground floor serve as refuse collecting chamber and storage basement, prefabricated slabs are joined to form the exterior wall system.

On the side facing Brunnerstrasse the only structural fixed points inside the apartments are a concrete support, a service shaft and a short piece of wall. The concrete ceilings are stretched ten metres from one separating wall to the next by means of joists. The interior division of this spatial volume is effected by light block partition walls that may basically be moved. In the standard solution the hall areas and passageways were minimized in such a way that the primarily rectangular plan is livened up with slight splays and kinks, yielding an optimum of living space. Like the extremely thin exterior wall slabs, the large windows and sliding glass doors to the loggias and terraces likewise extend undivided from floor to ceiling. The tangible principles that characterize the building are a reduction of material and components, a transparency of space and structure and clear relationships throughout. What is spectacular in this row of buildings that is oriented towards the west are the sound insulation and circulation systems. Richter arranged exterior corridors along the pavement and left ample free space between them and the building mass, so that access to the individual apartments is by short transverse bridges. This spatially very effective structure of leading from the public to the private sphere is shielded from the street by a frameless plain glass wall. Due to two or three subtle kinks, caused on the one hand by the building line and on the other by a slight bending back in the upper part, this 150 metre long and several storeys high glass membrane achieves spatial tension. Thus the residential area is distanced from the street noise, while at the same time it does not confront the traffic space with a separating wall but instead a semi-public structure of footpaths enveloped in transparency. To get such an innovative concept accepted within the constraints of subsidized housing meant, frankly speaking, a tough struggle. The difference between the technological demands of the architect and the ability and cooperation of the reality of building cooperatives has clearly left its marks. The result is a mixture that oscillates between precision and improvisation, a merging of high-tech and low fit.

Florian Riegler and Roger Riewe. Wolkenstein Cultural Centre, 1990

This building does not provide any aesthetic sensations, but it

communicates a very precise, sensitive, future-oriented attitude.

The art of minimal intervention: Wolkenstein Cultural Centre by Florian Riegler and Roger Riewe.

Hall

Helmut Richter. Housing development Brunnerstrasse, Vienna 1991

This is neither staged cosiness nor trendy

designer chic, nor a living machine, but a

building as a cool and subtle instrument.

The space that has been opened up: the housing development by Dieter Henke and Marta Schreieck.

Inside the housing development Frauenfelderstrasse

Dieter Henke, Marta Schreieck. Housing development Frauenfelderstrasse, Vienna 1993

Elsewhere Ernst Beneder has clearly
shown that today architecture can only
be free of untainable global, regional
or formal ideologies while yet being
contemporary and in the right place,
"if it provokes the respective problem
manneristically in order to resolve it in
a modern way". In this regard and as a
yardstick to show how far it is possible
to exceed the boundaries of the conventional even within the financial
constraints of publicly subsidized
housing, the Brunnerstrasse building is
a pioneering achievement for the
housing situation in Vienna at the end
of the 80s.
In direct comparison to the building
just shown; housing development in
Frauenfelderstrasse in Vienna; architects:
Dieter Henke and Marta Schreieck,
completed in 1993. While Richter's
building still communicates some of
the pointed pathos of Modernism this
building - with comparable intentions -
displays laconic calm and pleasant
harmony. The means by which this is
achieved are similar: a concrete load-
bearing structure, disks, supports and
ceilings, everything kept to a minimum.
The housing development is divided into
two wings - a southern one (with a front
garden) that takes up the rhythm of the
façade of the adjoining buildings with
two-storey maisonettes, and a western
one with apartments and shops on the
street level. In between - the corner area
which always provides difficulties in
terms of its plan has simply been cut
open - an open entrance hall and
stairway provide access and function as
a hinge. The maisonettes have outside
corridors on every other storey on the
courtyard side (north) which are set
slightly apart from the building and
connected to the apartment entrances
by means of bridges; they are stepped
back towards the uppermost storey,
thus providing more air for the courtyard.
The apartment entrances show individual
features. On the southern façade there
are two-storey loggias: their inner
membrane is entirely glazed while the
outer one serves as a visual and sun filter
with two-storey-high aluminum sliding
shutters. Inside the apartments there

The purpose of the building is fulfilled optimally; and beyond

that it clearly communicates an intellectual and artistic dimension.

Artistic Matter-of-factness: Research and Development Centre Leykam in Gratkorn.

Research and Development Centre of the Leykam Mürztaler Paper Mill at Gratkorn; architect Klaus Kada, completed in 1991. In Austria, too, the late 80s and early 90s show indications of regaining lost territory in industrial and administrative buildings in terms of their architectural quality. I want to present Klaus Kada's building as an example of this important branch of architecture which has long been neglected in Austria, since despite a very limited budget he realized a compact building with a considerable interior flexibility, the possibility of expansions and a technological finish that can well hold its own in the contemporary international scene. The building is also symptomatic of Kada's position on the lively Styrian architectural scene. I think that in particular his consistent concept - in a great diversity of building tasks - of dissolving the spatial programme into clear spatial blocks, of disentangling them, providing distances between them and reconnecting them with the copiously glazed intermediate zones of access and daylight illumination has early on brought to the expressive architectural climate in Graz a stringency that has today become general there. What else can be said about this building? It is determined by a system that permits alterations in function and size. The large percentage devoted to services and installations in this laboratory building resulted in the decision of using the vertical shafts as parts of the load-bearing structure in order to achieve both an economic building structure and all the necessary installation lines. The glazing of the central part of the forked building results in natural lighting of all working rooms from two sides and provides sufficient light for the circulation areas and public zones, as it were, in the building: short internal passages, inner transparency, visual relationships between the laboratories on the ground floor and the offices on the upper floor. A clear rhythm of the design and the outer shell; the laboratories on the ground floor are as transparent as possible towards the outside with natural lighting, while the EDP offices on the upper floor are more protected and hermetic. The building is made up of a few materials: smooth exposed concrete, shiny aluminium, large glass areas, finely perforated plate. The purpose of the building is fulfilled optimally; and beyond that it clearly communicates an intellectual and artistic dimension. Not by means of any stylistic gimmicks but by permeating the dangerous bottleneck of calculating matter-of-factness with an even more precise artistic matter-of-factness.

The Church at Aigen by the architect Volker Giencke was completed in 1992. Giencke is one of the few architects in Austria who consistently undertakes technological experiments in his buildings, even though this often poses the danger of failure due to outward circumstances. Giencke's subtle technologies, however, never lead to the commercial blandness of many well-known high-tech buildings, but instead serve as a very sensual, playful expressive potential. The church at Aigen is for me an example of the theme of artistic transcendence of the technical experiment. The lot is a free space in the centre of the village, separated from the village square - which is not really a square but a rather uninviting shapeless free area - by a crudely regulated stream. At some distance to the south is the thoroughfare. Giencke chose the building site himself, he fought for it, and he heightens this island-like location into a spatial centre, into a cheerful sacred region that can be reached from the street through an avenue of old fruit trees and that is connected with the secular village centre by three graceful new steel footbridges across the stream. The theme of the church was originally a polygonal space covered by a large roof. The spire and the rectory were added only during the planning phase and now combine to form a tension-filled ensemble. The large roof also awakens associations with ships and the ark; it is also built with wooden ribs like a ship's hull, with a keel leading from the entrance to the altar area. The height of the construction is also due to the considerable loads, for the roof is covered with grass, with a thick layer of humus. It returns to the earth the piece of meadow that was taken away from it by the building. The interior of the church seems to lean against the solid chancel and the massive northern wall next to the entrance. In between there is a sculptural part in exposed concrete - the front of the vestry, into which the confessional, a niche for an altar of Mary and space for the organ are integrated. The exposed concrete is covered with a translucent coat of paint in subdued pink. This wall gives the impression of an unfinished fresco or old parchment. The concrete obtains a very delicate, skin-like warmth and aura - in reality the result of a coincidence since the architect decided to simply leave the adhesive layer for the plaster that had originally been planned. On the south and west side the exterior wall is formed by polygonally shifted walls of coloured glass in steel frames. These four disks lean against the interior space like a transparent coloured house of cards, flooding the interior with colour and light reflexes. The cross section of the spire is an oblique trapeze with a slightly splayed base; the steel structure is covered with panels of rough rolled glass, which results in an extremely atmospheric and light appearance. In contrast to this the rectory is a cube with timber-faced façades and minimalist glass elements on top of an interior steel structure. In short we find here contemporary building technology, partly advanced, partly ingeniously put together, turned into the playful - a place that radiates a special atmosphere.

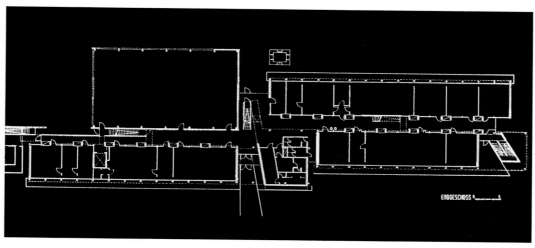

Ground plan

Klaus Kada. Research and Development Centre Leykam, Gratkorn 1991

The glazing of the central part

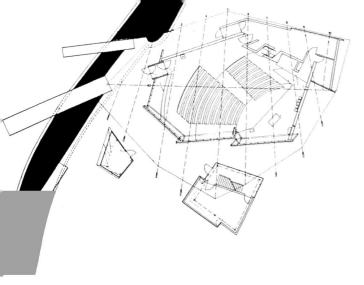

Church at Aigen, ground plan

Church in Aigen, interior view

Volker Giencke. Church at Aigen, 1992

Giencke's subtle technologies serve a very

sensual, playful expressive potential.

An experiment in lightness: Church at Aigen.

In contrast to this elaborate manifestation I am now going to show you the alteration of the church in Welzenegg, Carinthia, by the architects Franz Freytag and Felix Orsini-Rosenberg, completed in 1993. In the economy of its means and its fitting and cohesive result it is perhaps related to the intervention by Riegler & Riewe which I showed you earlier, although the context is quite different. The particular achievement of this alteration is the fact that a conventional and cramped aisle-less church of the 50s, an absolutely provincial situation, was turned into a dynamic, open space articulated in various ways. To quote Friedrich Achleitner: "This achievement has to be valued all the more highly as the intervention was done using practically only the resources of the existing building substance. By intelligent utilization and by transcending the constraints of the given situation something very specifically new has been created that could hardly have been achieved under unlimited design conditions."

The alterations were in the entrance area, in the enlargement of the covered space in front of the church (redesigning the entire area in front of it), in moving the access along the glazed exterior wall equipped with slatted blinds, a continuation of the path to a christening area which, placed around a support of the pierced exterior wall, not only creates a symbolic relationship between outer and inner world, but also opens up the altar area towards the spire that is visible from the inside. The proscenium-like closed chancel was turned into a spacious area flooded with light and expanded on the inside by an entire spatial layer. This spatial expansion responds not only to the opening of the opposite wall, but also permits another access to the free-standing altar for the congregation. Since in this spatial layer marked by thin, tall columns, the tabernacle is mounted on the last pillar analogous to the baptismal font, the constellation of the "sacred fixed points" (baptismal font, altar, ambo and tabernacle) leads directly into the chapel used on workdays which in turn was very

clearly developed as a spatial quality of its own. The rigid symmetry and blocked spatial flow of the old building were turned into a new spatial structure in which complex relationships between various axes act in a multifarious balance with each other. This profound alteration is certainly no sensation that will make the popular Top Ten. However, it is certainly exemplary in its attitude of contemporary recycling of that which already exists. What is sensational here is "only" something that no photograph can adequately communicate, namely with what simple means and subtly integrated "art embellishing buildings" a space can be brought to a liberated and spiritual dimension.

Franz Freytag and Felix Orsini-Rosenberg. Alteration of the Church at Welzenegg, 1993

The particular achievement of this alteration is the fact that

a conventional church of the 50s, was turned into a dynamic, open space.

The art of simplicity: alteration of the Church at Welzenegg by the architects Franz Freytag, Felix Orsini-Rosenberg.

Konrad Frey. Kunsthaus Mürzzuschlag, 1991

Section

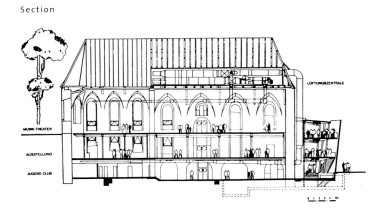

Alteration of a church from the 17th century

A building, very serve, without any subjective

gesture, intended as a technical instrument.

The building as an instrument: Kunsthaus Mürzzuschlag by Konrad Frey.

An analogous theme, but quite a different solution: Kunsthaus Mürzzuschlag, alteration and expansion of a church dating back to the 17th century, by Konrad Frey, completed in 1991. Frey is probably the only designer-architect in Austria whose involvement with high-tech designs is an integral part of his biography - through his inter-disciplinary work with Ove Arup in London. Konrad Frey, who is almost 60 now, has built very little, since he has been working chiefly in technically optimized ecological building research. I am showing you his Kunsthaus in Mürzzuschlag, since it is unique in Austria in the radicalness of the relationship between the old and the new building: a building, very severe, without any subjective gesture, intended as a technical instrument. The task in this case was to make a Baroque church space that had been secularized 200 years ago and was almost in ruin, useable on its three levels for a wide range of cultural events. The basic concept was to stabilize the existing building, to repair it carefully, and to keep it free of built-in features so that it would be useable in its entirety. Entrance, lobby, administrative offices and secondary rooms are con-centrated in an annex which is added to the old building as an external layer. Frey wanted this new layer to be like a scaffolding except that it is covered by a glass membrane instead of a dust cover. The scaffolding with platforms, stairs and ramps keeps its distance from the old building. The access corridors, the elevator and the comprehensive ventilation and energy supply system are freely placed into the remaining spaces. The outer membrane of insulating glass without any muntins was developed in cooperation with Austrian companies before the now common planar system was commercially available. The striking slanted lines of the annex might easily tempt one into fashionable formal interpretations. However, they originated quite rationally on the basis of spatial considerations and keeping in mind the local situation. From the point of view of the building code the façade could have been moved forward as far as the building line of the adjacent building on the right. It is, however, clearly set back in relation to this adjacent building. The latter is a very beautiful Baroque building, whose façade continues beyond the corner, and by setting back his building the architect allows a view of this beautiful corner next door, at the same time creating a free space in front of the Kunsthaus entrance. However, on the left side of the annex Frey moves as far forward as he is allowed to - thus creating the inclined plan. The inclined elevation has two reasons: Frey wanted to recover vertically at least part of the space that he gave away in the plan; the interior room arrangement is very tightly packed and 40 to 50 additional centimetres on the second storey help greatly. Moreover there is a noteworthy 10 % ramp from the second platform to the third level, the main level of the old building. The skylight of the annex is arranged parallel to this incline - and the glass wall in the front is at a right angle to it. For rational, economic reasons almost all façade glasses have the same rectangular format. At the line of intersection with the level of the space in front of the entrance these rectangles even reach below street level in a finely detailed slot: a very logical intersection of the membrane with the topos, since here the interior of the lobby also leads a few steps below street level to the level of the jazz club. As always the photographs are deceptive. The entire building is relatively small, strikingly refreshing in the street ensemble, yet quite undramatic.

Roland Gnaiger. Elementary and secondary school at Warth, 1992

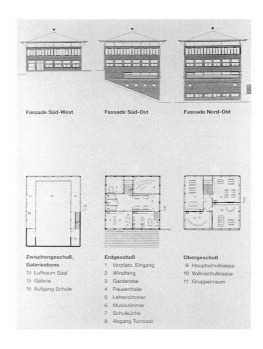

Fassade Süd-West   Fassade Süd-Ost   Fassade Nord-Ost

Zwischengeschoß,
Galerieebene
14 Luftraum Saal
15 Galerie
16 Aufgang Schule

Erdgeschoß
1 Vorplatz, Eingang
2 Windfang
3 Garderobe
4 Pausenhalle
5 Lehrerzimmer
6 Musikzimmer
7 Schulküche
8 Abgang Turnsaal

Obergeschoß
9 Hauptschulklasse
10 Volksschulklasse
11 Gruppenraum

Interior view

The building is inseparably rooted in its site and

yet is characterized by a universal attitude.

Building for a specific site (first example): the school building at Warth by Roland Gnaiger.

Building for a Specific Site: Elementary and secondary school with community hall at Warth, province of Vorarlberg, architect Roland Gnaiger, completed in 1992. Warth is originally a small village in the mountains, located more than 1,500 metres above sea level, that recently became a fashionable skiing resort and has grown and exploded with many new hotel buildings - and many problems. This new building at Warth is a type of school that is unique in Austria. It contains an elementary school as well as a secondary school that has only one (!) classroom but all the necessary special rooms: arts and crafts room, kitchen, gym, rooms for EDP and foreign language teaching. An essential aspect of the design is the fact that it defines the relatively great space requirement - in relation to the number of pupils - in such a way that space has also been created for hitherto non-existent public facilities for the entire village. The new school is situated next to the old community center on a steep hillside on the edge of the village and on the edge of the only and thus very valuable plane in the entire community. In order to preserve and even increase this level surface for games, sports and other events the new building was set into the adjacent steep hill. Between the new building, the old building, and a hill across them the playground forms a space that is situated on the level of the village, protected from road traffic, and providing level access to the school. Seen from here, the new building appears to be a two-storey counterpart to the old building. On the other hand, the northeast side of the

school reaches 10 metres further down, for there the terrain drops abruptly to the street. This difference in level is used to advantage by three more storeys inserted below the main level of the school. Through a gallery, the gym which also serves as a multi-purpose room and the level of the lobby the building steps down to the lower space in front of the building. There is the street entrance for larger events and the public use of the multi-purpose room. Gnaiger stacked the different functions vertically into a very compact, cube-like massing that is very structural and flexibly useable. As far as the building is embedded in the soil (up to the ceiling of the multi-purpose room) the construction is massive with insulation and outer roof boarding. Above the ceiling of the multi-purpose room is a prefabricated wood construction. The two-storey wall panels which are 2.5 metres wide were put up within five days. The 15-metre-long exterior walls each consist of six such elements. The most striking external characteristic is the large roof, a flat pyramid of timber with cantilevered projections that are pulled upwards on all sides. In Warth with its copious snowfalls in winter this roof shape is of elementary importance. The loads of snow there can reach enormous proportions - three metres high and more, and often unevenly distributed to boot. Gnaiger wanted to keep the plan of the school open and free of static forced points. He therefore had to design a roof that although itself weighing as little as possible will support up to 500 metric tons of snow (!) and spans the building

freely in such a way that the snow remains lying on top to prevent dangerous curtains of icicles and even more dangerous roof avalanches. The result is a building that is tailor-made for the topos, the programme, the climate, the available technology and the cultural situation of the site and whose structural, holistic concept has been refined to include even the details of the specifically developed furniture. For me this school is a model of precise building for a specific site. The building is unique although that is not what it intends to be. In many components it is conventional, but in their sum total it goes far beyond that which is usual. The building is inseparably rooted in its site and yet is characterized by a universal attitude. In addition this work is exemplary for a general new trend in the noteworthy architectural scene in Vorarlberg: to move beyond the theme of the single-family house and timber construction to more complex and larger tasks.

Prohazka's buildings are highly energetic and at the same time minimalized site-specific event machines.

Building for a specific space (second example): residential building near Wiener Neustadt by Rudolf Prohazka.

A quite different topos, other means and another signature. Residential building near Wiener Neustadt in Lower Austria, architect Rudolf Prohazka, completed in 1993. The commission in this case was originally to alter a do-it-yourself bungalow from the 50s and 60s on a very beautiful forested lot. Prohazka eventually preserved only the oldest core, a square room in log construction, the chimney as well as the platforms framed by natural stone walls. Around this wooden core the architect composed a new building into the surrounding splendid trees and onto the adjacent clearing: it is extremely delicate and airy, guiding one's movements around and across the space, opening and directing the eyes, enveloping the surrounding space, leading to a meditation in nature. The plan is structured into the rather compact eastern part with kitchen and dining area in the core, children's room and bathroom, in the west the living room which is open towards all directions, with its fireplace. Above the fireplace is a narrow, separate working storey with a bedroom that reaches out onto the large meadow in the back. A tall glazed hall serves to connect building and nature; a water trough has been placed transversally into the meadow to indicate its edge and also to frame the back courtyard; the entrance turns both towards a high birch tree and away from it. The way through the house leads in a wide curve towards the spiral staircase in the glazed corner, then upstairs to the upper floor - into the top of a spruce, out onto the roof and across a delicate bridge to the large roof terrace, below the top of a pine-tree and down again to the water trough.

Four reinforced concrete columns bear the main load of the roofing slab, otherwise white walls, undivided glass surfaces, sliding elements, all metal parts are left in the raw zink plating, no polished detail is in sight. This is clearly a continuation, a bringing up to date of White Modernism. In contrast to the hermetic and geometric formalisms of White Neo-Modernism of the late 70s, however, this building derives its power from the enormously sensitive and precise spatial interpretation of the site. Prohazka's buildings - and he has built several in similar locations - are highly energetic and at the same time minimalized site-specific event machines. It is the architecture which itself has been reduced to pure abstraction that creates the complex location of nature in nature.

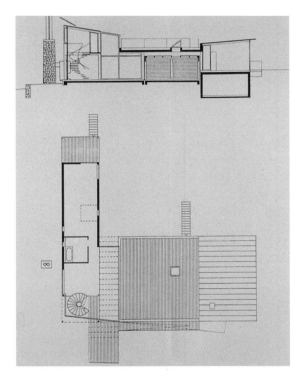

Section and ground plan

Rudolf Prohazka. Residential building near Wiener Neustadt, 1993

Analogous in the emphasis on spatial tension and the tendency towards Minimalism, and yet quite different in the means, in the signature. Commercial and office building Schillerpark in Linz by architect Adolf Krischanitz, just completed, to be opened soon. What is interesting about this for me? In his recent buildings Krischanitz has increasingly dealt with a risky and explosive problem. What he is concerned with is not experimental high-tech or the subjective detail nor the sculptural side of architecture. The challenge is to lift the existing technical, structural and detailed standard onto an unusual level of complexity and create an architecture with no striking details - while yet achieving very strong spatial effects and creating a spatial energy which transcends the material sphere, heightened by the colours of Oskar Putz. Moreover this building is an example of a topical and particularly urban building task. On the two lower levels the building is strongly and suggestively linked to the public space, and it transforms this response to the various movement directions of the lot into the overall sculptural shape all the way to the roof. The passageways structure themselves into a rhythm of narrowness and width, horizontally and vertically. The ground floor is relatively low in order to have a short passage to the second business level on the mezzanine with its ample room height, which is of particular advantage for the upstairs room of the restaurant/cafeteria overlooking the park. The strict grid of the position of the supports is brought into oscillation by the sinus curve of the courtyard roof planted with grass; there is a very generously dimensioned stairwell that is open towards the square. An existing regulation about the building line is adhered to at the ground floor façade, but in the upper storeys the building with its shading devices with integrated working grids for cleaning the façade ignores this slight kink and is flush with the neighbouring building, thus creating its own strong frame. Krischanitz has just carried out an almost identical programme at the Steirerhof hotel in Graz. These urban building tasks are subject to the specific dynamics of the world of business and merchandize and are confronted with the aggressive sign systems of advertising and the contemporary townscape. Usually architecture responds to these either regressively - by quoting traditional urbanism, a nostalgic typology of the passageways or by attempting to overcome urban entropy by means of so-called signature buildings designed by star architects or by retreating to the pure structure which willingly accepts the changing decorative facings - video façades etc. Krischanitz' building in Linz (like the one in Graz) is located between these extremes. It is sharply and clearly articulated, allows room for the free play of the world of merchandize outside and inside the building, and develops from the marginal conditions of the site an incisive space that clearly maintains the autonomy and the resistance of architecture while wearing the magic cap of the standard and the garb of its immaterial colour aura.

What Krischanitz is concerned about is not experimental high-tech nor the subjective detail.

The energetic space: the commercial and office building Schillerpark at Linz.

Commercial and office building Schillerpark at Linz

Site plan

Adolf Krischanitz. Commercial and office building Schillerpark, Linz 1993

Elevations and ground plans

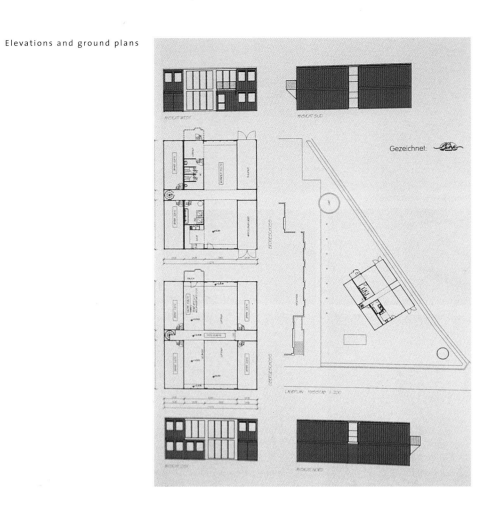

Team ST/A/D. Prototype house, 1993

Today the greater challenge is in the

limitation, the creative handling of

the standards, of the scarce resources.

The potential of the standard: the Prototype house by Team ST/A/D, architects Gerngroß, Höller und Schwan.

Prototype of a building that can be erected rapidly, designed by the team ST/A/D architects Gerngroß, Höller and Schwan, erected in the exhibition "SOS Aufbau" at the Vienna Secession last summer as part of an initiative of ideas by more than 70 architects who presented concepts for fast and cheap residential buildings for refugees, especially from the war regions of Austria's neighbouring states to the south. Not much needs to be said about this "fast building" by Heidulf Gerngroß & Co. It is put together from ten modules and can be erected in three days, providing 220 square metres of useable floor space at a price that is only one third of a conventional building. Yet it does not consist of schematic cells but has a generous interior quality. For me it is representative of this entire initiative by young and in some cases well-established architects who have supplied a number of new approaches for this urgent topic of cheap housing that does not seek to impress but to supply living space for fringe groups. The media have tended to report not too favourably on this event - the general tenor being that ideas for such modular housing existed already in the 60s, and nothing came of them - and anyway, isn't it almost cynical, such huts for the refugees...

Instead of such ignorant brushing off our media that are otherwise busily reporting on social and popular activities ought to have applied their influence to make further steps towards realizing this committed impulse on the part of the architects possible. For me this SOS-Aufbau exhibition was very important and positive evidence of the fact that in our architectural debate we are slowly getting away from this fixation on problems of superstructure, that architecture is once more coming down from its often vain desire to present itself as a so-called image carrier or fast road to corporate identity, that we are returning to other, more fundamental issues of building and that architecture is re-gaining its social reference, this time in a manner that is without pathos and non-moralizing. Today the great challenge is no longer to create architecture out of wealth, drawing on abundant resources. The greater challenge is in the limitation, the creative handling of the standards, of the scarce resources. "Peace to the huts" - I remember this title of a text by Dietmar Steiner, it was several years ago, the text has long been forgotten, unjustly forgotten. This is where we should start from and continue this train of thought: the future of the world, seen globally, will not be found in palaces, but in com-fortable huts - if there is any future at all. I am both happy and sad with this list of examples. Sad, because time and space are so scarce: one could easily analyze each of the projects presented for an hour or more. And that would really be rewarding, not just to sing praises but also to voice qualifications and ask questions. I am sad, because the time is too short: I or a few other people could immediately talk about 13 or 26 other current examples of buildings from

Austria. It would be a different but equally interesting range, and it should be done in the near future. I have a whole list of names and buildings that were not even mentioned today but would equally belong into such a stock-taking. Starting with the big names, the true candidates for the Top Ten, which I have withheld from you today. But there are at least thirty other names and buildings. I am not going to read them to you now. And this is the reason why I am at the same time very happy and very confident. There is still a building boom in Austria, and despite all complaining and griping there is a very efficient competition system, there even is - after decades of effort - an Architektur Zentrum in Vienna, yes in Vienna of all places, where these days European architecture is gathering for a festive event. Today in Austria a rich variety of high quality building activity is going on, a range of individual signatures, a scene as varied as the natural topography of the country itself that is so rich in contrasts.

Prague, as every other European city, is confronted with the problems of urban development.

10 | BUILDING WITH CHARACTER.
VLADIMIR ŠLAPETA.

Czech Republic

Form of State: Republic since 1993, **Area:** 78,864 km2, **Inhabitants (1992):** 10,325,700, **Capital:** Prague
Gross National Product 1992, per capita: $ 2,450, **Gross Domestic Product 1992:** $ 26,187 Mio, **Unemployment (Average, 1993):** 3.5%

In 1990/91, whilst the Czech Pavilion was being built in Seville, great changes were taking place in the Czech Republic. Architects began to leave the state planning offices, which quickly collapsed, and founded their own studios.

No other profession - with the exception of lawyers - underwent such a rapid transformation. At the same time, the effects of foreign investment started to make themselves felt - first in Prague, and subsequently in other cities too. Now, four years after the "Gentle Revolution", all of the popular cafés and restaurants have disappeared from the centre of Prague, including the "Fish House" ("Rybárna"), President Havel's favourite haunt. On the other hand, foreign capital has visibly had a positive influence: internationally renowned representatives of contemporary architecture were invited to submit designs for the development of the city of Prague. In 1990, after receiving a commission from a Dutch initiative, Jean Nouvel designed a project for the reorganisation of the Smichov industrial estate. The President's Office, together with Prague's chief architect, staged the "1991 Prague Workshop" in which architects such as Jean Nouvel, Vittorio Gregotti, Riccardo Bofill, Vojcek Ravnikov, Komomen-Heikkinen and two other groups of young architects from Prague and Brno participated.

However, during the first competitions in 1990/91, tendencies already started to become apparent that did not only confront Prague with the positive aspects, but also with the reality of a society based on a market economy: the construction of Hotel Penta, which is situated in an exposed position near Masaryk Station, proved to be mere façade architecture. Following the competition for the conference centre and Hotel Atrium-Tešnov, differences arose between the property developer and the architect, Martin Rajmiš, who had been awarded the first prize. As a consequence, attention turned to the conventional design which had taken the second place. In the competition for the development of the Myslbek gap site, the French developer imposed strict limitations on the possibilities open to the architect.

Internationally renowned representatives of contemporary architecture were invited to submit designs for the city of Prague.

Prague after the "Gentle Revolution".

Since the beginning of 1990, the architect Vlado Milunič has been planning to develop a gap site close to the residence of Václav Havel on the banks of the Vlatava. In the preliminary design, he had already begun to work with the composition of a gently rolling façade. The developer, a Dutch insurance company, insisted on bringing in an internationally renowned architect to collaborate on the project. Frank Gehry was chosen, in accordance with the agreement reached with the planning architect. A heated discussion ensued, both among experts and among the general public, over the new design, which was known as "The Dancing House". Some members of the public and a few experts involved in the preservation of historical monuments vehemently opposed the design, whilst Václav Havel, the owner of the neighbouring house, the chief architect and a few theoreticians gave it their full support. This house is most certainly a symbol of the American influence on Prague life in the wake of the revolution. (Some 30,000 Americans now live in Prague.) Without a doubt, this house represents a courageous step in allowing modern architecture to penetrate into the core of this historical city. That controversial reactions are invariably unavoidable goes without saying. Without questioning the qualities of Frank Gehry, I nevertheless feel that it is crucial to ask whether this design was not intended for Weil on the Rhine or for a suburban area in Los Angeles. It is a completely different issue realising such a project in a historical city like Prague, which has been completely preserved. Prague needs reflection rather than sensations. The early 90s represented the opening-up of the city on an intellectual level too. Richard Rogers, James Stirling, Josep Lluís Mateo, Christian Norberg-Schultz and Daniel Libeskind are just a few of the architects who came to Prague to hold lectures here. In this way Prague was able to make up for the failings of the past 40 years. The world looks on Prague in the hope that this city will once more come to play an important role in architecture. And for this reason, the ceremonial presentation of the Pritzker Award for Architecture was again held in Prague in 1993. Today, in the reality of everyday life, architects have to fight hard for their prestige in society. During the past 40 years, ten times as many civil engineers (those specialists in prefabricated construction) have been trained in the Czech Republic as architects. The pragmatism of the market economy is a great danger which the architect must confront by making public appearances. He has to successfully explain the designer role of the architect in society. Pilot buildings can be a very convincing argument in this respect.

Vlado Milunič and Frank Gehry. "The Dancing House", Prague 1990

Martin Němeč und Ján Stempel. Pavilion of the Czech Republik, EXPO Sevilla 1992 - photo: Pavel Stecha

The examples presented here show that modern

Czech architecture is again beginning to apply

the standards of the inter-war tradition.

The Czech architecture of the 20s and 30s, between New Objectivity and the example of
Le Corbusier, has not lost its model character.

Jaroslav Šafer. Office Building for the East-West-Group, Prague 1991-92

I should now like to present some examples of such projects: After a 15 years' stay in London and Australia, Jaroslav Šafer, who was born in 1946, returned to Prague. Since 1992, he has been professor for architecture at the Technical University of Prague. Whilst abroad, he gained valuable, extensive experience. Thus, during his last five years in Melbourne, he worked as design director at the architect's office of Daryl Jackson. In 1991-1992 he completed his first building in Prague. This project consisted in converting the courtyard block of a house (constructed in the 18th century and standing in Lilien Street in the Old City of Prague) into office buildings for the East-West Group. In the 20s, three storeys were added to the court block to accommodate a small factory which manufactured lifts. Jaroslav Šafer redesigned the interior rooms of the courtyard building and added a communications tower. His heavy steel structure reflected the Victorian Anglo-Saxon tradition of construction.

In comparison with the monolithic character of the original building, this new interpretation established a contrast, by means of transparency and reflection, between the exterior and the interior and vice versa. It seems like a volary, like a cage, which is spatial - three-dimensional - but not two-dimensional like a façade. The transparency and the spatial impact are not only visible on a horizontal plane, they also permit the transparent design of a part of the ceilings as well as translucency, on a vertical plane, through all the storeys. The colour-scheme is also derived from the Victorian tradition: dark green and lead grey are combined with black and green. In the substance of the old building, the arrangement of the windows takes its orientation from the original industrial character of the building.

The newly designed administration rooms were supplemented on each floor by a sanitary unit and a foyer. The foyer has been developed as an independent cube separated by a gap from the ceiling, i.e. in the form of a "house within a house".

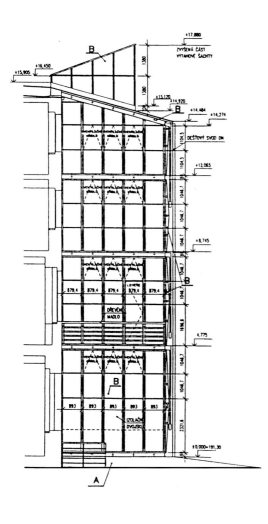

In comparison with the monolithic character of the

original building, this new interpretation established

a contrast, by the means of transparency.

A new conception of content, reflecting to the outside, too: the reconstruction of the centre of Prague by Jaroslav Šafer.

Section of the annex

Factory, interior view

Sections

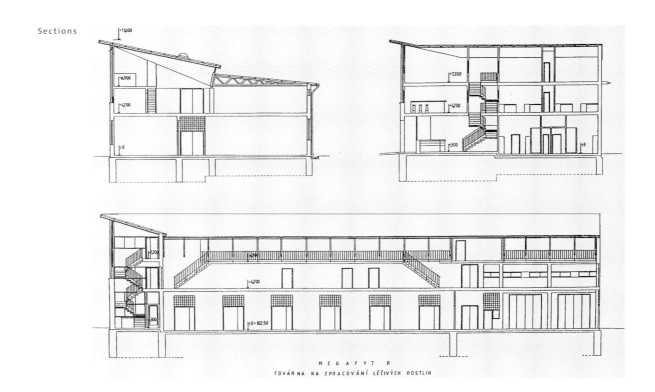

MEGAFYT R
TOVÁRNA NA ZPRACOVÁNÍ LÉČIVÝCH ROSTLIN

The next example I should like to present is the factory designed by Josef Pleskot. Josef Pleskot's first buildings dating from the early 80s revealed his unique feeling for a special kind of solemn modesty. The architect, who was born in 1951, has constantly succeeded in lending his works a personal intimacy, in reflecting regional inspiration and combining them in a generous concept.

The factory for processing medicinal herbs is located in the middle of the landscape on the banks of the Vlatava. Its front faces towards the stratified rocks on the opposite bank, whilst the south façade of the enterprise opens up to the sharp silhouette of the weir designed by the well-known Czech architect Kamil Roškot in the early 30s. The cubistic forms of Roškot's architecture, the individual rock strata and the rhythm of a row of poplar trees are reflected in the architecture of the factory, which Pleskot designed in collaboration with Radek Lampa, a young graduate from the Technical University in Prague. On the ground floor, the first level is formed by a masonry plinth, which absorbs the original garage section. A second, horizontally aligned level is intimated above this plinth. A coat of horizontally laid, grey Eternit slabs gives this level its texture. Further rooms are concealed behind the south façade. These rooms do not serve production, they constitute the staff common rooms and those for the management. The pleasing quality of this project is, above all, the sensitive and human dimensions, features which are so frequently neglected. It is apparent that the complex will be extended along the bank of the Vlatava.

Josef Pleskot. Factory, 1992-93

The pleasing quality of this project is, above all,

the sensitive and human dimensions, features

which are so frequently neglected.

Jirí Adam & Martin Pánek. Supermarket and Restaurant, Brno 1992-93

Restaurant

Initially, the impact of the process of change on

Brno seemed to be very slow. Today, however,

it is evident that this town is less bureaucratic

and hence more efficient than Prague .

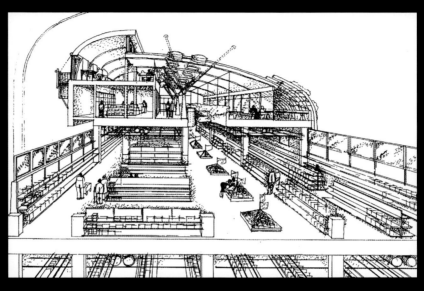

Axonometry of the Supermarket

Any further consideration of the architecture of the Czech Republic leads us to Moravia, or to be specific, to Brno. Initially, the impact of the process of change on Brno seemed to be very slow. Today, however, it is evident that this town is less bureaucratic and hence more efficient than Prague. As in the 20s and 30s, this is also reflected in the architecture. Brno is again demonstrating a close relationship to Vienna. Young architects such as Aleš Burian, Petr Pelčak, Jiří Hruša, Jan Sapák, Petr Křivuvka and others worked in Viennese planning and development offices during the first years after the "Gentle Revolution". Major building projects are currently being planned, such as a bank in Česká Ulice, the hospital in the district of Židonice and further projects which are sure to provide the basis for broader

discussion. While these projects are still awaiting realisation, I should like to present a new supermarket, designed by the architects Jirí Adam and Martin Pánek, in the district of Vinohrady. Just like Pleskot in his factory, Jirí Adam and Martin Pánek had to include the existing carcass in their design: the heavy reinforced concrete skeleton of a factory hall provided the starting point for their work. Two new storeys were constructed on top of this carcass in the form of a steel skeleton structure. At the side, the original building was adapted to the new requirements. The axis of the steel structure is aligned to the original module of the factory hall (6 x 9 m). The roofing consists of H-beams which were given a curved, circular and elliptical form during manufacture. The beams are supported by circular columns and by

diagonal struts. The original light well of the factory hall was used as an optical link between the individual storeys of the supermarket and the restaurant. The colour-scheme corresponds to the stock colours of the LERK company: green and yellow, combined with ochre. This supermarket is the first stage of a larger complex - consisting of a convalescent home and a hotel - for this district.

The final design reflects the diverse

character of the streets ending here.

Reacting on the rhythm of the city.

OMICRON K. Buisness-Center "Pexider", Prague 1991-94

My final example takes us back to the city of Prague. This building is the English "Pexider" Business Centre. The building, designed in the OMICRON K studio (architects: Martin Kotík, Václav Králiček and Vladimír Krátiký), occupies an important position in the centre of Prague. It is very close to Wenceslas Square and the National Museum and is also located at the prime access routes to Vinohrady, a district dating from the latter half of the 19th century. Following the demolition of the Baroque city wall, this district drew its atmosphere from the rows of rented houses and Functionalist buildings erected during the 30s.

The regular plan calls for a monumental solution of symmetrical form. The final design reflects the diverse character of the streets ending here. Belohradská Street is a city axis with pedestrian and road traffic. The architects reacted to this feature with a specially designed façade accentuated by a geometrical stone tile grid. In Anlická Street, by way of contrast, heavy road traffic prevails. At the planned location of the new building, the road widens to form a small square, to which the design reacts with a rounded glass façade. The second to the eighth upper storeys - with an area of almost 3,000 square meters - were designed for office rooms, and the arrangement of the floor-space can be varied. The ground floor is intended to be used by a bank, whilst the ninth floor houses a penthouse flat. An underground garage in the basement floors provides space for 75 vehicles.

In the inter-war period, Czech architecture was strongly influenced by the two poles of "New Objectivity" and a French architectural language that was represented by Le Corbusier. However, neither of these two approaches ever found extreme expression here. Nevertheless, Czech architecture did profit from a well-chosen standard, a sense for sound, craft composition and progressive technology which was made possible by domestic production. The examples presented here show that modern Czech architecture is again beginning to apply the standards of the inter-war tradition. Even though we are living in a chaotic and very difficult age, one which is characterized by many contradictory problems, I have not given up hoping that the development of both architecture and the building sector in the Czech Republic will move in a positive direction and that we will be able to reach to the European standard without, however, abandoning the smaller and more intimate, yet self-confident and independent character of Czech architecture.

Site plan

The country's cultural development has

always been rooting in admixtures and

influences, not on original conceptions;

on contrasts, not on unity.

Henrieta Hammer Moravčiková and Matúš Dulla on the character of the Slovac culture.

11 | ARCHITECTURE ON THE COUNTERPOINT.
HENRIETA HAMMER MORAVČÍKOVA, MATÚŠ DULLA.

Slovakia

Form of State: Republic since 1993, **Area:** 49,035 km2,**Inhabitants (1992):** 5,346,000, **Capital:** Bratislava
Gross National Product 1992, per capita: $ 1,930, **Gross Domestic Product 1992:** $ 9,958 Mio, **Unemployment (End of 1993):** 14.4%

It is certainly not easy to choose the five best buildings in any country, and even more difficult for Slovakia, a small inland country sharing borders with many neighbours. Its landlocked position has led to its exposure to various external influences which have often been stronger than the country's own creative potential. Slovakia is therefore a point of overlap amongst various layers of cultural values. The resulting mixture followed the progressive development in cultural centres inconspicuously but often relatively successfully. Predominant cultural trends never originated here. Slovakia has always been overshadowed by Vienna, Prague, Budapest and Krakow. The greats of European culture touched it slightly from time to time.

The country's cultural development has always been rooting in admixtures and influences, not on original conceptions; on contrasts, not on unity. We do not intend to present the so-called best of architectural practice, but to talk about dispersion and intermingling of impetuses. We will find numerous remarkable and, at the same time, inconspicuous cultural achievements and architectural works. They attract our attention by their simplicity which is conjoined to a plethora of influences and a fundamental humanism. The cultural situation resembles that in the countries on Europe's periphery. Here, on Europe's Eastern edge, the cultural expression is affected by the struggle to make a place for itself on this continent and by the permanent presence of differences, but most of all, by the consciousness of its own cultural self-sufficiency. All this has to be taken into account in the selection of the best architectural works. The first question which emerges is whether the work which best reflects contemporary demands on the current architectural work is in fact the most successful, consistent and credible. A positive answer has almost always meant following the more advanced model of Western Europe, where the orientation towards innovation has always been more pronounced. Such an answer assumes that techno-logical inventions promptly push the

architecture forward. In Slovakia, the ever-rich display of "other" and "better", which arises through confrontation with highly developed cultures, regularly generates uncertainty and hesitancy in choosing the appropriate direction.

The danger here is schizophrenia, so that architects often close themselves to influences, following instead their own line, their own logic in the con-struction of a building. They often succumb to resignation in matters of style, and sometimes also in their aesthetic ambitions. What should be given preference when choosing the best buildings: accordance with external inspirations or fidelity to one's own independent conceptions? A further question: should the works based on some eternal values be chosen? That would mean choosing the architecture which avoids stylistic classification. If its authors avow their creative inspiration (which is not always the case), then this inspiration is usually located in stable, persistent and generally recognized values. In Slovakia, modern architecture has served as a model to which indigenous architecture turned in its search for constancy. Returns to Modernism en masse were more frequent here than elsewhere. Comebacks took place after the World War II, after the Stalinist architecture of the 50s, in the second half of the 60s and, finally, in the 80s. These comebacks were especially pronounced because the opposition to Modernism has always been strong, even though it has always been political first and artistic only later. It has not been hard to subscribe to Modernism, which has been frequently renewed and understood within a wider context. Modernism has always lacked an unambiguous stylistic profile. It has always been a somewhat wide complex of loosely combined attributes belonging to a quasi-architectural style. The question we faced was: are we to follow this line, or should we undertake experiments which test the limits of free creativity? Experiments that based upon Modernism's provocation gradually lose their original effect. The mystery of the

new spirit disapperars and, in the con-servative community, to attribute even a short-term importance to such experiments is dubious. Of course, experimental works cannot withstand comparison to first-rate standard architecture. Are we to take this path, which has so often been used to introduce new experimental works from the domestic architectural scene, or are we to favour the country's indigenous architecture, although architecturally uncertain and unconvincing? Should we pay attention to the latter simply because it is authentic and bound to an inner responsibility that sometimes outweighs international perfection? This would be a very attractive way through a very imperfect Slovak architectural landscape. The other question is: are we to concentrate on the objectively best buildings in order to compile a "top five" which reflects only the works' inner quality and neglects their wider contexts? Or, are we to concentrate on a selection of buildings which is not completely divorced from the category: "the best works ever", but nonetheless expresses more general trends? This selection presumes a scale, although not necessarily of the buildings themselves but of the types they represent, of which they are examples with an overall architectural situation.

Maximum reduction and purity, in which

each form and proportion serves one

idea - the superb crystallic abstraction.

The new design for the Treasury is fascinating by a maximum of reduction.

In Slovakia, as well as in many other post-communist countries, we must answer the question, how to face the social transformation which began at the end of the 80s. Even if, on one hand, the decisive step was taken towards freedom and democracy based on the Western model, then on the other hand, it is obvious that this reorientation could only subtly change the depth of the whole creative potential. It nonetheless revealed a number of problems, limits and barriers in the architectural community. From this point of view, architecture is not only a system of buildings, but also a system of spiritual dimensions. Our selection is limited to five architectural works of good quality which represent stylistic currents of the last five years. Two works (one, an archaeological museum in the castle's treasury and the second, a villa, both in Bratislava), which reflect the effort to achieve a perfect architecture, start from technological quality and end in the pure brilliant appearance.

A third work included has similar ambitions within a purist new-modernist approach. It can even be said that this work, a small church in Vrakuňa, Bratislava, one of the most recent buildings of this type in Slovakia, probably reached the outermost limit in its effort to achieve pure simplicity. We were strongly intrigued here by the problem of counterpoint - on one hand, a pure simplicity, and on the other hand, the complexity and the human scale of the building. The human scale contradicts the original design, but at the same time originates from the fundamental architectural idea. The building is full of opposites, not only in its conceptual content, but also in its technological solutions. It materializes the never-ending conflict between exclusion and inclusion, the conflict between the clean,

purist work and that which has been marked by human traces.

One pronounced and deep trend in Slovak architecture is represented by another work, a small church in the small East Slovak village of Vojkovce. It represents an attempt to transpose narration into architecture, an attempt to tell the story. This work combines the post-modernist interest in narration with the old Slavonic world of fairy tales. Finally, we will present a temporary structure intended to manifest of the idea of friendship, a bridge designed as decoration for a celebration. It belongs neither to an eternal architecture of stone, nor does it represent the newest style (its construction was based on the study of architecure's internal organic co-ordinates), on the contrary it reflects the transience of this period.

The archaeological museum - the Treasury in the Bratislava Castle - by architect Ferdinand Milučký (co-operation architects Bouda and Masár and glass-maker Askold Žačko) was built in 1988. Those greatly-prized archaeological treasures - ivory, silver and gold treasures found in all areas of Slovakia and dating from the Paleolithic to the Middle Ages - which remained in Slovakia (some of the findings are in museums in Budapest, Vienna and Prague) are exhibited here. The Treasury is situated where the Hungarian coronation treasures had been kept - in the main tower of the castle - and is housed in four rooms, connected with a light staircase running through the lower space of the tower.

It represents an architecture based on modern certainties tested by time. Ferdinand Milučký limits his expressive vocabulary to the utmost in the spirit of Mies van der Rohe to access archetypal form. He inserts granite paving, glass display cases and flood-lights into the

pure white interiors from the 15th century. The central pyramidal display-case protects the archaeological collection's prized piece, the Paleolithic Venus from Moravany. All other cases are prism-shaped, oriented either aslant or perpendicular. Besides the archaeological finds, there are not many other artefacts which make up the exhibition: the entrance door, a balustrade and staircase in the first hall, the illusionist fillings of gothic portals and two pairs of half-cylindrical pilasters in the passages between halls. Maximum reduction and purity, in which each form and proportion serves one idea - the superb crystallic abstraction. The atmosphere of the exhibition is, of course, set by the archaeological findings: the most precious archaeological finds are exhibited here, Paleolithic statues, the gold treasures comprising ", Roman and Great Moravian jewels. Thus, the architectural solution only frames the projection of the history, to which the authors included the theme of projection in architectural solution. The pure abstract projection of the light coming from the flood lights offsets the scenographic spaces from the items exhibited in the dim light of the rooms. Several red-filtered flood lights at the castle tower create a dream-like atmosphere.

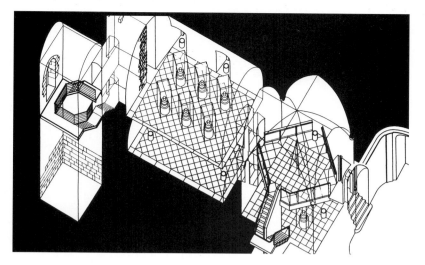

Axonometry

A new design for the permanent collection

Ferdinand Milučký. Archaelogical Museum
(Treasury), Bratislava 1988 - photos: I.Bacik

The structed mass does not disturb by an immodest

monumentally; rather, it grows naturally from the landscape.

Natural materials and an impressive use of llight: the Church in Vojkovce.

Vojkovce is less a small village than a settlement spread over the Spiš hills in Eastern Slovakia. The St. Bartolomej Church, built at a site of a small chapel from the last century whose capacity no longer satisfied the needs of the community, was completed by Albert Rybarčák of Prešov. Situated on the hill near the local cemetery, in the heart of the village, the church consists of three basic interpenetrating masses: a rotunda, an ark, a bell-tower. The untraditional entrance to the church is situated in the rotunda's arch. The ark's longitudinal body, with its pronounced vertical glazing and impressive wall painting, cuts the rotunda. The composition of the inner space is closed by the small apse of the bell tower. The altar as central celebratory space is emphasized by the light coming

from a skylight. The inner space is extraordinarily impressive: it tries to tell one of the oldest biblical stories, that of Noah's Ark, as if the Ark had run aground in Vojkovce. We see the ship's inclined body, rocking on the stormy water of the Flood, and the sun, whose beams penetrate grey clouds as a promise of God's grace. This unique retelling of the Ark story in the paintings on the main nave's wooden walls is the work of Vladimír Popovič. The Vojkovce church is noted for the humility of its natural materials and its impressive and ingenious use of light. The architects succeed in making a clear statement by using a system of simple archetypes. The church's outer appearance makes it a pleasant companion to the simple houses of the neighbourhood. Its structured mass does

not disturb by an immodest monumentality; rather, it grows naturally from the landscape. From the distance, it resembles a group of smaller objects rather than a huge monster.

Albert Rybarčák. St. Bartolomej Church in Vojkovce, 1993 - photo: A.Jirousek

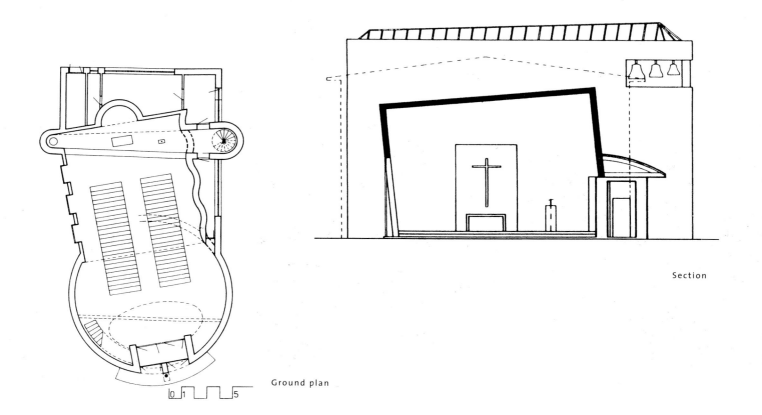

Section

Ground plan

0 1 5

The elegant rounded volume, lense-like in ground plan, is connected in a very pure and natural way.

The Church in Vrakuňa, an effort to expunge shallowness.

Michael Bogár, Lubomír Králik and Ludovit Urban. Church in Vrakuňa, 1992

The parish church and the St. Maria chapel in Vrakuňa were reconstructed and expended in 1992 by young architects from Bratislava: Michal Bogár, Lubomír Králik and Ludovít Urban. The small original one-nave church no longer met the demands of a parish church. The task was to provide space for the mass, and, when necessary, to offer facilities for other public gatherings. Today, the church can indeed serve as a lecture or concert hall. The elegant rounded volume of a new tabernacle, lense-like in ground plan, is connected in a very pure and natural way with an object of new and original style. The puristically clear mass of the new architectural elements represents an analogy to arms which open towards a small square. Simple smooth walls and grandiose glass surfaces mark off the building from its surroundings dramatically. The original Franciscan principle of the purified church is carried forth in ascetic pureness and formal sincerity. The church interior consists of a large hall with an elegant empora curve. This central hall is supported by a series of columns, whose disposition echoes the building's rounded glass wall. The simple wooden single-run staircase is linked to the glazed peripheral arch. An iron balustrade defines the emporia and lends a feeling of lightness and capaciousness. The connection of a new and an old church space naturally culminates in a smooth white prism, a house in a house. This prism serves simultaneously to support the emporia, and to house the staircase, a room for a priest and a confession box. The church's abstract form resembles the famous works of great Modernists. But the minimalist architectural language seems not to dovetail with the sacral theme.

The architects hesitate a moment before continuing in the same tenor: they introduce the works of various artists into a cold object bereft of all decorations. The mosaic, the peculiarly shaped capitals and the entrance portal, all works by a young Slovak "expressionist", Svetozár Ilavsky, lend the building an artistic expression somehow close to the fragments of Gaudí's park Güell, or to the aesthetics of Niemeyer's Brasilia. The altar is dramatically lit not only by a roof skylight but also by the cut-glass rosette in the front part of the space. The pews again reflect an effort to humanize the coldness which is so characteristic of Modern architecture. The organically curved form of the supporting iron structure resembles the biomorphological ornamentation of Victor Horta; the wooden seats made of natural unimpregnated oak-tree wood look, perhaps, too profane. This work controversially combines the greatest architectural simplicity and artistic richness. It seems to materialize the contrasts present in contemporary Slovak architecture: its effort to achieve purity and to expunge shallowness.

The villa represents one integrated unit, from the overall architectural compositions to the perfect detail.

Simple elegance and clarity: the Villa in Bratislava by Jozef Ondriš und Juraj Závodný.

Jozef Ondriš and Juraj Závodný. Villa in Bratislava, 1993 - photo: J.Králik

The architects of the villa, built in 1993 in the hilly outskirts of Bratislava, are Jozef Ondriš and Juraj Závodný. It is probably the first building in Slovakia that consistently exhibits the qualities of first-rate architecture, not only in the architects' intentions, but also in its final realization. The house is inspired by the constructional-technological quality and the architectural spirit of the architecture of the 20s and the 30s. This quality is a value in itself, which of course cannot improperly interfere with the artistic character. In a presentation of this villa abroad, one must emphasize that quality like this had only been a dream in Slovakia. The villa represents one integrated unit, from the overall architectural compositions to the perfect details. It is equipped with modern technology, including a small pool on the ground floor, a sauna, air-condition units in the main room and built-in ceiling lights. Although the site is no larger than 400 m2, the villa seems capacious. The building's two wings are slightly shifted against each other and linked by a bowed single-run staircase. From the street, the house appears to be two storeys high, and from the garden, four storeys. To the left of the entry is a garage, to the right, a space which runs along the whole length of the house and which is divided into the rooms for a studio. These rooms are accessible from the street through a separate entrance. A big ring-shaped window which offers a panoramic view of the centre of Bratislava and the Castle is a highlight of this space. The gallery above the main dwelling space is accessible from the rear. Under the gallery, there is a well-equipped kitchen, whose bar counter and stools rather resemble a bar. On this floor are three bedrooms, each with its own bathroom. The lowest floor, with its small pool, sauna, fitness room and boiler room, is at ground level at the rear of the house. The top floor has a smaller ground plan - the continual space can be used as a studio, or can be divided into two rooms, again with their own bathrooms. There are two terraces on this floor, one oriented towards the city and the other towards the garden. The garden terrace's circular roof not only corresponds to the ring-shaped window in the study, but also creates "the crown" of the whole building. Both the architecture and the disposition of spaces are noted for their simple smartness, lightness and clarity. The architectural means used here - interrupting or dividing of planes and surfaces, iron balustrades, wooden stairs -

are all set perfectly in relation to one another. The authors succeeded in reaching a very fine balance between two extremes: on one hand, almost uncontrollable complexity and, on the other hand, a provocative simplicity. The building consciously manifests decisive architectural experiences of this ebbing century. An examination of the details exposes the Villa's design as a retrospective study of the 30s (that is why the authors called it phonetically "Srti's"). They are dominated by simplicity, horizontal balustrades and glazed walls, all characteristic of the style of these years. If one seeks a precedent in the modern heritage, the villa slightly resembles Rietveld's house for Mrs. Schröder in Utrecht. The buildings resemble each other not only in their sequence of opaque and glazed planes but also in the principle of flexibility relative to partition walls. The vertical double chimney evokes the Douglas house by Richard Meier in Harbor Springs. Its wealth of colour is again slightly decadent - a combination of blue and pink, which are the architects' favorite colours.

View from the first floor - photo: J.Králik

Bridge of Friendship

Albrecht Mokovíny and Martin Somora. Bridge of Friendship, model - photos: A.Mikovíny, M.Somora

This architecture expresses a need to return to nature
and to the archetypical, which offer orientation to the
human being in the complexe world.

The Bridge of Friendship at Middletown by Albrecht Mikoviny and Martin Somora.

The Bridge of Friendship and its motto "Bridging the Gap to Friendship and Understanding" exemplifies the shift of architectural practice from utilitarism towards free creativity. It was designed by Albrecht Mikoviny and Martin Somora for a festival in the American city of Middletown, which was held in September 1993. The bridge represented the three new states, the Czech Republic, Slovakia and Ukraine, to which in 1993 the festival was dedicated. The bridge paraphrases the famous Charles' Bridge in Prague, a popular meeting place for artists and peddlars, and transposes its model into the formal language of the wooden bridge. The tower's form is closely related to the original Gothic stone architecture. Decorative ornaments were inspired by the folk architecture of the North Slovak village Čičmany and by the local Indian culture. All these elements are combined in a simple, constructionally pure and clear expression. The authors express a rich world of ideas in this relatively simple work. It reveals a need to return to nature and to the archetypical, which offer orientation to the human being in the complex world of his own existence. These are the works that, in our opinion, represent the most remarkable achievements in the Slovak architecture in the last five years. Despite the reduction of civil engineering as a result of serious social transformations in post-communist Slovakia, much has been built, which we only reluctantly excluded.
Finally, some words about those buildings that are not in our list. First of all, it is necessary to mention the buildings which represent the boom of contemporary architecture, i.e. banks, buildings of insurance companies and savings

companies. This architectural type was naturally very rare under the former political system. Nowadays, these financial institutions have financial sources, so that the number of such buildings is increasing dramatically. Their architectural contribution is, however, obviously small. They are conservative and conformist, and merely fill the white spots on the map but not the white spots in the field of architecture.
Let us return to the last of the buildings included in our list, the bridge in the USA. In it the main themes of East Slovakian architecture are represented. This part of Slovakia has always been slightly different from the Western part of the country. Its closeness to Hungary and the vast basin of the Tisa river brought the influence from Budapest, while the Western parts are rather influenced by Vienna and Prague. The current East Slovak architectural regionalism is reflected in the creative work of Imre Makovecz. Unfortunately, this approach is still waiting for built projects in which the architects could materialize their statements. We don't mention Post-Modernism, either. It often exhausts itself in conventional allusions to historical elements which it believes to be sufficient in creating a stimulating architecture. Perhaps, it is a way to enliven the greyness and monotony of our cities and villages which have been "cultivated" for decades; but it cannot fulfil higher architectural criteria. In Slovakia, the rigorous, cold and rational minimalism, observed e.g. in the Czech Republic, is almost entirely absent. It seems as if the narrative tendencies of the Slovak provenience, which are pronounced in Dusan Jurkovic's past

work, remained deeply rooted. The key problem of contemporary architectural discourse is a deep cleft. On one hand, there exists the ideal of a valuable architecture, for which the free and the democratic society offers good preconditions. On the other hand, frustration characterizes the reaction to the newest architecture, both in its projects and its realized form. The architectural community expects this divergence to disappear soon; it may, however, take several decades. Perhaps, this controversy can be productive, and can drive creativity towards new ideas and ideals. If so, then the effort to mitigate this controversy could lead most certainly to a new mediocrity and destructive complacency.

Political disappointment has lead to apathy; an

apathic society, in the midst of a shrinking

education budget and growing media wars, demands

spectacular events, and a staged architecture.

Akos Moravansky on the disillusion following the end of communism in Hungary.

12 | THE DRAMATIZED BUILDING SITE: THE POETRY OF BUILDING BEFORE
AND AFTER THE POLITICAL TRANSITION. ÁKOS MORAVÁNSZKY.

Hungary

Form of State: Republic since 1989, **Area:** 93,030 km2, **Inhabitants (1992):** 10,278,000, **Capital:** Budapest
Gross National Product1992, per capita: $ 2.970, **Gross Domestic Product 1992:** $35,218 Mio, **Unemployment (Average, 1993):** 1993):12.1%

The building site is, for Janáky, architecture's most important topos: an assemblage of materials,

forms and constructions better illustrating Hungarian reality than a completed edifice could do.

Hungary four years after the political transformation.

The debates on the fate of the monuments from the socialist past, in which a moralizing iconoclasm struggled with an enlightened irony, seem to have ended with the victory of the latter. The monuments have already become distant, their absence accentuated by empty pedestals and crossed-out street names. The stone heroes will be gathered into a new park in Budapest, where their hollow pathos shall be revealed by their multiplication. Already in 1988, someone proposed as an attraction an open air museum, a sanctuary of socialism. Even then, such ideas did not seem too surprising; many hoped that the relics of the "soz-real" of the 50s would end up at antique dealers' and not on heaps of rubble. And since that time, everyday reality has produced continuous ironies. A monument from the socialist past has, for example, been transformed into a Western car dealer's showroom. New buildings in Hungary - one could report on them in the way of the plan fulfillment report, an important rhetorical model from Stalinist times. But, in the first place, it is awkward to justify the heroic genre with good buildings. But more important, irony hinders any positive action that is now so necessary. The horrible jokes told by the inhabitants of Sarajevo over the radio demonstrate the triteness of endorsing the central European "apocalypse joyeuse". The newest architectural arrangements in Budapest, both the planned and the (almost) coincidental, either provoke irony or else are ironic themselves. The car showroom demonstrates the newly-attained freedom from a double perspective. Nestled in the monument, it contains the promise of a better quality of life for a segment of society while, with unconscious cleverness, the monument gestures towards a utopia shifted ever further into the distance. Or is it simply the pathos of the granite cubes, which appears authentic in comparison to the colourful artificial material of the shop, and which may well outlive numerous other temporary uses? The vertical addition to an old residential building in the centre of Budapest (1993) by Imre Makovecz is certainly not an intentionally

ironic gesture, but despite this it can only be read as an ironic commentary on the historical situation. In an environment where social consensus, modesty, and the conscious subordination of individual forms to the overall image of the street were formidable, something new and individualistic appears, orgiastically rich in detail. The unusual poetry, the white towers of the new storeys, make the restraint, the architectural prose of the gray, neglected houses on the street seem ridiculous and unimaginative. They certainly long for more than a decent repair job, cleaning and painting; they dream of towers.
Imre Makovecz is seldom ironic in his remarks, and often speaks about community, about home, about God, but most often of the drama of building. "The essence of building, I believe, is not its material, its strength, its construction, its style, but rather its drama. Of this I am convinced", he wrote in 1988 in an essay entitled "The Drama of Village Cultural Centres". Péter Reimholz, an architect whose cultural centre will also be discussed here, speaks similarly of the drama of the building site.
Irony and drama, like tragedy, poetry and prose, are purely literary concepts. Why should they be used as metaphors for architecture? What does the "drama of building" actually mean? Such terms, I believe, should not present the work merely as the result of the architect's formal intentions but, rather, explain it as the consequence of the genre's inner laws. When a writer narrates something, the fundamental structural laws of the genre of literature - tragedy, comedy, satire, etc. - determine his statements as much as does the content of the sentences he writes down. When architects speak of the drama of building, they raise questions regarding dramatic heroes, the dramatic situation, the conflict, and the structurally conditioned possibilities of the conflict's solution. Which form the architectural imagination chooses - whether irony or drama - determines a lot: deus ex machina as a dramatic solution would seem out of place in a comedy. Further indications of genre as a key to the explanation of

architecture might also be found in the fact that Hungarian architecture has no theoretical tradition equivalent to the developed exegeses of modern Western architecture. The writings of such significant Hungarian architects of the 20th century as Ödön Lechner, Béla Lajta, and Farkas Molnár are purely factual descriptions of their buildings set in a biographical context rather than programmatic texts. To dramatize the building site, predetermining its reception and programme, interprets the intentions of these architects somewhat unconventionally, but one hopes the works will demonstrate the legitimacy of such an approach.
Instead of proceeding chronologically, I am tracing my theme backwards in history from the present to the past; as the point of departure for the story is determined from the beginning by the anticipated final destination. Firstly, there is a project whose realization is still doubtful; the second one is an office building just completed. Both these projects show that good architecture in Hungary for the moment has to dispense with ideologies and great models. Instead of ideology one finds a search for spontaneity and heterogeneity. The next two specimens date from the last years before the political transformation. These are quite different. These buildings are loud, they are ideological, they refuse the status quo and the architecture of the officially controlled offices. Nevertheless, the two buildings follow contradictory strategies. The last project I am going to mention here stems from the 80s.

> **The building site is, for Janáky, architecture's most important topos: an assemblage of materials, forms and constructions better illustrating Hungarian reality than a completed edifice could do.**

Fragmentization as an architectural strategy.

The competition entry by István Janáky and György Major for the Pedestrian Walkway of the 1996 EXPO in Budapest, my first example, was awarded a prize in 1993 even though the architects had proposed, in place of the pedestrian bridges demanded in the competition announcement, two main focal points on each riverbank connected only by ship. On the Buda side, two large university buildings mark the north and south sides of a large square; in its centre, an artificial hill forms an auditorium, designed like a shell with rows for an audience. An assembly hall is placed on the riverbank; its lower storey serves for ship moorings while the terrace of the stone-clad cube projects far over the Danube, like a gesture in the direction of the Museum of Modern Art on the Pest side of the river. The hill with the assembly hall marks the centre of the EXPO, with a circle of pavilions and radial rows of trees around it. The current buildings are all horizontal, both in order not to distort the monumentality of the river and to emphasize the spot as a new border between capital and periphery. The Pest side follows this creative concept further. Here, two 40-metre-high tower-like structures form a kind of gateway, with the Museum of Modern Art as the third element. The link to the riverbank is secured by an underground construction open to the Danube. The connection between the riverbanks, hinted at by bridge-like structures, exists only in the movement of the ships and not in a fixed, built construction. Motivated by the suspicion that the prizewinner needed a symbolic bridge for the international exhibition, the architects erected markers with no inherent meaning. Janáky avoided a large-scale solution in the

spacious Interior Hall of the Budapest Electricity Works (1988-89). Instead, he surrounded the hall with another shell, which resists any appearance of a container, or of constructed bravura. Thus the building looks like an accidentally formed shed. The building site is, for Janáky, architecture's most important topos: an assemblage of materials, forms and constructions better illustrating Hungarian reality than a completed edifice could do. The poetics of the unfinished, as expressed in both Janáky's remarks and designs, has a genealogy that reaches back to John Ruskin's critique of perfection. Ruskin rejected an architecture that aimed to the appearance of perfection with simple means and unified, undecorated form. Such monumental forms were not to be found in nature, he thought, since the Creation was perfectly conceived and then left to natural erosion. The honest work of men should remain fragmented, undecorated, and incomplete. The hope of the building site, of the half-finished building, stands in opposition to the melancholy of the decayed, completed building. Janáky employs the metaphor of the wanderer invited to the wedding celebration: one enjoys speaking with him, laughs and cries over his stories, and listens to his "remarkable prophecies", yet as soon as the house is finished, he is sent away. The romantic image of the wanderer, the essential attributes of which are estrangement and discomfort separating him from the completed work, emphasizes the importance of authenticity; the possibility of decision-making; the rejection of the finished, unified, and systematic solutions offered by politics, the media, and design; and

votes in favour of nomadic life. For Janáky, the hopefulness of the building site has nothing to do with the avant-garde constructivist pathos of the "building site of the future". The objects, flotsam on the great river of time, can only be brought into an illusory relationship by a deceptive completion. The short summary of Janáky's competition project, called a "dedication", used an archaic form; it was written in the style of the old Improvement Committee of the Biedermeier period. In 1911, the first article appeared in the paper "A Ház" calling attention to Budapest's domestic classicism of this period. Janáky's dedication conjures up the atmosphere of this time when Archduke Joseph and Joseph Lechner decided on new streets and squares and granted licenses to building plans. The EXPO design by Janáky without citing this past, shows the architects' interest in an architecture of hybrid forms and coordinated heterogeneity. His design could become important for Budapest, if only it will be realized. At the Seville EXPO, hisdesign won the first prize, but, nevertheless, someone else's design was realized. The Budapest EXPO was cancelled in the mean time.

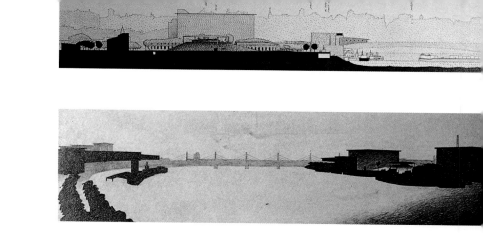

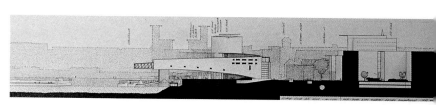

István Janáky. Competition to the pedestrian walkway of the EXPO 1996 in Budapest

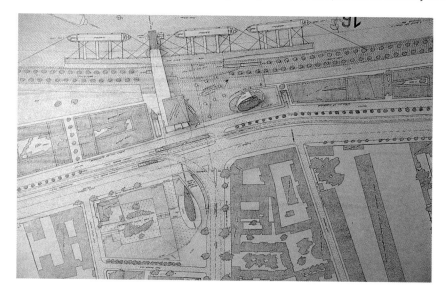

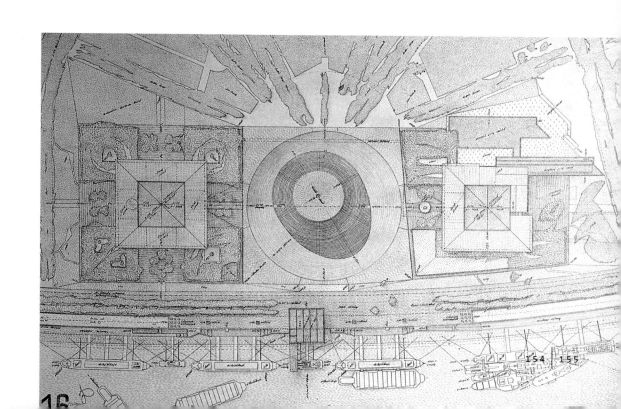

Gábor Turányi. Office building, Budapest 1993

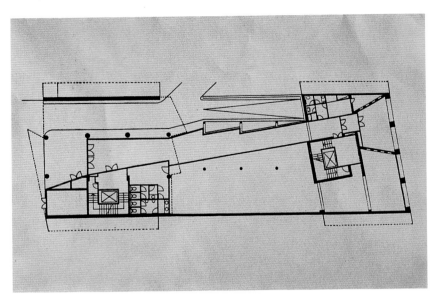

Ground plan of the office building

The minimalism of Turányi's position is didactic and educational

bringing him in the vicinity of the Biedermeier period with its

demand for continuity, modesty, and an awareness of context.

The temptation of referring back to the past.

Gábor Turányi. Holiday Centre Badacsonytomaj at lake Balaton, 1983

A similar attitude to architecture is to be found in Gábor Turányi's designs. His new office building in the centre of Budapest between Károly Ringstrasse and Asbóth Street was completed in 1993.

The point of departure for Turányi, as for Janáky, was the question of spontaneity. He made use of this idea earlier with his Holiday Centre in Badacsonytomaj at Lake Balaton (1983), an ensemble combining planned and already existing buildings. What apppears "readymade" is in fact designed, and the entire arrangement takes on the form of spontaneously enlarged holiday homes.

It is disconcerting that this playful language, originally intended for the holidays, here served a paramilitary organization: the workers' militia. The layout is especially interesting for the contradiction between the organization's proclaimed heroic traditions in the labour movement and the design's feigned spontaneity of form. It is a good example of the increasing withdrawal of political representation into an almost private space in the last years of socialism. Significantly, the current owner, who opened a hotel here, considers the layout too unattractive and plans to modify it.

Turányi's Expansion of the Roman Catholic Parsonage in Obuda-Ujlak, Budapest (1987), follows further the game of spontaneity and structure. Turányi placed a small school in the new wing - an entrance hall, two classrooms and a large attic room with open rafters, used as a students' hostel. The long wall with the large gabled roof lends the environment a faintly provincial, almost rustic tone. By upgrading and adapting such banal motifs as fence and gabled roof, the house assumes a healing function, it is cautiously renovating the district. The wedge-shaped space between wall and façade has something fort-like about it, protected by the large cantilevered roof and its visible wood construction. The minimalism of Turányi's position is didactic and educational bringing him in the vicinity of the Biedermeier period with its demand for continuity, modesty, and an awareness of context. "Biedermeier as Educator" was the title of an essay by Joseph August

Lux, written about 1910. Lux maintained that Biedermeier interiors were the same from the Kaiser to the middle classes: a unified interior for the whole society. The Kádár era aspired to exactly this reconciliation. Introversion resulted in seclusion towards the exterior. In a short essay written in 1986, Gábor Turányi emphasized the importance of pursuing this kind of architecture: "This architecture accepts the given facts, the modest possibilities, rather than disguising them; it has a clear and intelligible design, so that it demonstrates unambiguous and correct solutions rather than hints and indications. Its intellectual resources are complex enough to carry multilayered meanings. Having clarified its purpose and resources, it employs building technology in an objective manner. Instead of believing in the omnipotence of technology, it experiments with a new, sober modernity. It strives for full continuity; it wishes also to make use of the lessons of the last fifty or sixty years. For Turányi this architecture is especially important since "the chain of continuity appears now to be broken".

Many architects at the beginning of this century, such as Paul Mebes and Adolf Loos, have made use of this metaphor and argued for a reconnection to the place where the chain had been broken: the domestic architecture of the Biedermeier period. That was the lesson announced by Mebes in his influential book "Um 1800". Turányi's new office building in the Károly Ringstrasse fits well into the context of the unified street front. The most important and dominating element within this context is the large headquarters of the Council of Public Works, erected in 1938 as the main building on a planned new radial street called Mádach Avenue.

The architect was Gyula Wälder, a professor at the Technical University who was influenced by Fritz Höger's brick buildings in Hamburg.

There had been building projects earlier, for the gap in the Madách Ringstrassen's front, employing only vertical bands of brick in order to establish the connection to Wälder's building. Turányi's solution is

more in keeping with the old building; the façade is a pared down version of Wälder's. The plasticity of the main entrance building, with its rows of arcades, becomes a two-dimensional street façade; the vertical brick profiles throw diminished bands of shadows. In lieu of the rows of arcades, Turányi designed a two-storeyed commercial façade not of expressionist character but slightly reminding of Budapest and Vienna shop façades of the turn of the century. The "well behaviour" of this façade displays a virtue seldom found in contemporary Budapest architecture, but this alone would not be worth a remark. The façade on Asbóth street achieves tension through a very well orchestrated confrontation of motifs. In continuation of the generally very high quality of the Hungarian achitecture of the 30s this façade exposes good proportions, attention to detail, carefully selected materials and a fine finishing. The quiet, stone-clad screen of this façade, developed from inside, carries over to the middle section, which itself seems like a fresh implementation of the theme of the main façade clad in brick. The parallelism of this area of the façade to the main street appears as a resonant, aggressive motif, equipped with iron girders, further emphasizing verticality. The acute angles, borrowed in an altered form from the apartment house architecture of the 30s, confirm that Turányi's references to continuity here comprise a continuity with the avant-garde.

**Building is a drama whose arch spans between
potentiality and realized facts.**

Imre Makovecz on the tragedy of the building site.

Reference to the avant-garde is the main theme of my third example as well. In 1987, Gábor Bachman and László Rajk designed a Bar in Szigetszentmiklós, a workers' suburb south of Budapest. The bar is named Munka-Tett: work-action. This example's significance lies in the fact that it confirms the heroic image of the avant-garde and uses the existing structure of power to finally demask them. But it is worth to note that this design does not alone use hammer and sickle for bar stool back rests, but at the same time Moholy-Nagy's light space modulator. The avant-garde is part of the surroundings. Discussed much more in foreign publications than in Hungary, the tradition of the Hungarian avant-garde is even less present in Hungarian architectural debates. After the Second World War, in the era of socialist realism, it was condemned as "cosmopolitan"; in the late 70s and 80s it was associated with an architecture of prefabricated concrete slabs. The beauty of this sensitive architecture could be experienced only in reproductions. The bar is a disenchanted place today. It is shrilly lighted; someone has composed the name of a German brand of beer with the letters of MUNKA TETT. The back rests are gone, as are the intellectuals that had a taste for this ambience. In the 80s the avant-garde tactics so nearly approached the edge of appropriation that it aestheticized the objects of its criticism and made them fashionable. Contemporary ambivalence, rejection and nostalgia in the face of the socialist past is in part an unintentional consequence of this tactic. Some of the guests of the Work-Action-Bar can, in fact, reconstruct the irony perfectly, but others cannot, and as a result the forms of "socialist realism" have today been assimilated to mass culture. The architecture of Imre Makovecz follows another trace, rejecting the ironic tactics of the avant-garde of the 80s.

His architecture lives on the pathos of opposition, and its tragedy lies in the fact that after the disappearance of the communist system it became the official architecture. Imre Makovecz needs no introduction; his fame today results mostly from the myth of his internal exile. His Catholic church in Paks is the fourth example I would like to mention. I have to explain why I selected it though I dislike his approach. Experience has proven that a conscious refusal of this architecture reinforces the myth of its suppression. And, doubtlessly, Imre Makovecz's architecture is at the moment the only point of reference for Hungarian architecture. These buildings divide the public: on the one hand there is enthusiastic support, on the other there is an emotional refusal of their formal language. The location of Paks, where the church stands (built in 1990), is symbolic. As a city, Paks is hardly worth a thought (although Hungary's only atomic power plant is located there). The building's tale of woe corresponds, in the discussion of the church, to the architect's personal fate and to his exile in the early 70s from the state system of architectural planning. He has been the dramatic hero in a struggle against large office bureaucracy and the first to be aware of alternatives. This architecture contradicted to the reigning ideology; it voted for handicrafts rather than industrial production, for wood rather than reinforced concrete, for organic forms rather than grids, and for transitoriness rather than the illusion of stability. It opposed the avant-garde not only in its rhetoric, but also in its conscious rejection of the use of existing institutional structures. In an essay of 1989 the sociologist István Magyari-Beck described Makovecz's reference to anthropomorphism in the following words: "The traditional wood constructions, the beams, no longer recall their original, living forms. Makovecz

apparently wants to make his houses look more organic, more vivid, but instead he builds images of death. The debarked tree reminds one less of the life-serving beam than of a tree killed for the purpose of building. Let us think of painting, or of photography, to confirm this interpretation. The leafless tree, killed by a lightning bolt, is there, too, a symbol of destruction. It is an astonishing truth that architecture, even against the artist's intention, expresses the truth of its age." Building is a drama whose arch spans between potentiality and realized facts, Makovecz once said. That the drama ends, in this case, as a tragedy is perhaps no contradiction to the architect's intention - Makovecz's conception of history and of life is essentially tragic. The church in Paks is a building expressive of this tragedy, this "culture of frustration". The effect of this position, the opposition of the conjured up ideal of an organic society and the tragedy of its realization, is to set free powers that in their turn will thwart the process of recovery necessary today.

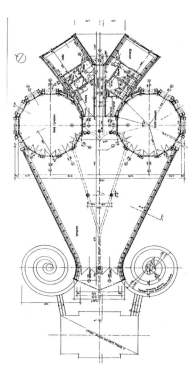

Ground plan

Imre Makovecz. Church in Paks, 1990

This example's significance lies in the fact
that it confirms the heroic image of the
avant-garde and uses the existing
structure of power to finally demask them.

Avant-garde as a means of enlightenment.

Gábor Bachman und Lászó Rajk. Munka-Tett Bar in Szigetzentmiklós, 1987

My last example emerged in the 80s from the state system of the planning office. Here, as well, the idea of drama is predominant. The city of Székesfehérvár, where Péter Reimholz's Cultural Centre Videoton (built in 1984) stands, was the coronation city of the Hungarian kings in the Middle Ages. After the Second World War the large electric company Videoton was established there; the households of the Eastern Block countries were supplied with television sets and their armies with communications technology. Videoton could then afford to build a cultural centre on the city's edge. The drama was interpreted by Reimholz in an interview as a dualism of materials; simultaneously as a dualism of massiveness and transience. He wanted to give material proof that there was an architect who "in a given place and under given circumstances, would achieve forms that would not be works formed by hand but rather the result of an interaction of strengths, imposed and held together by a formative spirit." What is described as "an interaction of strengths" leaves an open space. Reimholz said:

"The whole brick façade is a dialectic game: someone decided to put gigantic reinforced concrete pillars at intervals of three and nine meters, let light fall between them, and placed ceilings - life - in the areas in between the pillars. If one builds a large wall in front of them, the imprints of fragments of life will show upon it. On the north side of the building this method has produced a democratic façade, I think. On the main façade, I took advantage of an exciting opportunity: I let everything its own will, from the engine room to the WC-window; from the cloakroom to the spaces for central heating. On the entrance side, this kind of populism, or this democracy, flushed the façade into the house. The front garden and the row of buildings in front have turned this façade into an internal one, into a façade where borderlines are experienced."

The back façade, facing south, should "behave properly", and looks therefore a bit pathetic and monumental. The relief effects on this façade, exposed to the sun, turn it into a text legible for those strolling past. Reimholz explained that this contradiction between the north and south façades is acceptable to him - and it is impossible to ignore the political content of his explanation: "If this house has a message, it is exactly that it is democratic in front, monumental in back, and that both sides are the results of the same course of events."

Asked about the precise meaning of spontaneity and democracy, Reimholz had to admit that for him reality is only what he accepts as such, and that, in the final analysis, the architect's taste and talent are the last constants on which to rely. The house has three sections: one for culture, one for sport, and a middle connecting section with a saddle roof. The brick wall also covers this section, but, out of an obligation to honesty, he used here a curious, triangular window form. It is a "weak" and "powerless" solution, but a pleasure to imagine that the visitor will understand the hint. The circular windows find no explanation at all: "This arbitrariness increased in the course of the planning, and my desire for an honest statement became less powerful. During the building process, I decided to let the forms live, in order to understand their intentions and also their effect on me."

Reimholz also described his "favourite vision" : his house as a half-destroyed ruin, with the two longitudinal load-bearing walls still standing and, at each end, the crumbling kindergarten and garage, with cables and drainpipes visible in place of the collapsed façades. Soon after the political transition in Hungary, this vision was fulfilled; the VIDEOTON was on the verge of ruin, in an economic sense. An entrepreneur bought it and began its renovation with the dismissal of hundreds of employees. The cultural centre now belongs in part to a sports club, and even recently its fate is still unclear. But above all it is the "pluralistic model" of society that has become ruinous.

The argumentative culture of the 80s was replaced by public political struggles. Political emancipation and disappointment have lead to apathy; an apathic society, in the midst of a shrinking education budget and growing media wars, demands spectacular events, and a staged architecture.

Péter Reimholz. Cultural Centre Videoton in Székesfehérvár, 1984

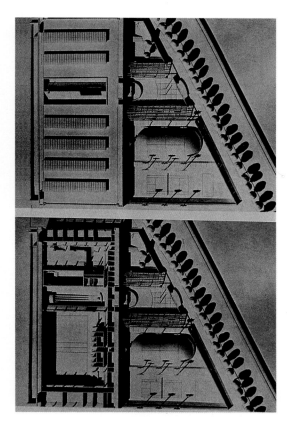

Model

Péter Reimholz had to admit that, in the final

analysis, the architect's taste and talent are

the last constants on which to rely.

Searching for constant points of reference.

Interior view- photo: Ákos Moravánsky

Jože Plečnik's architecture completely ignored

the architectural development of the time.

Modernism and International Style - without any influence on Slovenian architecture between the two wars.

13 | NEW THEORETICAL DEBATES.
| ANDREJ HRAUSKY.

Slovenia

Form of State: Republic since 1991, **Area:** 20,254 km2, **Inhabitants (1992):** 1,996,000, **Capital:** Ljubljana
Gross National Product 1992, per capita: $ 6,540, **Gross Domestic Product 1992:** $ 10,655 Mio, **Unemployment (End of 1993):** 15.5%

> The post-World War II generation of architects was able to establish direct contacts with contemporary developments in Switzerland and particularly in Scandinavia.

The lack of Socialist Realism in its dogmatic form and contacts to foreign countries helped to reestablish architecture in Slovenia after World War II.

Architectural evolution, at least in Europe, cannot happen outside the Zeitgeist of its own era. So when speaking about contemporary architecture in Slovenia, we must be aware that it cannot be discussed outside the European context. Nevertheless, the architecture of each nation or region has its own particularities. This is also true for contemporary architecture in Slovenia, and it is exactly these differences that are of special interest. For me they are not interesting in themselves, rather what is important is why and how they occurred. To understand this, we must recall some historic circumstances which are not evident to the average reader. Slovenia is often compared to Czecho-slovakia and Hungary. These countries were once part of the Habsburg Monarchy, and all were until recently part of the Eastern Block.

These commonalities, however, do not mean that the status of architecture in each country was the same. In fact, in recent history, it was completely different. Until the Monarchy's end, Slovenia was a small province on the route that connected Vienna to its port, Triest. After World War I, it became an institutional part of the new Slavic state, Yugoslavia. Architects turned away from Otto Wagner and others with whom they had studied in Vienna. As in the other newly formed Slavic states, the Vienna School was considered an expression of Germanic culture. Architects tried to create national architecture in their countries. In Slovenia, it was Ivan Vurnik (1884-1971), also a Wagner student from Vienna, who tried to establish a Slovenian style, but soon the architectural scene

was dominated by the strong personality of Jože Plečnik (1872-1957). He returned to Ljubljana in 1923 to become a professor at the newly formed Faculty of Architecture. He rejected the ideas of a national style and opted for his own "architectura perennis" (eternal architecture) based on regional and historically classical principles. His architecture completely ignored the architectural development of the time. As Slovenia's dominant architectural personality, both in practice and especially in the important role as a professor, he almost completely blocked the influence of Modern Architecture in the development of Slovenian architecture between the two wars. When Avgust Černigoj (1898-1985), the only Slovene student to study at the Bauhaus, prepared an exhibition in Ljubljana in 1924, he was completely rejected by critics as well as by the general public. Plečnik's rejection of modern developments in architecture led to opposition amongst his students. It was only after World War II, when Plečnik's influence declined, that they could realize their ideas under the new Socialist Regime. In 1948, Yugoslavia's president Tito opposed Stalin; consequently other Eastern countries organised a cultural and economic blockade of Yugoslavia. This meant that in architecture, as well as in the broader Yugoslavian culture, Socialist Realism was not the officially sanctioned style. Led by professor Edvard Ravnikar (1907-1993), the younger generation of architects took full advantage of this situation. Ravnikar, a student of Plečnik, also went to Paris as one of several Slovene architects who worked in Le Corbusier's office. In the

early 50s he became professor on the Faculty of Architecture in Ljubljana. He emphasized international contacts and the exchange of theoretical ideas. For this reason he initiated the architectural magazine "Arhitekt" (Ljubljana 1951-1963). With the help of this magazine, the post-World War II generation of architects was able to establish direct contacts with contemporary developments in Switzerland and particularly in Scandinavia. The new architecture, soon known as "The Ljubljana School", was not purely functional in the sense of a pre-war Bauhaus tradition but was influenced by the architecture of Alvar Aalto and by developments in Scandinavian public housing. One can also trace in their work the tradition of Plečnik's consideration for material and detail. This school prospered until the mid-seventies and finally dissolved with the retirement of Edvard Ravnikar.

Western examples were often too easily copied, and

forms were transplanted without clearly understanding

their concurrent generative design theories.

Restrained contacts to the Western countries and the isolation of the East European Countries left their marks on Slovenian architecture.

A building which wins the attention.

Housing development in Ljubljana by Božo Podlogar.

Typically, all Eastern European countries after World War II lacked information. The border to the West was more or less closed (in Slovenia fortunately less than in other countries); excursions and literature were relatively expensive. Architects were aware of this un-favourable situation, which led to an increased interest in foreign architectural developments. But political and economic differences prevented a theoretical dialogue on a common basis. Thus, Western examples were often too easily copied, and forms were transplanted without clearly understanding their concurrent generative design theories. An awareness of the importance of architectural debate led to the founding of "AB Magazine" in 1974. Young architects gathered around "AB Magazine" and directed the architectural debate again towards architecture itself. Again, the importance of theory was conditioned by international connections. The activity of this group broadened with the organisation of an annual international architectural symposium in

Piran eleven years ago, with the foundation of the DESSA architectural gallery in Ljubljana five years ago and finally with the publication of the journal "Piranesi". Supported by these institu-tions the group expanded the range and breadth of the theoretical debates which have generated the basis for the five representative projects presented here. The common reference point of these projects is that they consider architecture a rational act that should solve concrete problems. In this respect, the form itself answers the problem, while the solution always respects the historical and spatial context. The buildings always try to establish an appropriate connection to the site where they stand.
Architecture in Slovenia always refers to its context. An example of this is the residential building by Božo Podlogar (born Ljubljana 1947) in Kotnikova Street in Ljubljana. The building is part of a larger scheme which was divided among the architects who won the competition (Jurij Kobe, Janez Koželj, Peter Pahor, Božo Podlogar and Jurij Sadar). The housing lies

in the old town and refers to the Church of the Holy Heart and to the historically preserved gas station, both built in red brick around the turn of the century. This explains the theme of red brick which appears on the elevations facing these two buildings. This building also refers to the neighbourhood architecture of the late 30s, the period in which the surrounding neighbourhood was built. These buildings were planned rationally and then decorated with small details, such as round windows or horizontal stripes, to soften their appearance. This is the primary reference point that Podlogar used as a generative design concept in his project.

Božo Podlogar. Housing development, Ljubljana 1989-92

Architecture is a rational act that should solve concrete problems.

Andrej Hrausky on the task of architecture.

Connecting wing between the staircase and the Baroque Villa

A dialogue between the old and the new.

Museum of Contemporary History in Ljubljana by Jurij Kobe.

Jurij Kobe. Annex to the Museum of Contemporary Art, Ljubljana 1990-91 - photos: Damjan Gale

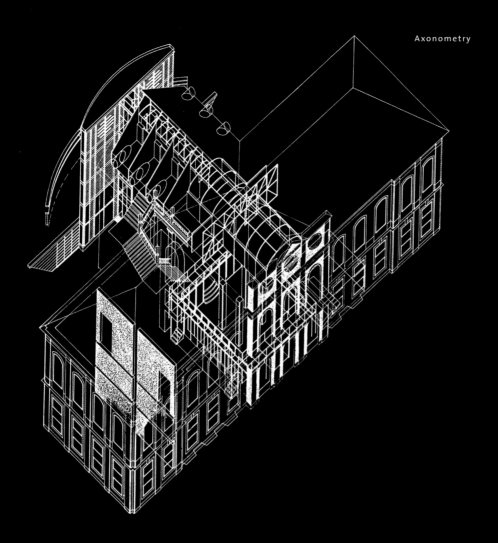

Museum of Contemporary History in Ljubljana by Jurij Kobe (1992): This project deals with the dialogue between old and new. The Baroque villa, in which the museum is located, has been rebuilt several times. Jurij Kobe (born Ljubljana 1948) therefore first tried to remove or rationalize the various earlier interventions in order to return the building to its original splendour. His own interventions, which were needed to house the new programme, are done with contemporary means and materials while referring to old principles. By adapting the attic, deepening the ground floor and adding a new stair on the back, Kobe succeeded in doubling the building's useable space. Thus the museum, its offices and the Historical Institute were successfully accom- modated which allows each to function separately. The stair at the back is built in steel and glass but it is attached to the building in the same way as the front façade, the villas's blind windows are echoed in the blank frames of fixed blinds at the back. The entrance hall is surrounded with built-in cabinets

housing reception, equipment and elevator for handicapped persons. Above them is a corridor that connects both mezzanines in the wings; its principle is derived from the design of Baroque balconies but executed in a modern way. Only at the grand stair does Kobe use traditional materials. But even here he invented the balustrades and furnished the staircase with his own lamps.

Vojteh Ravnikar (born Nova Gorica 1942) is the oldest member of the group and the author of the annex to the town hall in Sežana from 1978. It was a turning point towards new architecture in Slovenia and the first major project realized by this generation. The office building from 1986 is not his latest building, but it may best characterize the influence of "architettura razzionale" in Slovenian architecture. This influence in Sežana is direct since the town lies on the border with Italy. Vojteh Ravnikar, who is not related to the above- mentioned Edvard Ravnikar, also comes from the Italian bordertown of Nova Gorica. The building is sited along the

city's main street which also leads to the border crossing. Thus, the building's commercial programme generates its orientation towards the city's most important business, pedestrian and vehicular corridor. This is achieved with the help of arcades and mezzanine balconies which open the building towards the street. While this openness gives the building a light and transparent character, the back façade is solid and creates a wall that guards the Sežana cultural centre which stands behind it (also by Vojteh Ravnikar).

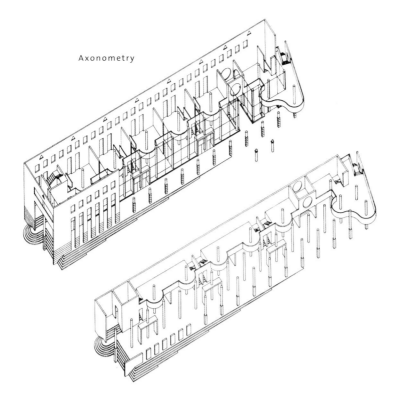

Axonometry

It was a turning point towards

new architecture in Slovenia.

The architecture of Vojteh Ravnikar - an important part of contemporary architecture in Slovenia.

Vojteh Ravnikar. Office building in Sežana, 1986 - photo: Damjan Gale

Residential building in Ljubljana by Janez Koželj (1988): No Slovenian architect, especially in Ljubljana, can ignore Plečnik's tradition. The dilemma is how to respond to it. An interesting solution to this issue is the residential building in Poljanska street in Ljubljana. Its architect, Janez Koželj (Ljubljana 1945), was asked to design a gymnasium on the site. Because the street is a historical entrance to the old part of Ljubljana, he considered this type of building culturally, formally and contextually inappropriate to complete the street wall. He convinced city officials to move the gymnasium off

the street to a site behind the narrow residential building, which now defines the street line. The narrow triangular site created the same problem that Plečnik had to deal with in 1933 on the same street only 500m to the west. Koželj intentionally derived his solution from Plečnik's "Peglezen" (a slang expression for the German term "Bügeleisen" - "flat-iron"). Perhaps the most important architectural element that Koželj was able to understand and realize in this project was the preservation of a small portion of façade at the site's pointed termination which,

in spite of its narrowness, creates a recognizable view along Poljanska street. But the small triangular site was not Koželj's only problem; he also succeeded in solving the architectural issues generated by the street's curve and its substantial elevation change. In this respect, Koželj was able to upgrade and even supersede Plečnik's project, which was only a starting point.

Janez Koželj. Housing development in Ljubljana, 1987-88 -photo: Damjan Gale

No Slovenian architect, especially in

Ljubljana, can ignore Plečnik's tradition.

The dilemma is how to respond to it.

The residential building in Ljubljana by Janez Koželj responds to Plečnik's influence without surrendering to it.

Aleš Vodopivec succeeded, however, in creating

a synthesis between the local building tradition

and contemporary architectural expression.

A hotel annex, not built in the ordinary manner of "alpine kitsch", but with an autonomous architectural language reflecting on traditional forms.

Hotel annex in Bohinj by Aleš Vodopivec (1990): One problem architects in Slovenia must adress is strict building regulations in historically preserved areas. These regulations are usually based on national historicism and favour Post-Modern, "alpine kitsch" architecture; this leaves little freedom for contemporary architecture.
This is the case of the area around the alpine lake Bohinj, which is part of the Natural Monument Area. The gabled roof and wood were prescribed. Aleš Vodopivec (born Ljubljana 1949) succeeded, however, in creating a synthesis between the local building tradition and contemporary architectural expression. The building is divided in two parts. All rooms are oriented towards the lake, while the recreation facilities, swimming pool and fitness room face the back yard. This is why the roof on the backside almost touches ground.
The parts are divided by a corridor that leads from the old hotel to at a garden on the edge of the wood.
The prescribed wood on the façade is designed in a rational grid which regulates the main elevation and its balconies in front of each room. The wood is painted grey, which recalls the colour of old, unpainted pine.

Stairs to the swimming hall

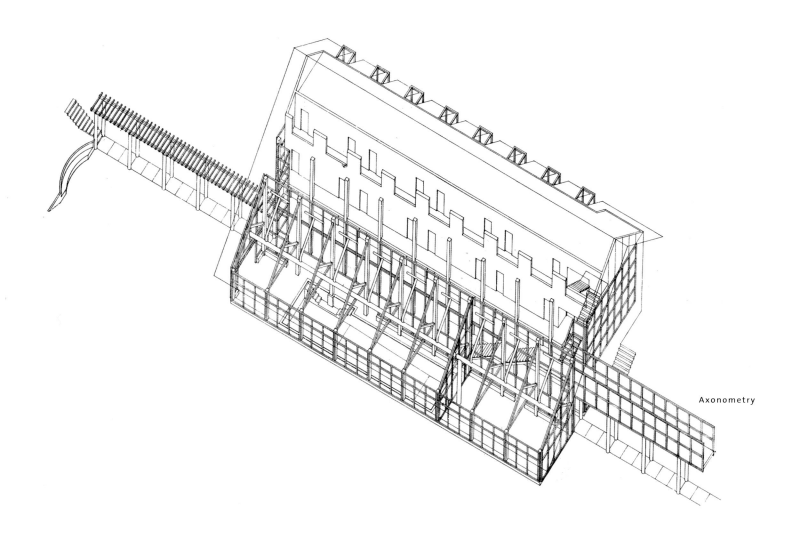

Aleš Vodopivec. Hotel annex, Bohinj 1990

Most changes occur quietly without

attracting much attention.

Aleksander Laslo on the changing socio-economic as well as socio-cultural "landscape" of Croatia.

14 | To Return to the Modern or Back to the Future. Alexander Laslo.

Croatia

Form of State: Republic since 1991, **Area:** 56,538 km2, **Inhabitants (1992):** 4,789,000, **Capital:** Zagreb
Gross National Product 1992, per capita: $ 1,900, **Gross Domestic Product 1990:** $ 24,395 Mio, **Unemployment (end of 1993):** 16.9%

I admit, when I was about to prepare my lecture for the 2nd Vienna Architectural Congress in November 1994 I was almost puzzled with the task. For some time I thought that I could cope with it through capricious terms such as "reassembled fin-de-siècle" or "a new belle époque", then in fanciful abstract terms of borders, boundaries and frontiers. Obviously neither worked. When I subsequently returned to the particular theme of transition I confronted the multitude of turbulent transformation processes we are facing in my country, to which I would like to apply the term "landscapes of transformation". Some of them are rather well known places such as, for instance, the changed geopolitical landscape, including all the violence and disgrace that is connected with it. But the greatest changes occur quietly without attracting much attention: there is a changed socio-economic landscape with decisive effects of some new, so to say, primordial accumulation; the architects operate within a completely changed but not yet legally regulated professional field; the changed educational landscape creates too many experts for too few things to build, not to mention the changed physical landscape with all wounds and scars caused by the aggression and warfare to which we were exposed during the last few years. Although all the points mentioned here surely deserve an elaboration, I will limit myself to the question: What are the prospects for architecture under these uncertain circumstances? Perhaps they can be found through investigating traditional values of Modernism. One can say that the history of Croatian architecture, as it has been conceived and built between the turn of the century and World War II, bears the stamp of a coherent evolutionary cycle, made up of influences and their assimilations, yet consciously relying upon the idea of

an independent participation in the cosmopolitan distribution of the modern architectural programme. The greatest virtue of this architecture lies in an aesthetic of purposefulness: in the transformation of the programmatically formal and ideological rules into the criteria of efficiency, durability, economy and constructional feasibility. Furthermore, it concerned not only the synchronous correspondence of local circumstance with the plurality of international occurences, but was also an attempt to reexamine avant-garde style patterns, while taking into account specific real architectural problems. All of this certainly came from the intention to create a particular inherent spatial order. It was also a highly integrative process with the ultimate objective being the development of a general architectural idiom with a universal capacity of identification. This particular architectural strategy testifies to - at the crossroads of many different regions and the most divergent geopolitical aspirations - a vigorous internal mechanism, a self-protective impulse to preserve its own integral identity equally from atomisation as well as from local or regional self-sufficiency. Croatian architectural Modernism crystallized somewhere in 1906 with Viktor Kovačić (with his Oršić-Divković apartment house in Zagreb). A student of Otto Wagner and a close friend of Adolf Loos, he freely amalgamated the functionalist teachings of Wagner with the skepticism and purism of Loos. Further development led to International Style modernism during the 30s, and ranged from the universal architectural language (in the first high-rise apartment building - the Radovan flats by Slavko Loewy, 1933) to the regional one (in the Deutsch villa by Frane Cota, 1936). The extent of experiments with form can be startlingly ascertained through the

examination of the work of a single architect: Ernest Weissmann, who was not only capable to unify the principles of Plan Libre with the principles of Raumplan in the same building, but also able to act at the same time in terms of pure abstraction and of clear figuration (as in his villas Kraus and Podvinec in Zagreb, both from 1937). One can finally trace the fading away of modernism in the late 50s as signalized in the work of Drago Galić and Ivan Vitić. After the dull period of the self-conscious and false economic productivism of the so so-called self-governing socialism during the 60s and 70s, also after some sporadic flashes of Post-Modernist ambitions, one can find the first marks of a turning back to the modernist sources. Proof of this is the dialogue between new abstraction and new representation, as in the works by Radovan Tajder and by the partnership Juračić-Kincl, or in the efforts to stress some crucial events of the Modern Movement, as in the works by Ivan Crnković (evoking Viennese grand housing estates), or in the works by Branko Kincl (evoking modest Dutch housing). All of these projects date from the early 80s.

Zagreb Fair, 1986-91 - photo: Damir Fabijanic

The building displays its

stability by frankly showing

its structural system.

The office building for the Customs Department on the Zagreb Fair.

After the framework for investigating recent architectural production is established, it is easier to choose reference points to support the thesis quoted in the title - Back to the Future. First I selected my favorites: architects who can respectably represent the dual nature of Croatian architectural heritage: the continental tradition of tectonics and the mediterranean tradition of stereotomy. They are Edvin Šmit, born in 1943 in Osijek/Esseg (in Croatian Slavonia where Otto Wagner designed his famous steel structured parish church), then Boris Duplančić, born in 1942 in Split/Spalato (in Croatian Dalmatia where the Roman emperor Diocletian built his world-known summer residence), and finally Djivo Dražić, born in 1951 in Zagreb, in whose heritage both traditions are united. I browsed through their most recent designs (an apartment block, a small housing estate and an urban villa by Duplančić, competition entries for a hotel and for a church by Duplančić and Drazic, all in Zagreb). I also walked through their built architecture (Vrbik apartment block in Zagreb by Duplančić and Martial arts gymnasium in Samobor by Šmit). In the end I decided to highlight the following five examples.

Customs Department Headquarters and Extension to the German Pavilion at the Zagreb Fair, designed in 1990 and built in 1991 by Dražić and Šmit: Both buildings are fragments of a huge development plan that was elaborated 1986-1990 for the restructuring of the Zagreb Fair compound into an international trading and business centre (WTC). Mixed use development was conceived as a city within the city, on limited grounds, and the restructuring began with the new main gateway in 1986. The office building for the Customs Department, located on the outer corner of the compound, displays its stability by frankly showing its structural system. The Pavilion extension, on the other hand, indicates its protected position through the delicateness of a fragile envelope. Unfortunately, further development was cancelled due to the dramatic events of the fall of 1991.

Two apartment houses in Zagreb, designed in 1988-1989 and built in 1993 by Boris Duplančić: These two urban infill projects, sharing almost opposite locations on a very long city street, play an amusing "even-to-odd" game. The "even house" lies just within the regularly planned city district, the "odd" one in the adjoining irregular town pattern. The "even house" is quite even in plan, the "odd" one quite the opposite, but not less efficient. Both of them interpret a traditional way of building, and both of them belong to the so called "city completion programme". Each of them, in its own way, aims at a new form of representation.

Djivo Dražić und Edvin Šmit. Extension to the German Pavilion, Zagreb Fair 1986-91 - photo: Miljenko Bernfest

Elevation

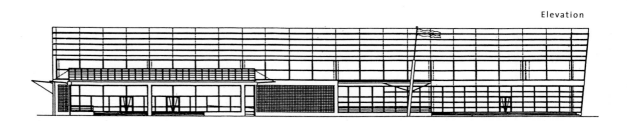

Boris Duplančić. Shopping Centre "Črnomere", Zagreb 1993 - photo: Damir Fabijanic

Apartment house in Zagreb - photo: Damir Fabijanic

Boris Duplančić. Apartment house in Zagreb, 1988-93 - photo: Damir Fabijanic

The apartment houses by Boris Duplančić interpret a traditional

way of building, but aim at a new form of representation.

Dwelling as city completion programme.

Edvin Šmit. Partner Banka, detail of the façade, Zagreb 1994 - photo: Damir Fabijanic

Elevation/Section

Shopping centre "Crnomerec" at the bus
terminal in Zagreb, designed in 1990 and
built in 1993 by Boris Duplančić: This simple,
flat and expandable structure is meant as a
focal point to help systemize a suburban city
district. With its regular, although casual
geometry and its modest architectural
detailing, it defines the other face of the

completion of the city.
Bank building "Partner Banka" in Zagreb,
designed in 1992 and built 1992-1994 by
Edvin Šmit: This building, although a
relatively typical urban infill project, is
with its building programme an example
for the representation of a new usage - it
is probably the first in the series to express

the transformed socio-economical values. Its
values lie in flexibility and speed, so its plan
must be clear, its structure must be literally
supporting, and the entire architecture must
be highly efficient.

The "Partner Banka" building is probably

the first in the series to express the

transformed socio-economical values.

Flexibility and speed, the new values for the representation of a new building usage.

In a group of recent works modernist

experiments flash again.

The experiment "Modernism" is present again in Croatian architecture of today.

A rental office building in Zagreb, designed in 1994 by Boris Duplančić, now under construction: It is a sophisticated, neutral, tailored-to-fit scheme that observes the rules of a market-oriented economy. Although the concept is not yet going to redefine traditional ways of conceiving contemporary city life, its programme parameters, like its architecural detailing, are designed to be advantageous to the needs of small business enterprises.

The above-mentioned architectural productions are clear and consistent in their concept as well as in their final appearance. They are characteristic of the main direction of new construction in Croatia. This way of professional thinking, however, would not be convincing enough without a view to the broader material "background" which is not only to comment on but also to confirm the very pragmatic content of the actual operating methods. Here I would like to point out a group of recent works where particular flashes of considered modernist experiments are to be recognized

At the four "Rudeš" apartment buildings (1987-1990) in Zagreb by Mladen Josic (born in 1953) and Teufik Galijasevic (born in 1951), a standardized dwelling programme was successfully distinguished from a rather anonymous satellite neighbourhood by the skilful manipulation of the geometry of the building and through the discrete association of De Stijl colouring schemes. At "Zelengaj" housing estate (1991-1994) in Zagreb by Zoran Boševski (born in 1959) and Boris Fiolić (born in 1959), urban villas of a higher living comfort were developed as pure serial products, that are nevertheless individualized by modifications of the building envelope. A small "High Fidelity" retail store in Zagreb (1990-1991) by Krešimir Kasanić (born in 1941) and Dragutin Gašparović (born in 1954) exposes its neutral building structure, it acts like a bubble, and its double-coded (solid vs. void) flat surface stresses the simplicity of the "container-architecture". At the "Stobreč" primary school (1991-1993) in Split by Ante Kuzmanič (born in 1952), a particular formal language with a clear ordering

of platonic solids was used and the linking space created between the main building elements became a stage for this architectural articulation.

Modest in its spatial program and small in volume is an addition to the existing gymnasium (1990-1991) in Samobor by Edvin Šmit. Here he achieves a counterbalance to the architectural minimalism through the clarity of structure, subtle detailing with durable materials and an overall balanced composition. Two works by Nikola Bašić (born in 1946) built on the Adriatic coast manifest a specific regard to the highly inspiring Mediterranean landscape.

Urban villas of a higher living comfort.

The "Zelengaj" housing estate in Zagreb by Zoran Boševski and Boris Fiolić.

Typical housing unit - photo: Damir Fabijanic

Zoran Boševski und Boris Fiolić. "Zelengaj"-housing estate, Zagreb 1990-1994 - photo: Damir Fabijanic

Nikola Bašić. "Zlatna luka", Nautical Centre in Zadar, 1987-91 - photo: Damir Fabijanic

The project makes reference to the highly

inspiring Mediterranean landscape.

The "Zlatna luka" nautical centre in Zadar by Nikola Bašić.

Timoslav Ćurković, Zoran Zidarić. "BML"-Office, Zagreb 1992
photo: Damir Fabijanic

Multilayered composition methods as a model for remarkable interieurs in Zagreb.

Timoslav Ćurković, Zoran Zidarić. "Zrišort"-shop in Zagreb, 1994
photo: Darko Bavoljak

The service facilities at "Zlatna luka" nautical centre (1987-1991) in Zadar, with their ambiguous "ephemeral vs. eternal" design, precise in detailing in a sort of shipbuilding manner, are meant to establish a cultivated but restrained dialogue with the powerful natural scenery. "Betina Marina" (1990-1991), on the contrary, was planned as a condensed enclosure for a mixed-use architectural programme with the intention, however, to achieve the commensurability of a clearly divided building volume with its direct environment.
I believe that the selected projects, clearly supported by additional examples, when observed from the point of view of regained modernist progressivism and positivism, aim to span the factual gap of an architecture in transition. Also concepts of social consciousness, particularly concepts of an "architecture of chez-soi" are still very intense.

Although I am not sure for how long these efforts and their inspiring aura will last, several fresh solutions realized in the so-called small architecture practice of interior design certainly offer promising starting points for future developments in architecture. The rigid reductivism and naked objectivity of "BML"-office, "Agrooprema" and "Zrišport" shops (1992-1994) in Zagreb by Timoslav Ćurković (born in 1961) and Zoran Zidarić (born in 1962), followed by attempts to bring in the entire modernist experience (from Adolf Loos to, let me say, Louis Kahn) within a single spatial framework, as at "Jobis" shop (1994) in Zagreb by Mira Tadej-Crnković (born in 1959), seem to be the most appropriate preface for the multilayered composition method performed at "Collage" shop (1994) in Zagreb by Marko Murtić (born in 1958) and Vedrana Ergić (born in 1966).
Short-living by its very character thus

generally considered as less significant, interior design may, however, at least indicate, while not anticipating some new strategies of present-day Croatian architecture. Yet, the most exciting discovery met in analyzing its recent production is the fact that one can still trace some lasting task-orientated and metier-awared way of architectural thinking.

What we can hardly find in this architectural situation is

the drive to search, to investigate, to accept the challenge.

Romania between expectation and resignation.

15 | **EXPECTATIONS VS. REALITIES.**
ANA MARIA ZAHARIADE.

Romania

Form of State: Republic since 1991, **Area:** 237,500 km2, **Inhabitants: (1992):** 22,760,449, **Capital:** Bucharest
Gross National Product 1992, per capita: $ 1.130, **Gross Domestic Product 1992:** $ 24,865 Mio, **Unemployment (Average, 1993):** 10.2%

The opportunity to discuss the achievements and the potential of Romanian architecture almost six years after the 1989 Revolution both fascinates and intimidates me. The main danger in making a value judgement is the impossibility to detach oneselves from the situation, therefore distortions of meanings are hardly to be avoided. The subject oversteps the usual boundaries of architecture and becomes an issue of cultural discourse and of history, especially contemporary history. It is this almost physical contact with history, the feeling we are called upon to contribute to the making of history, to choosing among possible futures, that leads me to refer less to the built work than to the phenomena and conditions surrounding contemporary Romanian architecture. One of the most distressing aspects of this subject is the discrepancy between our expectations and the actual overall image which can be perceived at a first glance. No doubt, such general political turmoil as we have witnessed, must impress itself in architecture, first of all through a period of stasis. But we would have expected this to be only apparent stasis: to represent a period of relief during which to ponder and to mull over our heritage, and to establish contact to the architectural world we had been able to observe only through barbed wire. We expected to experience the eruption of a creative activity which would force new cultural dimensions upon architectural production, dimensions based on the rediscovery of the meanings of urbanity, on the search for the essential, on authenticity, on a balanced local identity, in a word, upon the recovery of the values obliterated by the dictatorship. Such a phenomenon did not need to materialize in a tremendous building activity, but at least in projects, theoretical research and fruitful debates on the most important themes. The results of six years of architectural activity are, however, disappointing when compared to our overestimated expectations: First, although the number of vernacular buildings grows disquietingly all over the country, escaping any control, real architectural

production, including theory and paper architecture, is scarce. Second and most upsetting, the overall image is chaotic and incoherent; it is not the image of an inquisitive eclecticism (eclectic culture has its inner coherence), it is the image of a hesitant disorientation governed by an obvious apathy. What we can hardly find in this architectural situation is the drive to search, to investigate, to accept the challenge. Could this strange anomaly be the effect of some extrinsic circumstances too difficult to bear, or is it more deeply seated in the mentality and psychology of the architectural profession, or its biased understanding of its own position? One cannot deny that, from an economic point of view, times are difficult. Major investors are extremely few, public investment is absent (although basic necessities are imperative), the property rights over urban land are not clear (and the legal provisions to clear them up still missing), the technological level is low. The radical change in the way the architectural profession is organized, which led to the etablishment of small private design studios produced bewilderment and real difficulties in the corporate body still accustomed with the old, huge, state-owned design institutes. In fact, this drama is emphasized by the absence of any law regarding the statutes of the profession, the right to signature, the copyright. All these aspects need to be seen against a background of disastrous building heritage. I shall not refer to the so called "House of the People", but to the general condition of our cities, destroyed by both a total lack of maintenance practically since World War II, and the implementation of political decisions, fortunately not fully realized. Under these circumstances, the media's total lack of concern in this respect is quite absurd. Again, the only exception is the same "House of the People", discussed much more than it deserves. In the 60s, when Bruno Zevi blamed the media for their disregard for architecture, the future of the cities could not have been more dramatically threatened than they are now by the spasmodic power of an incipient market economy and

uncontrolled real estate speculation. For critics educated exclusively within Materialistic dogma the above-mentioned aspects could seem sufficient motives for the actual lethargy. I, however, believe that such a judgement is a very dangerous trap. The economic and political factors primarily affect realized work rather than research or conceptual projects. As a result, the illusion takes shape that once these factors were overcome, the problem of architecture would already have been solved. Such an attitude allows us to indulge in the present apathy, waiting for a solution to come from outside. Thus, it becomes an alibi endangering the future of both the architectural profession and production. To have overcome the economic and legal difficulties does not mean the real menace to architectural production has been removed. For this reason, we have to uncover the real problems influencing Romanian architects, their consciousness and their approach. We can not yet see with lucidity and without complexes our own architectural history in all its aspects: benevolent and malevolent, positive and negative.

According to Martin Heidegger, history is a causal concatenation which comes from the past and passes through the present towards a future. Therefore, the past has no particular priority. This is precisely the meaning of history we neglected, even avoided in viewing our own architectural evolution. We are instead repeating a collection of slogans, or wallowing in delusions either pitiful or aggressive before a past we wish to glorify or damn. There is no attempt to search earnestly and thoroughly. It is a perverted perception which perceives the past either as ineffectual or as determinate for the present, and, therefore, as an alibi. In both cases, relationships are arrested in an everlasting present. There is no projection towards a future because the concatenation of the historical becoming is broken. There are certain formative aspects which govern the historical becoming. There are also key moments, belonging to the historical development of architecture, which could serve as reliable reference points. The dictatorship knew to aim precisely at these aspects and moments in order to arrest or to pervert a natural evolution. Thus the chain of history was broken, and stable values obscured. We were alienated from our own history. The central formative aspect of Romanian architecture is a remarkable osmotic capacity of a society situated at the crossing of very different, even contradictory, cultural influences. Architectural creation is thereby based on the purest meaning of the "syntagmic cultural" exchange, it gave birth to architectural expression and identity. The prohibition of certain approaches, the enforcement of others (e.g. the Stalinist architecture in the 50s, the high-rise high-density dwellings since the 60s, etc.), and especially the gradual exclusion of all that could have represented an organically necessary influence succeeded in disequilibrating the inner mechanics of the cultural exchange as a sine-qua-non condition of a valid synthesis. That above-mentioned osmotic capacity and the organically adjusted cultural exchange led to a remarkable achievement in the 19th century. Romanian society and culture experienced a spectacular and explosive evolution from a late medieval status to

an integral part of European culture. The original synthesis which took place in the Romanian Modern movement reached a climax between the two World Wars. This period is to be considered a key moment in our architecture for many reasons: It embraced passionately the new language and its expressive potential - and for substantial reasons assumed the character of an avant-garde. This architecture became not only unusually popular, but made its mark decisively on the Romanian city. At the same time, it made no pronouncements and adhered only minimally to the Modern Movement's radical ideology, especially with regard to urban development. It rejected that "progressive ideological model" (Françoise Choay) in the name of an urban tradition which architects did not want to aggress, but to modernize and adapt to the new society's needs and ethos. We can speak about that period's solid and specific approach, a kind of "Critical Regionalism" avant-la-lettre, which would have been worthy of continuation. Because, however, it did not accord with the communist ethos, even less to that of the Ceausescu dictatorship, it became increasingly obscured and was replaced by the very ideology it rejected. It is an historical paradox that this occured during the 60s, when the Charter of Athens was already a target of sharp criticism and the CIAM dissolved.

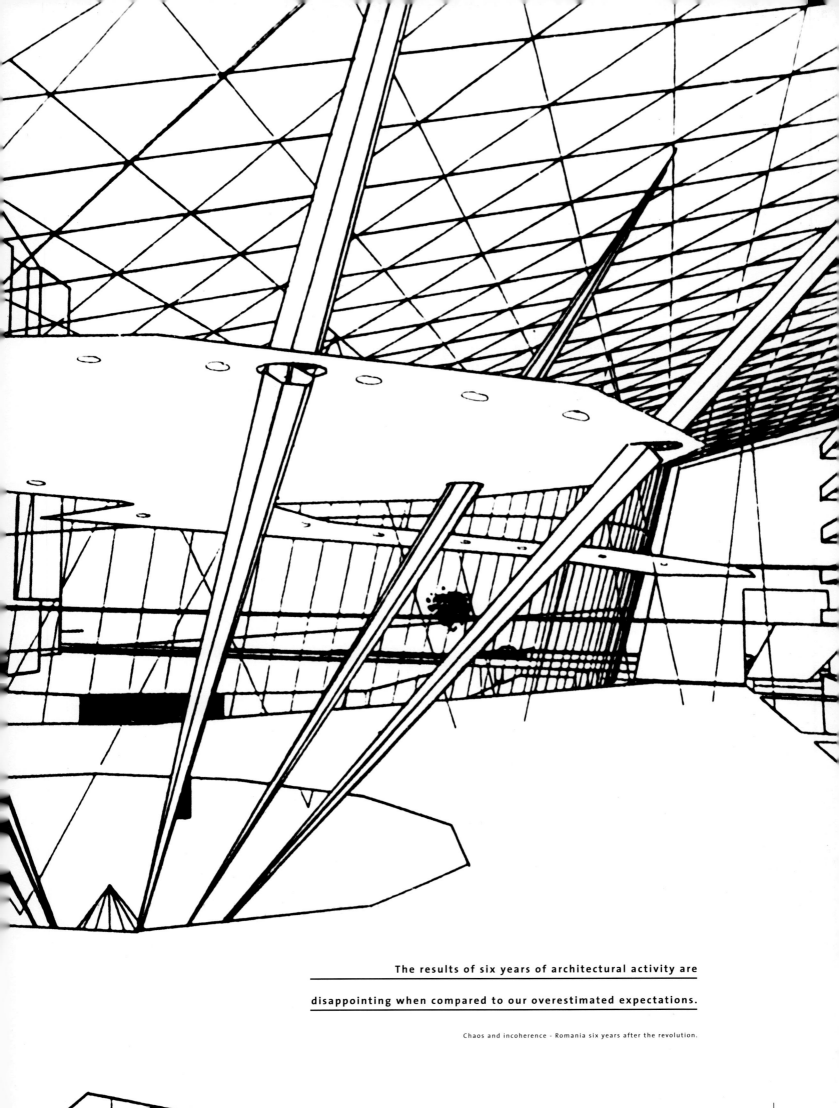

The results of six years of architectural activity are

disappointing when compared to our overestimated expectations.

Chaos and incoherence - Romania six years after the revolution.

Prodid Studio, Stefan Sturza. Modernization of the Orphanage of Timisoara, 1991

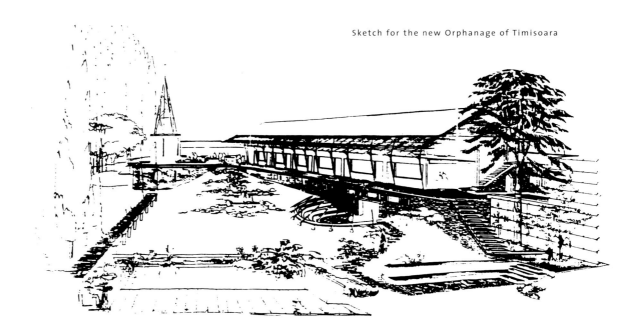

Sketch for the new Orphanage of Timisoara

Stair construction

Sturza used neither imported materials nor technologies,

he created a timber structure instead, partially covered

with glass and supported by the dendromorphous pillars.

Renovation and annexe should be near to the nature - this was the idea for this project.

Romanian architects were always very pragmatic. They built, but explained very little. Theoretical contemplation was weakly developed. This was mainly due to an academic education, based on the Beaux-Arts model, within which little importance was granted to the philosophy of architectural creation. When the School adopted Modernism, approximately at the end of the 50s, the change was simply one of style. Real modernization after 1968 never took place, since in the 70s education became one of the principal tools of manipulation. Within this kind of instrumental approach, it was easier to condition the architect to be the effective and manageable performer the system needed. Thus, on the basis of conviction, or just deprived of information, the Romanian architect ignored the primary questions which tormented the Post-Modern world, or perceived them distortedly. Feelings of fear and guiltiness regarding collaborationism find a peculiar expression in a quest for theoretical substantiations; we become accomplices by masking that trivial, empty, futureless architecture behind the name of Romanian Post-Modernism although it bears no relation to a true Post-Modern approach, except - if we want to be malicious - by a certain stylistic libertinage. From a theoretical point of view, this cheap sophism might seem harmless if it did not contribute to the general confusion. Obviously it is convenient for those who chose to collaborate, but, unfortunately, it also relieves the culpability complex of those who were compelled to collaborate. Hence it is a generally accepted excuse. The growing confusion is extremely unfair for a young generation searching for a point of reference. This alibi has already proved its sterility: it is not accidental that some significant movements or approaches - as scarce as they are - crystalize at some points of defiance or amongst personalities that tried and sometimes succeeded in

resistance. We must understand our historical condition, and we must react. I expect that our architecture will evolve under the motto: Towards an architecture and towards an architect. It is extremely difficult to select the five most representative projects. Representativeness is not a value in itself. It refers to something which can potentially be generalized, which displays common values or a coherent search for specific aesthetics. I shall select the few points of agglutination which can be observed in the generally deceiving overall image. These points might represent the inception of worthwhile directions. They might be the missing link in our architectural evolution. The remarkable efforts centred around the Union of Architects and its president Alexandru Beldiman aim at recovering its corporate status, self-consciousness and will. The Union has organized the First Biennial of the Romanian architects with participants living in the country and abroad. The theoretical and critical debate raised by the magazine "Arhitext Design", proves more and more successful. This kind of cultural nuclei could give an important impetus to architecture. The scientific approach to urban development based on "sustainable development", has crystallized around the Department of Urbanism of IAIM (the research studio Urbis, led by Alexandru Sandu). Such work is very important because, to quote Bernard Huet "the problem of the relation between architecture and the city is the core of the debate started by the end of the 50s [...] a real point of reference which gives the measure of the distances between schools." The individual, almost clandestine studies, based on a systemic approach, which were carried out by the members of the department in the last years before the Revolution, made the quick consolidation of their research studio possible. The group's prestige continued to grow and it became an institution in its own right, consulted by the municipalities in order to

substantiate their decisions. Within architectural design, the most representative movements are concentrated in Timisoara and Bucharest. In Timisoara the school of architecture works - in the sense of a group sharing common preoccupations, attitudes, believes. In Bucharest, everything is still focused around the work and charisma of Dorin Stefan, an architect and lecturer at IAIM. The approaches which are taking shape are more important than the projects themselves. They could demonstrate the birth of an architectural elite.

Dorin Stefan. Project for an Office centre in Bucharest

Dorin Stefan considers himself a rationalist: the forms and spaces he proposes are always motivated and try to investigate new expressive possibilities in the existing stylistic and technological context.

Rebellious as Dorin Stefan is, arises his charisma from his permanent friction with the old dogmas.

Model

Born in 1950, Dorin Stefan is a rebellious, sophisticated, even anarchical personality, sometimes theoretically prolix. His charisma arises from his permanent friction with the old dogmas and order, but most of all from the insatiable hunger of his open mind, and from his natural and profound architectural sensitivity. Ever informed and attracted by novelty, he always tried to push things forward. That is why students have always loved him. There is sometimes a distance between his statements and his drawings. In his words, there is an intention to shock, even to displease and to offend, in order to incite the spirit.

His architecture is never governed by this intention, although it is an evocative architecture. It is provoking and sensitive in its attempt to bring a new spirit into the surrounding apathy, and to explore new expressive means, although not through an affiliation to a style. He has been considered a Deconstructivist, which is obviously not true, although his work's idiosyncrasies do share common ground with Deconstruction. He considers himself a rationalist: the forms and spaces he proposes are always motivated and try to investigate new expressive possibilities in the existing stylistic and technological context.

One year ago he opened a manifesto exhibition which he called, with surrealist irony, "Coachworks". He displayed his latest projects, all of them about to start construction. The title referred to the fact they might remain simple, empty shells, due to the clients' lack of understanding for architecture.

I would like to focus on a project that I deem most representative because it attempts to revitalize an important place in Bucharest which had been seriously disfigured by Ceausescu's interventions. This project was made possible by the sale of a huge, amorphous block of flats which fronts the south side of an important urban place, and handcuffs the visual axis from the lakes towards the crossing of two important avenues. The building's shape and dimensions also falsified enormously this traditional place's urban scale. The proposed project

is intended above all as an urban correction. All the architectural gestures derive from this idea in order to minimize this front's disastrous effects and to integrate the place in the city's real life. The building incorporates three under-ground parking decks (parking is an acute problem in Bucharest), two floors of commercial spaces joint to the subway station, three levels of offices, and a restaurant at the top level, with a skydome offering a vista over the existing park to the north. In order to correct the front's indecisive proportions and texture, a horizontal datum is introduced using 2 metre strip windows, alternating with 2 metre marble parapets. Thus the effect is maintained, in negative, at the night. The inclined tower, which opposes the horizontality, is motivated by the place's asymmetry; the symmetrical front is obviously shifted off the main axes from the north. Hence the tower becomes the focal point of this important visual axis. The glass wing, which covers the building and articulates the proposed slender slab and the existing front, creates a commercial arcade. The arcade was a traditional urban space in 19th century Bucharest. The project eliminates the inertial, alien effect of the existing front. It creates a dynamic and sensitive overall impression, as if something had begun to live again on the dead place.

Since the 70s, Timisoara has been an exceptional case contrasting with Bucharest's decay. This is connected with the emergence of a local Design Institute and a three-year school of architecture. Unlike in Bucharest, the confluence here of young architects from different Romanian cities gave birth to archi-tectural dissidence. There was an intellectual coherence among this new local elite, whose members joined forces when dictates had to be resisted. They enjoyed the advantage of a greater distance from the centralized power in Bucharest, and a traditional regional pride with marked cosmopolitan tendencies. Even when the school was dismantled by governmental order, the people continued to develop their research and design work. Thus, while in all the other cities

the destruction of traditional urban fabric began, the architect Mihai Opris published an excellent monograph on Timisoara's architecture, a bed-side book for all architects, and the city took action to restore its historical centre.

After the Revolution, the school was re-established as a six year programme. Old and new collaborators carry on with their explorations. There is an implicit consensus to hold course. This common background, from which their common architectural approach arises derives from the former school's architecture programme based on the Bauhaus model, and from the experiments done collaboratively with the artists Flondor and Bertalan. These experiments are very closely tied to an exploration of the artistic potential of traditional materials and techniques and to a search for a modern but lasting elegance in their use. The scrupulous attention to detail in these experiments is remarkable. They are especially fascinated by furniture perceived in terms of architectural detail: a rather artisanal approach, in fact.

Although Ioan Andreescu and Vlad Gaivoronschi differ in

architectural expression and language, they are tied by a

common design philosophy: each programme has certain

functional dimensions, suggesting a definite stylistic purity.

Reflecting function.

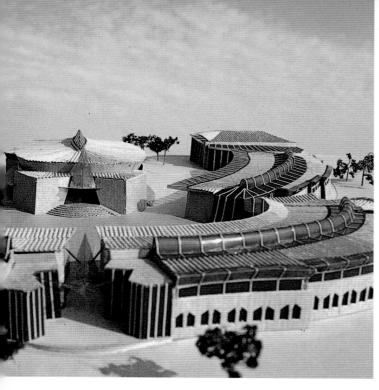

Ioan Andreescu and Vlad Gaivoronschi.
The Waldorf Centre at Timisoara

Ioan Andreescu and Vlad Gaivoronschi.
"Gold Tim" Store, Timisoara

Ioan Andreescu and Vlad Gaivoronschi. Market "Badea Cartan", Timisoara

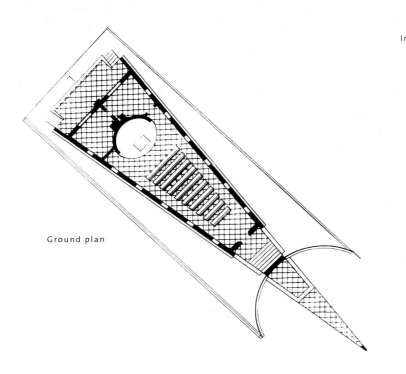

Ground plan

Interior view

Radu Mihailescu. Chruch in Vucova

The design philosophy of Prodid Studio is extremely profound, refusing any

ostentation. It is fundamentally characterized by a contextual approach.

Architectural genealogy between simplicity and Baroque dynamics.

The Church in Vucova was designed for a small village by Radu Mihailescu (born in 1959), the building exhibits an extreme purity, realized with the most elementary means of controlling form.

The expression, remarkably simple and dynamic at the same time, results from cutting a beautiful double-sloped roof with the converging planes of the walls. The wooden rafters and the light (natural and artificial) are the building's only ornaments. The project is a modern synthesis of Romanesque simplicity and Baroque dynamics, both traditional in the area. It is an example of formal austerity integrated into the landscape.

Serban Sturza, born in 1947, deserves special attention because he is, no doubt, the most remarkable architectural personality of the last 25 years.

His activity as an architect and urban planner and his moral support for the promotion of architecture have been prodigious. He was, in fact, the soul of the Timisoara resistance. He has been active both in the school of architecture and in the local design institute, and fought relentlessly to save the city's threatened identity.

Serban Sturza only left the design institute in 1993, after completing the general urban plan of Timisoara and the rehabilitation project for the banks of the Bega river, issues of central significance for the city's future.

"Market 700"- this project of Sturza was commissioned in 1991, following the competition for the modernization of the main market, located in the city's south-west, sectors adjacent to a ruined bastion and the military chapel, then unappropriately used as market annexes. The competition had a simple and pragmatic theme, but any idea related to the area's revitalization was also accepted. Therefore the project was based on an urban planning approach, focusing on this programmatic function's impact on the city. Grounded in a historic reading of the area and on urban studies of its relation to the old city, to existing typologies and to the vehicular circulation, the building synthesizes their

respective studies' conclusions. It is composed of a long slab (administration, hotel and commerce) which continues an important street on its interior, a three-dimensional structure which is formed by the covered market; and a second slab containing a general store and the underground parking levels for the entire historical centre. The project's particular value is its capacity to articulate the new volumes and functions as well as the old fabric and vestiges of the city and to retain its utterly modern and integrated appearance. Unfortunately, the chances of seeing this project realized are very reduced in this moment.

The project of the Orphanage of Timisoara which in fact led to the founding of the Prodid Studio, started in 1991 as a low-budget modernization of existing orphanage pavilions located in a neglected park. Because of a German foundation dedicated to helping Romanian orphans, it became possible to bring the buildings up to an international standard. Once the additional functional elements had been decided upon (medical and treatment premises, refectory, kitchen, chapel and dormitory), the architectural execution proceeded with extreme delicacy. The site, a park within the city, and the character of the 19th century pavilions challenged the architect to design a building which could compensate for trimming off a piece of the park. Therefore, the building "had to exist alongside and simultaneous with nature". The building moves from a renovated pavilion through a 3-storey tract to end at the vertical volume of the chapel, which becomes the built reference point of an axis created by an existing poplar alley. The horizontal organization creates a gently enclosed natural space, a sunny lawn for the children. Thus, the whole enclosed surface assumes the shape of a hill, with an amphitheatre covering the building's first floor (the therapy section and the refectory) and transforming it into an element of the landscape. The second floor, a long balcony accessing the dormitory rooms - a characteristic

typology for the houses in Timisoara - becomes a covered walk on the hill's ridge. All rooms, including those on the upper floor, are accessed from this walk. In fact, there are two buildings: a sturdy basement partially engulfed by the stones, the moss and the flowers which form the new hill, and a wall which defines a shelter moving from inside to outside. The building's transformation into a sheltering landscape has been accomplished by the richness and poetry of the walk and by the roofing system, which modulates the shadow of the wall into the light of the lawn. Sturza used neither imported materials nor technologies, he created a timber structure instead, partially covered with glass and supported by the dendromorphous pillars. The walk is protected by huge, transparent eaves, a reference to the eaves which are a very important architectural element in our vernacular architecture. Each rafter ends with a pointed stake. One could speak at length about this building's troubling poetry and humanism. It is not by chance that it has been awarded the Biennial medal for architecture.

The Prodid Studio has an offshot in the meantime, a studio specializing in furniture and interior design (together with George Ivanescu). It is another proof of their continuous search into the artistic use of materials.

Greek architecture continues to be *terra incognita*,

not only abroad but even in Greece itself.

Even nowadays, Greece is still not present in the history of modern Art.

16 | MALAKASA INTERCHANGE.
YORGOS SIMEOFORIDIS.

Greece

Form of State: Republic since 1975, **Area:** 131,957 km2, **Inhabitants (1992):** 10,300,000, **Capital:** Athens
Gross National Product 1992, per capita: $ 7,290, **Gross Domestic Product 1992:** $ 67,278 Mio, **Unemployment (Average, 1993):** 10.0%

Any attempt to describe the contemporary architecture of Greece, particularly the work of younger architects, founders immediately upon a lacuna historica, the historical absence of Greek architecture from the international, or even Western European, architectural scene and debate. In fact, Greek architecture is missing from almost all the classic and the avant-garde histories of modern architecture. Perhaps this absence is due to the "Eurocentric" approach of these histories. Greece appears in the body of European architecture only as the first step in the continuity of that architecture, in conformity with an Enlightenment system of thought and tradition. However, also within our own frontiers, any similar attempt is hampered by the lack of criticism or the theoretical cloud-cuckoo-land of the last fifteen years. Such attempts as have been made have endeavoured either to legitimate Post-Modernism as a late stage in Greek architecture (in unthinking acceptance of the evolutionary succession of styles and isms), or simply to verify the difficulty of distinguishing and evaluating by pointing out the similarities between "artful architecture" and mass-produced architecture. There has hardly been any critique not intended to prove a value assumed to pre-exist instead building a consensus among readers as to the status of a specific project. Greek architecture is not only, as has been repeatedly stated, in a state of semi-disrepute: it is also incapable of formulating a fruitful dialogue with any appeal beyond the bounds of the architectural community. I believe that a discussion must focus on specific projects as well as set out from an interpretation of the themes which today concern the architecture of Europe - of which, with all its individualities, Greek architecture consciously forms part. Greek architecture continues to be terra incognita, not only abroad but even in Greece itself. And yet, almost all the phenomena and characteristics of modernity and of its concomitant crises manifested themselves here. The mistrust and revulsion which Greek architects felt towards the system of thought and the ideas which accompanied the advent of Modernism - that is, towards Western

rationalism - led Greek architecture to introspection of its historical origins, a process which began in the inter-War years. The absence of any contact or dialogue with the work of the leading European masters and, in particular, with the historical avant-garde movements was, I believe, of catalytic importance for what followed. Greek architecture, cut off from international developments, developed a conservative and academic attitude which prevailed despite the ripples of the Inter-War period. Careful historical research would prove that even the famous IV International Congress of Modern Architecture, held in Athens in 1933, did no more than scratch the surface of Greek architecture. It would be foolish to suggest that the Post-War course of Greek architecture is unrelated to the turmoil of the Civil War and the subsequent political developments. The dictatorship of 1967 threw a veil of silence over the "architectural spring" which had begun to sprout in the late 50s and was to take more concrete form in the 60s, with architectural conferences and the flourishing of Neo-Brutalism which, let it be noted, was accompanied by a vision of society. Even more so, the dictatorship broke any continuity and interweaving that might have existed among the works of such architects as Mitsakis, Despotopoulos, Konstantinidis, Karantinos, Provelengios, Valentis, Krantonellis, Doxiadis, Hadjimichalis, Zenetos, Valsamakis who, despite their often obvious differences, had managed to filter the "tradition of the new" into their work. They were unable to pass that tradition on to the following generations unlike the case of Alvar Siza in Portugal on Europe's other periphery. It also isolated those who chose to follow the road of the "diaspora", such as Koulermos, Zenghelis, Porfyrios, Christofellis, Tsiomis, Manikas, Chlimintzas and others. Against this background of discontinuity, it is exceptionally difficult to seek out the evidence for influence or even trends which could be said to have contributed to the formation of a distinctive visage for Greek architecture. It is no coincidence that the only distinguished, if often misunderstood, trend is that which leads

from Dimitris Pikionis to Kyriakos Krokos by means of Aris Konstantinidis, Suzana and Dimitris Antonakakis and Dimitris Fatouros. I am refering to the Greek version of "critical regionalism". Contemporary Greek architecture is made highly unstable by a variety of social parameters, such as the under-estimated client relationship, the failure to apply quality control in construction, the absence of large-scale public projects and interventions in the cities, creeping mistrust in the architectural community, the inflexible mentality of the civil service and the discontinuity in its functioning. Although some Greek architects - such as Pikionis, Konstantinidis and Zenetos - have thinking of their own to propose (though always via their personal poetics), and though that thinking transcended the national frontiers, we have to admit that Greek architecture has contributed nothing to shaping that of the rest of Europe. Under these circumstances, the crucial question is how to approach the work of young Greek architects without resorting to useless stylistic categories or rhetorical constructs which would only produce bewilderment. An interpretative approach to contemporary architecture must involve a correlation to the shifting social and cultural setting. The panorama of contemporary architecture requires a different strategy of critical approach, a strategy of exploration, as Josep Lluís Mateo has rightly noted; historians and critics should not hesitate to travel in and map out its more "unknown regions".

Undoubtedly, one of the prominent landmarks is the "Ideas for the Greek Pavilion" exhibition, organized by the architecture, art and design review "Tefchos" as one of the three Greek contributions to the 5th International Architecture Exhibition at the Venice Biennale, held in September 1991. 18 teams (about 60 architects, including certain well-known professionals and many representatives of the younger generation) were invited to participate. The exhibition was conceived as an essay, an exploration indeed, on a specific theme: the exhibition pavilion. The relative freedom of the theme, without clear programmatic constraints, was meant to "stretch" unforeseen, not expected, movements, over and beyond the current conventions of professional practice. It was a risky and contradictory undertaking which immediately came up against the ambiguous relationship between art and architecture.

This relationship is not only one of co-operation, but also one of antagonism, particularly today, in the context of our broader cultural horizon, which seems to be trapping itself in the invincible "age of the triumph of the museums", in an age when "art cannot stand architecture, and architects get upset by the intoler-able presence of art", as Pier Luigi Tazzi reminds us. In touching upon the some-what obscure borderlines of art and architecture, the "Ideas for the Greek Pavilion" exhibition and its 18 projects raised a series of questions which dealt more with the investigation of the architectural than the ideological status of the exhibition pavilion.

The "Ideas" projects presented were marked by the game of repetition and difference with history, through the analysis of place, personal memory, episodic hints which are strictly auto-biographical. How else is one to interpret the hedonistic self-quotation of Gigantes/Zenghelis to previous images of their own architecture, in a pavilion which is an oasis/garden for resting art-lovers, or the entirely mythopoetic approach to the Venetian-Hellenic culture in the design of Koulermos, whose buildings articulated a "panegyric iconography". A totally personal "Mediterranean-ness" characterized the designs of Krokos and Kokkoris who approached the pavilion as a metaphysical or seasonal harbour for the mooring of art; eclectic affinities

(Terragni, Mies) were present in the distilled form of Patestos/Tsakalakis. The design team Kokkinou/Kourkoulas/Korres/Hadjimichalis/Paniyiris employed the idea of the floor-zattera alongside the canal, in which the rhythm of time of the exhibition is transformed. The dislocation of an exiled Greek landscape to the depth of the lagoon is the theme of Spanomaridis/Zachariades' project. Other projects proposed the strict materiality of their volumes and materials, incorporating into the design "some vibration, a slight gesture, an almost casual distortion, the fracture of some geometry". This is exemplified by Diakomidis/Fatseas/Haritos/Psarra's long raised metallic space in which parallel stratification and interweaving surfaces and transparencies define a space for art; by the floating perimeter walls in the design of Nicolakopoulos, who proposed a pavilion which is a support-wall for art; and by the detachment of the walls and their interposing with plate glass in Papoulias' pavilion-shelter. This last project could also be interpreted within the framework of the first category, since it elaborates an archetypal trace, the plan of the primitive Mediterranean house. It is apparent that these projects clearly belong to certain design "traditions". Their starting point may be a mental image, which lays claim to the artistic quality in architecture, according to the well-known saying that "art is thought in images", or an organizational principle, which insists upon its "architecturality", in accordance with the equally famous saying that "construction is a technical and not an aesthetic process", or, possibly, a combination of the two. The mental images all retain an echo of a classical Mediterraneity in the themes of the labyrinth, the harbour, the geometrical layouts and the archetypal forms, but, above all, in that of the theatre analogy. The organizational principles, on the other hand, approach programmatically, functionally and constructively such structural issues of the exhibition pavilion as space, materials, lighting, movement. In both directions, we can distinguish between a figurative and conceptual handling of the issue; between a more synthetic (metaphorical) procedure which invokes narrative and autobiographical images and memories and a more analytical (metonymic) approach which concentrates on the combination and the relations between

the separate elements, materials and themes (metal, transparency, wood, weight). The same distinction holds for designs dealing with the "Greek" character of the pavilion and its supposed incorporation into Venice: these projects hesitate between a more nostalgic and a more cold-blooded, almost "rhythmical", relationship between them. With this first viewing of the pavilion projects we can immediately single out those in which the personal reference to memory and history plays a decisive role, and those which are governed by a more abstract, extreme, logic. The same is true of the five buildings that I have selected to present here. I would like to start with a project by Kyriakos Krokos, the architect who achieved the capacity to realize a large public building, the Museum of Byzantine Culture in Thessaloniki. Thereafter, I want to present four projects by younger architects, built or in process of construction.

Drawing of Byzantine Museum

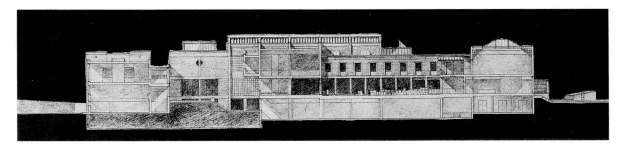

The panorama of contemporary architecture requires

a different strategy of critical approach, a strategy of

exploration, as Josep Lluís Mateo has rightly noted.

Re-evaluation and research as a first step towards a new orientation concerning the history of modern Greek architecture.

Kyriakos Krokos. Museum of Byzantine Culture, Thessaloniki

Inside view

The architectural idea focused from the beginning on a

pattern which we know from other modern museums:

a spiral in which galleries are arranged on either side.

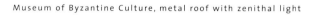

The Byzantine Museum: a turning point of post-War architecture in Greece.

Museum of Byzantine Culture, metal roof with zenithal light

My first project is the Museum of Byzantine Culture by Kyriakos Krokos. This project, which won the prize in the 1977 competition, suffered under the inability of the public sector to implement and complete large public buildings. The resulting delays coincided with the architect's increasing abandonment of an abstract concept of architecture as propagated by a Modern university training and his immersion in the qualities springing from the processing of matter. The result is faithful to the framework set by the designing architect, Kyriakos Krokos, who had the good fortune to encounter a builder-architect, Yorgos Yeorgiadis, with an understanding of that framework and an equal amount of boldness.
The Byzantine Museum was designed and constructed without reference to its valuable collection. The architectural idea focused from the beginning on a pattern which we know from other modern museums: a spiral in which galleries are arranged on either side. This museum differs from the others of the same archetypal rationale in so far that its exhibition halls lie off the axis of movement which runs across the museum. This serves to emphasise the building's other elements: its external appearance, the entrance gate, the peristyle atrium, the foyer to the main entrance hall, the numerous intervening spaces which are also passages, and the typical constructional section of the exhibition galleries, all of which are constitutive traces of the museum's architectural mentality. Krokos has in any case repeatedly stated his intention of leaving untouched the original idea of the design, the "initial frame", and working only on its details, on the processing of the "matter" of the building and on the interstices, most of them semi-open air). He wanted to try on a larger scale an approach which had already been tested in his Filothei house. The two projects have to be read in parallel and, in fact, were built almost in parallel. It may be that the ordering of random reality and the "ordinary" materials in which we build today, this trial and test, does not correspond to a common need. The approach which permeates Krokos' architecture and the Byzantine Museum is based in synecdoche. In synecdoche, the relationship between the parts and the whole exists for the purpose of attributing a predominant quality to the whole. Synecdoche is used representationally, as a way of giving

meaning to the phenomena which we perceive. Krokos frequently returns to Bracque's aphorism: "To construct means to assemble homogeneous elements. To build means to bind together heterogeneous elements." Perhaps, architecture today is moving more in the direction of constructing, of assembling, rather than that of binding together (despite the fact that both have a clearly artistic starting point). It is from "building", then, that the project's emblematic character stems, as does the organic dimension of its construction. Those features are also the result of the emotional atmosphere which emerges not only from the choice of building materials and their treatment, but also from their technical implementation, their "tectonic" binding together. The insistence on building, the organic aesthetics, the picturesque composition, the fact that the fundamental display areas for Byzantine art objects resemble basilicas, the metal domes which illuminate the halls, the trihypostatic division of the whole and often of the details, such as, for example, the tripartite division of the roof over the area surrounding the main halls, which transforms the plan of one of the apses of a basilica into a static and structural section, providing a simultaneous solution to the lighting and roofing of the building, all these features are signs of the work which has been done on matter and which drive into a blurred interpretative depth. This is the starting point for an underwater current in modern Greek architecture, a tradition of thought and not of forms, which has in the past been investigated by other architects, including Pikionis and Konstantinidis. It is a tradition which is sceptical with regard to positivism and abstract thought, but open, inclined towards a search for homocentric ontological guidelines. This tradition inspires the work of K. Krokos, one of the most prominent architects of the "intermediate generation". I have always advocated, and still do, the need for public architecture to have hardness, coldness and austerity, for it to be free from nostalgic impulses. Yet nothing can detract from the significance of this project, which - more than any other - testifies to a critical point of transition for post-War Greek architecture.
If we examine domestic architecture, we will find inscribed within it a complex variety of mentalities and practices which relate to distinctions between the sexes, parent/child relations, "inside" and "outside", "public" and "private".

These are recorded in the design of the spaces, and even in such individual features as furnishings. At this point, I believe that Greek architecture has a great deal to offer and can contribute fruitfully to the international debate. In most cases we will see that everyday life touches on the design of a central core, the "heart", the "esteia" of the house which usually forms a two-storey space. Here, one approach stands out for its empirical designing of an ideal solid shape and for its almost sculptural addition and subtraction of masses; another organizes buildings within the artful formulation of an "outdoor" space and the distribution of the various "indoor" spaces and functional units around it. The latter applies to the works by Dimitris and Suzana Antonakakis and Kyriakos Krokos. However, there were other approaches: the early work of Valsamakis and the work of Zenetos attempt to integrate a more modern, flexible open space within the conservative realm of the house. In this sense and regardless of their apparent differences it would be interesting to see whether the works by the so-called young architects actually do re-examine the basic assumptions within the conventional programme or whether they confine themselves to the unconscious repetition of a stereotypical organization of everyday life.

House in Neo Irakleio, living space

Athanasios Spanomaridis and Iannis Zachariades. House in Neo Irakleio, Athens 1990-93

Nothing in this house corresponds

to the conventional perception of

a suburban house.

9 x 9 metres of built reality, distorting the conventional perception of a suburban house.

The House in Neo Irakleio, Athens, was realized by Athanasios Spanomaridis and Iannis Zachariades. The site which fronts one of the main traffic roads of this suburb is small and, according to the building codes, has only the minimal space necessary to build a house. The building is free-standing and its façade 9 metres long. Nothing in this house corresponds to the conventional perception of a suburban house. The main façade is almost blind, whereas the side facing the house of the owner's family is more conventional, more familiar. The private space is delimited by a 9 x 9 metres square which is transformed in different levels through an always peripheral, external movement. The space is vertically relieved, where the movement from street to house and back garden is crossed by the movement from the submerged living-room courtyard to the first floor patio.

The presented projects by Dimitris Tsakalakis are situated in Siteia, Crete. These interventions constitute a unity of personal architectural style, the results of which are interlaced with a unified building system which in turn can be interpreted and formalized based upon each single design. The volume of the first house in the existing part of the city could be realized only by placing the staircase outside the apartment space. The project starts from an existing court-house typology but only in order to achieve a single volumetric form; in a certain sense it is rather a distortion of the typology. The same applies to the cultural centre project, where an existing building, a mosque transformed into a raisin warehouse, was renovated, so as to make the pre-existing immediately recognizable from the new. All the new spaces are created by horizontal and vertical light metal and plywood panels, which permit the space to be perceived as a whole. This minimal intervention is also characteristic of the open square,

facing the seaside, which is designed as a raised plateau, a loose rectangular shape of 20 x 20 metres. This shape can be read as a void urban block, in as much as its sides coincide with the existing urban layout. Finally, the last house shows the same tension, between a simple trapezoidal shape in the ground floor, placed on a base of 15 x 15 x 8 metres, and a complex first floor of four different volumes, designed in a more disordered arrangement. These two levels relate in the interior of the house where we find again the double-height space.

The natural surroundings enter the house through the two openings in the ground floor and then move upwards through the double-height space. Striking in this project is the deliberate will to merge in a single form two different spatial systems: open Modernist space and traditional space which is structured by volumes. One could even suggest that this house represents an abstract imitation of the mundane, conventional suburban context of "illegal" settlements. Although both projects depart from the double-height central space, they opt for a certain distortion: in this sense, the third house in Siteia sets a contradiction between an elongated ground floor space which stretches from one side of the building to the other, and a rather more enclosed upper floor of volumes, while the detached house in Neo Irakleio (where the two-storey space is always perceptible) speaks of a different life-style, especially in terms of the relationship between "inside" and "outside", the "public" and the "private", and thus alters the established per-ception of the detached suburban residence.

Pantelis Nicolakopoulos: House in Afidnai, Attica. The main and primary impression made by this project arises from its austere geometry within the apparent freedom of the landscape. The house organizes movement in a cruciform.

Longitudinal movement follows the topographic lines while lateral movement refers to their elevational differences. Surprising here is the reversal of the familiar relationship between exterior and interior spaces. This results from the interpenetration of movement and extremely careful detailing, for example in the floor level where the architect achieved a continuous flow. The detail is hidden, is not evident, additive or self-referential. It creates a sense of space because it is embedded in construction. The detail is always referential to construction, and related to the building's overall concept. Materials are used in their natural form and texture, the interior design of the interior bespeaks an integrated furniture logic, not a furnishing by adding casual pieces. Both metal and wooden elements share the same geometric characteristic, i.e. horizontality. It is a modern house made out of concrete, wood and metal. Particular care has been given to the floors and the naturalness of each element.

Catherine Diakomidis and Nikos Haritos: Project for a house and a private collection in Nea Vrilissia, Athens. The programme included a house and a space for the client's collection. The complex is a rather huge, approximately 2.500 m2 built space and a lot of open spaces as well. What is interesting about the project in the first phase of which Papoulias also participated is the decision to divide the programme into different parts arranged because of the client's requirements on a horizontal plane. All walls parallel to the primary retaining wall are blind, with no openings at all, while all the other sides are completely transparent with open views towards the city and the mountain. This horizontal transparency which follows the direction of the primary movement, is traced by a long wall, creates an interplay of volumes and change of scales. This fragmentation is counterbalanced by the austerity and simplicity of each part, of each volume, particularly in the use of materials: exposed unplastered concrete walls, wooden floors for the interior spaces and the main corridor, aluminium and wooden infills, white marble for the service spaces, stone paving for the open air public spaces, "terre battue" for the rest of the site surface and indigenous vegetation and landscape. Wooden roller blinds can close the open façades and create a wooden and concrete interior space when completely closed. The retaining wall becomes the spine of the dispersed programme's individual elements, while the surrounding landscape and all related areas are as simple as possible in order to receive new sculptural pieces. Some very interesting statements can be discerned in both projects: the vertical/ cross juxtaposition of the volumes to the existing topographic lines, and the overscaled dimensions of the openings and the structural sections, which relate not to an urban but to a natural context. This not immmediately perceptible scalar transformation creates a distortion of dimensions, of heights. The difference between these two projects rests in the familiar character of the first and the almost "uncanny" character of the second.

The detail is hidden, is not evident, additive or self-referential. It creates a sense of space because it is embedded in construction.

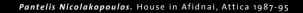

The house in Afidnai shows a rigid geometry.

Pantelis Nicolakopoulos. House in Afidnai, Attica 1987-95

Catherine Diakomidis and Nikos Haritos. House with a private art collectio in Nea Vrilissia, Athens 1992

House in Afidnai

House in Nea Vrilissia, Elevations

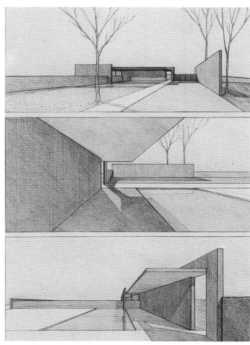

This fragmentation is counterbalanced by the

austerity and simplicity of each part, of each volume.

The house in Nea Vrilissia, containing a private art collection.

Dimitris Tsakalakis. House in Siteia, Crete

It is a landscape of isolated movements,

not one of collective endeavours.

The architectural landscape of Greece - *terra incognita* in the contemporary debates on architecture.

Northfaçade

The Spanish critic Ignasi de Solà Morales presumes the absence of a clear, collectively accepted system of evaluation as the foundation for artistic and architectural activities. He discerns two types of architectural experience which are formulated as personal answers to the crisis of values in contemporary architecture, which wavers in a "condition of weakness": the architecture of identity and difference (the subjective re-founding of architecture through references to its historical structures) and the architecture of the logic of the limit (a new system of foundations relying on the fundamental elements of experience).

The first of these two attitudes which consciously opposes the commercialized sentimentality or reactionary historicism of Post-Modern architecture is typical of the projects of those who have confined themselves to analysis of the site, personal memory and incidental allusions of an exclusively autobiographical nature: those who are in search for a trace, a simulacrum from which to start, which they subject to a process of differentiation, ultimately leading to a rejection of this starting point (for example, Rossi, Graves, Moneo or Botta). The second approach is typical of the projects of those who, at some risk, approximate an elementary architectural writing, who insist upon the severe materiality of mass and of building components, while incorporating into it a slight tremor, an almost imperceptible gesture, a nearly random distortion, a rift with the geometrical shape (for example, Herzog & de Meuron, Souto de Moura, J. Navarro Baldeweg, Venezia, Collovà). According to de Solà Morales, these two experiences correspond to the distinction between Arte Povera, which reworks an extant iconography, and especially that which stems from a knowledge of history and accumulated memory, and Minimal Art which sets out from rudimentary kinaesthetic experiences such as geometry, colour and space. In effect, we could call the two experiences "back to basics" and "back to the limit", the central difference between them being the

referential nature of the former and the self-referentiality of the latter. De Solà Morales perceives and accepts the significant impact of contemporary art on architecture when he alludes to the cultural diffusion of artistic discourse into numerous other practices. Other critics, such as Kenneth Frampton, have seen in precisely the same phenomenon the decline of contemporary architecture because this tendency moves away from its etymological roots in craftsmanship, and tectonics/tekne, and, consequently, from its inescapable integration in technical, economic and social evolution. These two views reiterate the familiar pre-War dispute between the claim to the functional dimension of a Modern international architecture and the claim to architecture's artistic nature, and to the distinction between art and technology. It should be noted that in these approaches neither critic comments on the work of those architects, who are open to the mass cultural phenomena of post-industrial societies (such as Jean Nouvel and Rem Koolhaas). Could this pattern be related to Greek architecture? If there is any such connection, can it be associated to specific projects, or only to one architect's "oeuvre complete"? We can find the search for a Minimal architecture which, by means of rudimentary geometrical manipulations and simple materials, succeeds in attaining a marginal and contemporary tension between a traditional urban and rural setting in the interventions in Siteia by Tsakalakis, the transformation of a square by means of movement into a space in relief, in the free-standing house in Neo Irakleio by Spanomaridis and Zachariades; and in the austere geometric positioning of the buildings on the site in the projects by Nicolakopoulos and Diakomidis, Haritos. These projects all distort the usual perception of the building. This interpretative pattern could in fact serve as a tool to excavate initially the landscape in which the younger generation of Greek architects moves. It is a landscape of isolated movements,

not one of collective endeavours. Yet it is equally obvious that the first category, the architecture of identity and difference, has become more important in Greek architecture than the architecture of the logic of the limit. Of importance in the projects noted above and in the work of other young architects is the fact that there seems to be a clear departure (or at least a desire to depart) from the easy answer of imitative Post-Modernism and architectural high-handedness. The latent challenge to contemporary Greek architecture is its confrontation with mass consumer culture. It should not content itself with a complacent embrace of the idealized world of "artistic architecture".

Today there is growing unrest in the Italian architectural

scene, a result of the extremely severe tremors which have

severely shaken Italian society.

Marco De Michelis on Italy, its society and its architecture.

17 | THE "INTERMEDIATE GENERATION" AND ITS SUCCESSORS.
MARCO DE MICHELIS.

Italy

Form of State: Republic since 1948, **Area:** 301,302 km2, **Inhabitants (1992):** 56,859,000, **Capital:** Rome
Gross National Product 1992, per capita: $ 20,460, **Gross Domestic Product 1992:** $ 1,222,962 Mio, **Unemployment (Average, 1993):** 10.2%

My contribution deals with the decline and crisis of Italian architecture; a decline inasmuch as the vitality of the critical reflection and experimental projects which matured towards the end of the 60s now undoubtedly seems to have disappeared, never to return; and a crisis because in those cases in which questions and investigation did not prove to be idle, they challenged precisely the system of relationships between architecture, town and country, as well as the status of architectural works in relation to their context, which had hitherto been characteristic for every urban project. Today there is growing unrest in the Italian architectural scene, a result of the extremely severe tremors which have severely shaken Italian society. At the same time, however, this also reflects a stagnation that cannot simply be blamed on Italian politicians and which has had a direct impact on the decisions and activities of architects. In 1991 Vittorio Gregotti wrote in the journal "Casabella" of a "decline in Italian architecture" (1) and also underlined its diminished influence abroad as well as the uncertainty of the planning opportunities being offered.

A few months later, in an attempt - in "Casabella" (2) - to document the works of younger generations of Italian architects, it was possible, with great effort, to pick out the grand total of six architects - half of whom at least had completed a long apprenticeship in the studio of Vittorio Gregotti. It was acknowledged that they displayed genuinely surprising, although - for young architects - not exactly disappointing, qualities and virtues: the realism and concrete character of their works, the further development of the lessons of the "master", an absence of avant-gardism, and a wilfully impertinent

architecture. The generation, which had played a key role in the theoretical debate surrounding architecture in Italy since the 60s (and certainly not as a monolithic block, even though it was homogenous in substance), began to belatedly harvest its first professional successes in the 80s (although it still, in hegemonic fashion, seizes for itself the rare opportunities offered to "quality architecture").

This generation comprising Aldo Rossi, Vittorio Gregotti, Gabetti as well as Isola and Gino Valle is now being confronted with the sum result of its own activities. Gregotti attempted to outline the most important aspects (3), self-critically and sometimes in a melancholic manner. Thus, for example, he accuses himself and his peers of the growing marginalization and specialization of architecture in relation to the overall context of cultural-political work as well as the incapacity of reforming a system which could organically pass on an architectural knowledge capable of coping with the new tasks facing future generations. At the same time, however, he sometimes aims too high and becomes omnipotent when he actually credits his "inter-mediate generation" with the honour of carrying out a critical revision of the dogmas of the "Modern Movement", of once again focusing on the relationship to context, history and the environment as well as having the courage to accept the unrest of subsequent generations together with the issues both raised and, of course, left unsolved by them. These issues include the practice of metaphorical inference between diverse languages, the experience of the immateriality and universality of the means of mass communication as well as the acceptance of provisional and fragmentary phenomena as natural components in the development of a

project. Speaking from the standpoint of this "anonymous" successor-generation, which is now around fifty years old, still lacks masters as well as recognition and no longer stands in the lime-light but looks in from the outside, Massimo Scolari responded with the grave accusation that they had deserted the battlefield after their first victory and thus renounced all critical reflection, all attention to the future and all solidarity with the younger generation just at that very moment when belated recognition finally interrupted a long period in which the profession conspicuously suffered from a shortage of orders. This "victorious party" had succeeded in swallowing up Italian architecture in its entirety by resolving the factional struggles that took place in the early 70s "in cynical drinking sessions in front of baffled and motionless footmen", who were reserved the privilege of having academic power in the mass universities, already on the verge of collapse, and in designing "cardboard-box architecture"(4).

Aldo Rossi's and Ignazio Gardella's Teatro Carlo Felice in Genoa constitutes a general metaphor for many of the episodes in this delayed yet inevitable success of Italian architecture. In this work, the two most important generations of Italian architecture of this century encounter one another: the generation of Ignazio Gardella who, since the 30s, has been a main representative of the "anomalous" Modern Movement in architecture, together with Figini and Pollini, Terragni and the BBPR group of architects on the one hand, and the group around Aldo Rossi, which developed around the project of issuing Ernesto N. Rogers' "Casabella Continuità" on the other. Here, the diverse subjects of post-war reconstruction, the fear of ruins and the longing for new directions collide. The Classicist building erected by Carlo Marabino between 1826 and 1828 was severely damaged during the bombing that occurred in 1942 and 1943. Paola Chessa prepared reconstruction plans in 1949. There was an attempt to realize a similar project by Carlo Scarpa in the early 70s. It was interrupted several times due to changes in the construction programme and by new legal regulations until the work was definitively abandoned following the architect's death in 1978. The destruction of the historical ruins and the attempt to more or less save large fragments of Marabino's building followed in an unresolved confrontation alternating between Modernism and history (5). In 1981 developments entered their final phase after the municipality of Genoa had invited architects to participate in a competition. Seven planning groups emerged victorious and, after being placed on the short list, were invited to participate in the second round in 1983. The project submitted by Rossi, Gardella and Fabio Reinhart was awarded first prize and was to have been definitively concluded in 1990. If it seemed that Italian reconstruction had finally been brought to a conclusion with the Teatro Carlo Felice by Aldo Rossi, so did a decisive chapter in the debate on Italian architecture, a chapter - full of endless polemics - which was dedicated to the character of modern architecture, its relation to history and to the concepts of the "monument" and "public architecture". Rossi took advantage of his opportunity to implement a rapid succession of architectural decisions. He employed Marabino's pronaos and portico and also turned the entrance towards the square. In this way, he

defined a system of references between the new building and the diversified urban structure, which is able to change existing hierarchies. He transformed the technical contingency of the light-tower projecting above the stage into a extraordinary typological invention. (In the past, the tower had frequently presented difficulties during the renovation of 19th century theatre buildings, from the Berlin State Opera to the Semper Opera in Dresden.) The tower was now turned into a public focal point of the new building, and refers to the surrounding town. Rossi enhanced the traditional room of the foyer with the surprising architectural figure of a pointed cone which cut through the foyer to the roof. He dispensed with traditional design "all'italiana", which he had still employed during the Parma competition, and brought Gardella's Vicentinian experiments into play, creating a terrace-like auditorium without boxes and circles. A surprising metamorphosis in which the stage and the auditorium thus pass into one another (6). "Casabella" gave its assent to the Teatro Carlo Felice from the very beginning. Even though it "certainly did not ... [correspond] ... with the Modernist examples" which the Milan journal generally supported, Rossi's project was nevertheless interpreted favourably in these pages as an extreme variation on that kind of urban architecture which may even assume the extraordinary forms of a monument in both its encounter with history and in its special programmatic function. The objections raised only concerned questions of architectural language, such as the cornice of the light-tower and the idealized metaphor of the city in the auditorium. The requirements of the context, the city and the laws of the architectural forms which prevail over them united the standpoints of the many diverse talents (Gregotti, Aulenti, Rossi, Tafuri, Tentori and a few others besides) that gathered around the "Casabella Continuitá" under editor-in-chief Ernesto N. Rogers. Throughout the 80s, the same requirements were to create a bridge uniting the independent paths taken by the main representatives of the "intermediate generation". This was a generation which had, at long last, been called upon to realize (abroad far more than in Italy) its own ideas and projects: from the Belém Cultural Centre in Lisbon by Gregotti Associati to the IBM headquarters in Paris and the Venetian houses on the Giudecca by Gino Valle, to

Modena cemetery and the residential houses in Berlin and Paris by Aldo Rossi himself. Cracks started to appear in this kind of orthodoxy as it began to lose its hold towards the end of the decade, as new impulses and experiences chaotically began to assert themselves. Sometimes they recalled the Post-Modernist motives of dissecting knowledge or the decadence of the "grands récits", yet in other places there was an awareness and experience of the impossibility of realizing a pure and simple reconstruction of the original urban-planning structure in a city like Berlin, a city which reveals contradictory, morphological traces and is marked by irreparable and destructive transitions, a city which became an international field of experimentation during the long years of the 1987 Internationale Bauausstellung (International Architecture Exhibition). There were also signs of research into styles based on open and dissected geometries, the rediscovery of the material and conceptual terseness of the architectural object accompanied by a decline in the importance of architectural regulations: this as yet vague and initial combination of diverse elements prevented the realization of many projects.

In this way, Aldo Rossi defined a system of references

between the new building and the diversified urban

structure, which is able to change existing hierarchies.

Aldo Rossi's Teatro Carlo Felice: an urban architecture between history and the forms of a monument.

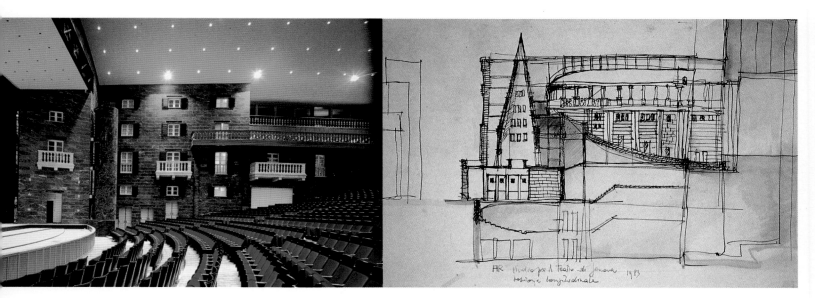

Auditorium   Sketch

The very word city has lost its capacity to evoke the complexity of current urban events. Megalopolises, metropolises of information are the new words which ought to be replacing the word city.

Piero Derossi on the difficulty of finding a term for the modern city between fragmentary context and recollection.

Pietro Derossi. Tower for Berlin, 1985-88

The high-rise building intended for realization in Berlin by Piero Derossi within the framework of the programmes of the Internationale Bauausstellung between 1985 and 1988 is an expressive representative of this approach. For Derossi, the modern city can no longer be reduced to a homogenous system of regulations, principles and designs. "The very word city", wrote Derossi in 1990, "has lost its capacity to evoke the complexity of current urban events. Megalopolises, metropolises, metro-polises of relationships, metropolises of the mind and metropolises of information are the new words which ought to be replacing the word city. (...) urban facts present themselves as a complex fabric of events. Each event is based on an opportunity and exists in the specificity of a space and a time". (7) Derossi's city is nothing but a frag-mentary context, rich in traces and

memories, in monuments and places which are reduced to remnants of greater and meanwhile unintelligible stories. Intervening in these locations means to reformulate a story there, to link the fragments in a new narrative structure: "It is as if one were inserting a novelette into the 'novelettes' of the city." In the Berlin tower, Derossi takes the traditional division of a high-rise building into the three design forms of the plinth, the shaft and the crest by availing himself of special situations and emotions for each part. The brick plinth ends at the traditional eaves height of Berlin's housing blocks, alluding to their solid strictness and only interrupting the regularity of their scale with unfinished compositional elements that underline the fragmentary and contingent character of the work. The shaft rests on the dripstone cornice, which is thus transformed into a balcony going round

the entire building and decorated by a light balustrade enhanced by a row of spherical lamps. The clearly rendered surface, upon which the window apertures are arranged in an orderly manner, is interrupted on the upper level by a series of "contingencies" - metal structures, aerials and fire escapes - which become increasingly frequent as one moves up towards the crest. Here, the building culminates in a pyramid-shaped figure made of a metal grid partly clad with colourful sails, and from which cheerful aerials and flag-poles rise into the sky.

Here we witness a truth of the building: a truth which

"traverses" it from the northern portico to the impressive

outline of the cathedral, and a second truth that is

silently enclosed in the interior of its constructed borders.

The project of Francesco Venezia for the centre of Amiens is a contribution to a new urban architecture which realizes
the dream of a dense and coherent city.

Francesco Venezia. Competition for the Centre of Amiens, 1993

One of the more recent projects by Franceso Venezia for the centre of Amiens confronts us anew - in a specific context, and again outside Italy - with the subject of the changing concept of "urban architecture". In 1984, architects were invited to participate in an international competition, in Amiens, on the reorganization of the central areas around the great Gothic cathedral. The aim here was to remedy both war damage and more serious cases of building reconstruction. Also involved were urban motorways and a debate, which had never ceased, on the adequate form for the square in front of the cathedral. Rob Krier won the first prize with a project that Bernhard Huet, a member of the jury, saw as "falling back on a simple view of the city as being divided into housing-blocks which, each representing a closed unit, observe an urban order consisting of streets and orders of magnitude. [...] Krier won because he knew and respected the rules. The others are mistaken in thinking that architecture consists of exceptions".(8) Almost ten years later, the dream of a dense and coherent city rich in picturesque perspectives, covered passages, small squares - perhaps already public, yet perhaps still private - seems to have vanished. A new competition, which ended in the summer of 1993, restricted the project area to one housing-block

wedged between a large, busy boulevard and the course of a canal bordering on the square in front of the cathedral. A library and the faculty of economics and law at the University of Amiens constituted the functional programme of the proposal.
Francesco Venezia emerged victorious at the end of the two-phase competition and rapidly set about completing the final planning within the framework of a project of unusual complexity. Here, as in his better-known accomplishments, the smaller buildings in Gibellina, Salemi and Salaparuta in Sicily, Venezia also tended to internalize the morphology, topography and building regulations of the surrounding city as immaterial concepts rather than adopt them at a material level. The Neapolitan architect has always preferred ruins, fragments and deep deposits to overtly evident geometries. As Alvaro Siza pertinently observed, "[his] eyes rapidly consume leaves, branches and trunks. They are searching for the root of things".(9) In Amiens, too, the large building complex planned by Venezia has been sunk five metres below street level. And in the surrounding cityscape, the level of the square in front of the cathedral has, like an ideal horizon, the function of a plane section, against which one can judge the heights of the buildings. The architectural form thus arising is low (the height of the

metres). It peacefully runs along the border of the housing-blocks. There is a more open and divided structure in the portico and in the small square linking the two buildings along the northern side. The closed structure of the wall, in contrast, points towards the cathedral. A cornice runs along its entire length thus underscoring the height of the ideal plane section with the descending slope of the square in front of the cathedral. Hence the typological essence of this work - the stratification of the different levels, the allocation of functions, the courtyards which allow sunlight to penetrate the lowest storeys, the entrances located below street level - seems to be internalized and inscrutable to the beholder. Here we witness a truth of the building: a truth which "traverses" it from the northern portico to the impressive outline of the cathedral, and a second truth that is silently enclosed in the interior of its constructed borders.

A comment recently made by Pierluigi Nicolin on the "Italian anomaly" is, I believe, of crucial significance. He stated that Italy had "entered the Post-Modernist phase, and thus left behind a weak and much criticized tradition of Modernism" (10). Italy had always seemed unprepared and indecisive vis-à-vis the three critical periods of the Modern Movement and had certainly been irrevocably slow in reacting. This had been the case with the issues of modernization and reform, which turned attention to social housing projects and the existence minimum as well as to the garden city and large estates. In Italy all these things had been dealt with in the form of "fascist modernization", in which some kind of avant-gardist "casa del fascio" and "casa del doppolavoro" (a type of public building for social events and leisure activities) tended to be built instead of houses for the benefit of the public. The same procedure repeated itself in the unsettled years of the post-war reconstruction period, in which a flood of property speculators and the violence of a modernization brought about by a chaotically expanding capitalism (which was devoid of any conception of how to relate to culture) played far too much of a central role. In the 60s and 70s, there still existed the exemplary building sites of the Italian economic boom, the city districts of social housing, the so-called ZEN district in Palermo and the Università delle Calabrie by Gregotti, the cities in Turin and Milan, and subsequently in Florence, the great plans for renovating old cities such as Bologna and Venice; everything had come to a standstill, leaving behind the scars of a dramatic defeat. The debate over the essence of Post-Modernism assumed the form of a "pathos-filled return to pre-modernist visions" instead of proceeding - as Nicolin noted - "from modernity". Thus an uninspired accumulation of new Arcadias and populist regionalisms arose, Post-Modernist "true-to-style" Historicisms imitating the American, or as we now know, the transitory original models, egoistic rediscoveries of the "authority of the star architects", which opened up small yet important market niches to the most famous names. Proceeding from such shaky premises, the discussion soon came to an end, leaving in its wake hopelessly divergent yet unavoidably pacified fronts once the commanders had apparently decided how to share consensus, recognition and the market. What was left on both fronts were, as Scolari put it, the dismal footmen returning home. These observations are intended to provide us with a few critical criteria required to analyse the character of the project realized by Nicolin in his successful participation in the scope of the 1991 International Competition (11) for the new city in Milan in the area of Corso Garibaldi - Piazza della Repubblica, as well as for investigating the reasons for the criticisms and the unrest which ensued. The terrain selected was a large rectangle which was left unused after the railway terminals had been shifted back at the beginning of the century. Today the huge gap thus created can still be seen from the various incomplete parts of the city surrounding the centre. Banks and hotels, offices and the seat of the regional government of Lombardy, trading activities and flats all formed the colourful functional programme of the competition.

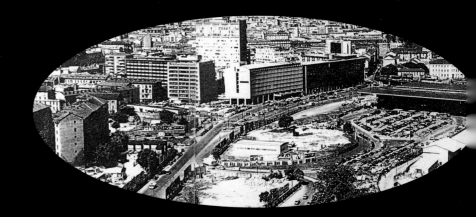

Nicolin provoked a scandal by refusing to repair the urban gap in a way that would have meant him simply filling it up with the functions of the proposed programme. Instead, he viewed the terrain as an "urban park".

Nicolin's project for Milan is the conscious refusal of dictating norms.

Pierluigi Nicolin. Competition for the new City in Milan, 1991

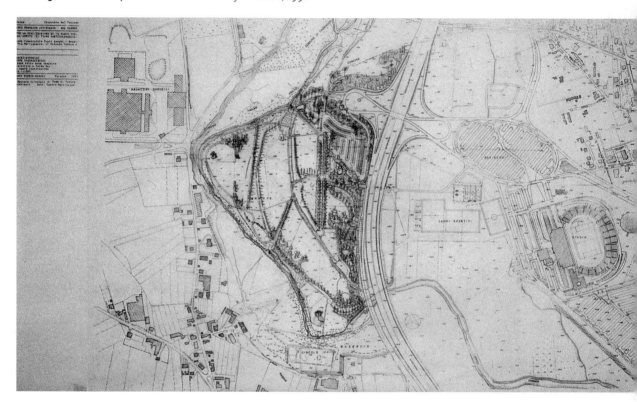

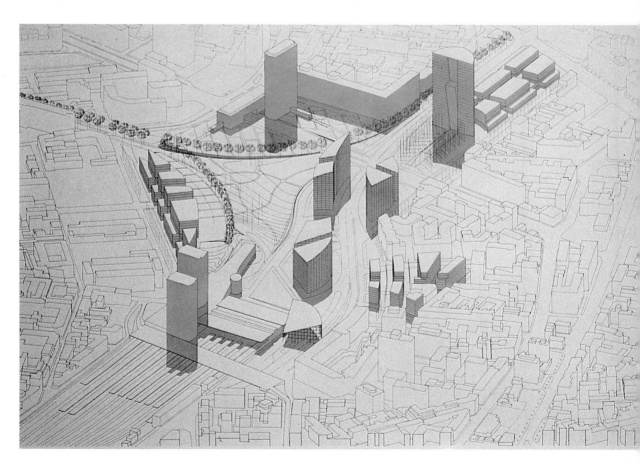

Roberto Pirzio-Birolo. Pavilion at the park along the River Cormor, Udine, 1993

This new cycle of deconstruction, re-use, renewal and transformation seems to

play a major role in the large territorial park realized by Roberto Pirzio-Biroli

Roberto Pirzio-Biroli defined by his ecology of re-use and reflection, and with modest financial means one of the most fascinating areas of work in the future.

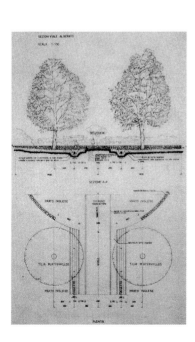

landscaping drawings

Nicolin provoked a scandal by refusing to repair the urban gap in a way that would have meant his simply "filling it up" with the functions of the proposed programme. Instead, he viewed the terrain as an "urban park", as an area unspoiled by careless construction activity and as one onto which various urban fragments look, to which differentiated functions are allocated, and where the functions of the traffic are optimized without disturbing the existing layout of the city. This decision resulted in a variety of solutions: the recomposition of the peripheries of the various urban structures - which look onto the gap - without re-creating the continuity or homogeneity eradicated by the course of the railway lines one hundred years ago. It also involved the creation of an urban landscape park, the realization of a few new housing blocks, the allocation of erected fragments on the area which had largely been left undeveloped, a few architectural structures, high-rise buildings such as that - over one hundred metres high - for the regional government, and the low-level building blocks of monolithic appearance. These are "Fragments" - writes Nicolin - "of a different city, more open to the expansive terrain and the landscape". Thus, the refusal to adopt a unified plan capable of re-uniting the irrevocably divided parts of the big city, the refusal to dictate norms, to draw routes and abolish differences has been replaced by a projection which manages to suggest both a variety of possible locations in the city and new standards, which can also conceive of the gaps and the incomplete fragments as subjects of urban architecture, as a kind of ecology of differences and contrasts and as an unexpected economy of symbolic values and means of expression (12).

This new cycle of deconstruction, re-use, renewal and transformation seems to play a major role in the large territorial park realized by Roberto Pirzio-Biroli along the River Cormor. He managed this by including the two thousand hectares of the periphery belonging to the city of Udine. The first 45 hectares were completed in the course of 1993 (13). The urgent requirements which give rise to such a project include the decline of the city periphery, the migration from the

The World's Fair in Seville and the Olympic Games in Barcelona

were to give Spain an impetus otherwise difficult to imagine.

After forty years of international isolation Spanish architecture is back to life.

18 | **THE ART OF REACTING. SPANISH ARCHITECTURE IN MOVEMENT. MARTA CERVELLÓ.**

Spain

Form of State: Parliamentary Monarchy since 1978, **Area:** 504,782 km2, **Inhabitants (1992):** 39,085,000, **Capital:** Madrid
Gross National Product 1992, per capita: $ 13,970, **Gross Domestic Product 1992:** $ 574,844 Mio, **Unemployment (Average, 1993):** 22.7%

The main characteristics of Spanish architecture are

a recurrent use of the Modern Movement as a source

of inspiration and a pragmatism of the solutions.

Taking Modernism and the practice of building as an example - contemporary architecture in Spain today.

Since 1977, Spain has been involved in a successful process of transformation that has changed the state from one governed by a single personality to an almost Federal democracy in which the different regions are beginning to manifest their autonomy culturally and politically (but not yet economically). That is why it is so difficult to present the five best buildings. Each region of Spain has different capacities and cultural interests. Nevertheless, the last five-year period has seen only large projects, the majority of them built for the events of 1992. The World's Fair in Seville and the Olympic Games in Barcelona, together with the fact that Madrid was chosen the Cultural Capital of Europe for that year, were to give Spain an impetus otherwise difficult to imagine, although each of those manifestations had a different origin and goal. Despite the fact that the architecture built in Spain during the past twenty years is known for its quality, we cannot pretend that everything realized for '92 was of the same caliber as earlier works. 1992 permitted all of Spain to show its strength in economic terms even beyond its actual capacity, and provided Barcelona and Seville with a great opportunity to carry out important infrastructural developments. It is impossible to explain here why the democracy has been bound to increased construction, but after a nearly forty-year dictatorship, the government agencies, especially some of the regional ones, undertook the task of building and rebuilding facilities and social housing.

The accompanying support of experimentation helped to develop local personalities which, once consolidated, comprise the spirit of the acclaimed examples of cultural manifestations. To choose the best five buildings of the last five years in Spain is not simple. I will try to select five representative buildings, and then quickly show several other major examples of recent Spanish architecture. Each embodies some of the very specific characteristics of Spanish architecture: The recurrent use of the Modern Movement as a source of inspiration, the attempt to avoid local particularities, as well as international trends or paper architecture tendencies; the attention to materials and details, mainly using native material and traditional techniques still in use. Respect is payed to the context and existing environment, coupled with a creative and interpretive point of view. In that sense, the historic heritage has not been passed on to supposed specialists, but to stimulating architects. Another main feature is the pragmatism of the solutions, due to the fact that the Spanish architecture is built, and is almost never a theoretical exercise. It is important to mention the responsibility which an architect assumes in Spain when he accepts a commission: from the design to the last built detail, he is legally responsible to user and owner. That fact causes Spanish architecture to be very conservative in some respects. The conditions for projects in '92 were somewhat different. Because commissions in the past years

have been public, construction schedules and budgets have been less strict than in the private sector. (Payment has also been less strict, causing great trouble for architects). We have now to cope with a different situation: public institutions need little architecture, and the public sector has little to spend. The interventions in Spain are often minimal in size: they are usually made in consolidated areas having structured urban fabrics. The location of the project therefore becomes strategic and should aid in developing local infrastructural needs. Most of the examples I have chosen are built by architects from Barcelona, Madrid, or Seville. All these cities are home to interesting architecture schools and have a longer architectural tradition than the activity associated with '92.

Court inside with zenithal light

d'Ebre, the hospital in Mora d'Ebre (close to Tarragona, by Elias Torres and José Antonio Martínez Lapeña, 1988) recalls a hidden fortress by virtue of its chromatic materials, similar to the colours of the surrounding geography. The building that includes all facilities required for a hospital programme occupies a vast surface. Taking advantage of the hill's section, the building avoids growing tall, and instead, expands over the land in a series of patios. In this way,

along the side that offers the best views, refusing any other less advantageous possibility. The emergency unit is situated perpendicularly, which makes the large unit look smaller, while it separates the garden from the parking. Circulation routes are also conceived from a functional point of view. They comprise two parallel but divided corridors that organize two systems: the public, and the personnel. Materials are simple, and the methods of construction traditional,

of the building. Careful attention is given to the details. In addition to functional requisites, natural lighting is guaranteed by transparent covered courtyards all along the building. This particular strategy relates to the landscape in which the building is located: open vistas effect a very orderly and clear atmosphere.

Located on the hill-top above Mora d'Ebre, the Hospital in Mora d'Ebre recalls a hidden fortress by virtue of its chromatic materials, similar to the colours of the surrounding geography.

Convincing functionally and conceptually: the Hospital in Mora d'Ebre by Elias Torres and José Antonio Martínez Lapeña.

Elias Torres and José Antonio Martínez Lapeña. Hospital in Mora d'Ebre close to Tarragona, 1988

In the first instance it was quietness we sought; material

uniformity dissolved the borders of our activity; dissolve

it into the earth and helped us finding that quietness.

Carme Pinós on the transcendental idea of the Igualada cemetery.

cate with the
throughout
erested in
s together
llel in their
alism. In the
erpiece of
tion, there is
d to the use of
the elements
e, and the
e second
mportance
similarity
y avoids
nages to
r-spectator
nventive, but
.

1 Entrance
2 Sliding door
3 Metal grille gate
4 Chapel door
5 Sacristy grille
6 Kneeling stands
7 Altar
8 Pulpit
9 Catafalque
10 Sacristy case
11 Skylights
12 Park stair
13 Sacristy entrance

19 Armarios

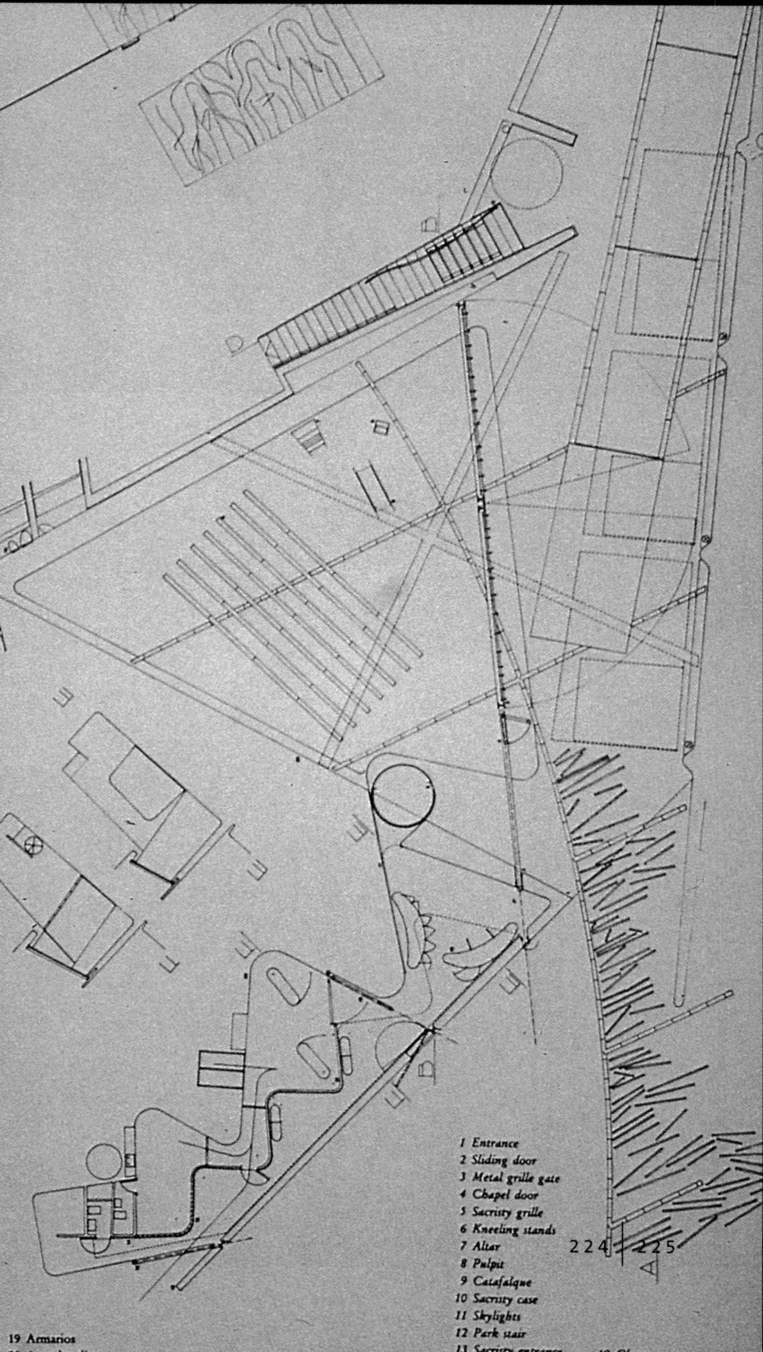

The site of the Olympic Basketball Pavilion in Badalona (near Barcelona, by Esteve Bonell and Francesc Rius, 1987-1992) was a sort of no-man's-land, a collection of heterogeneous and messy situations bordering speculative neighbourhoods of the 60s.

The programme was a basketball pavilion for 13,000 people that would be used for the Olympics, as well as for other activities. The building's intention is to lend a special image to this part of the city, to create the mechanisms which would guarantee its urban success by the precision and simplicity of the architectural solution. The building is composed of a central hall for spectators and players, and a series of functional subsidiary spaces (access, main entrance, and facilities, with training fields, changing-rooms, etc.). It is sheltered by a large roof that follows the radially positioned columns on the grounds of simplicity and austerity. It was impossible to systematize roof pieces to form the building's elliptical shape. The realized building's form focuses on the people.

The Housing development in Tharsis, Huelva (by Antonio Cruz and Antonio Ortiz, 1992) is located in a mining area, founded in 1820, which never truly became a town. Moreover, the building site is marginal even to this other, previous sparse development.

The programme called for 50 housing units of 70 m2 with three bedrooms, plus public amenities in five more buildings (a library, shops and an institutional building, the town-hall). The project appropriates the site by means of four branching rows of houses like streets that organize land by demarcating public and private domains. To give autonomy to the houses, each is elevated above a small platform. The houses appear as a housing experience of an almost superreal presence; above all, they represent a high standard quality.

The realized building's form

focuses on the people.

Preciseness and simplicity: the Olympic Basketball Pavilion by Esteve Bonell and Francesc Rius.

Site plan in Badalona

Esteve Bonell and Francesc Rius. Olympic Basketball Pavilion in Badalona near Barcelona, 1987-92

Navigation Pavilion

Harmony between interior and exterior.

The Navigation Pavilion, a symbol for Sevilla also after the EXPO '92.

Section

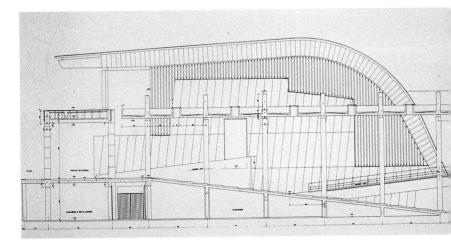

Guillermo Váquez Consuegra. Navigation Pavilion in Sevilla (EXPO '92), 1988-92

This may be the reason for the success of Spanish

architecture. Its capacity for response is more primitive

and authentic, and therefore, more enthusiastic.

Spanish architecture is based on a language which does not look back to the past, but forward to the future.

The Navigation Pavilion in Seville (EXPO'92, by Guillermo Vázquez Consuegra, 1988-1992) is one of the very few Pavilions built for the World's Fair '92 that from the beginning was planned to remain on the site after the Fair. It will house the Maritime Museum of Seville. The building is composed of three different elements that articulate the whole: the main building; the ramp and terminating pavilion; and a two-part observation tower that helps to balance the other horizontal shapes. The ramp is the element that guarantees the project's unity, by setting up its own interior/ exterior harmony while it assures a connection with the Guadalquivir. In addition to its formal roles, it serves as a covered waiting and queuing area. The main building has a large copper-clad curved roof that is, in fact, its main façade. It is meant to refer to images of hangars or harbour installations, and in fact, also to waves and foam. The interior is divided in two bars. The thin one contains amenities, and the large one,

covered by a wooden structure of 40-m-long beams, the exhibition hall. The interior scheme designed by Dani Freixes and Vicente Miranda for the Fair's duration did interfere with the normal way of using the space, but in exchange, it offered a wonderful collection of situations and experiences, the only valid place in the Fair.

one of these examples are in fact
presentative of anything other than
emselves. I could have chosen five
chers instead. I will quickly mention
ese other projects.

hree conditions prompted the creation
f the new Santa Justa Train Station in
eville (by Antonio Cruz and Antonio
rtiz, 1987-1991): the implementation
f the AVE (TGV), the need to bury the
ormer rails, and the development of
sable area in the site's vicinity.
he exterior is rather austere, while
he interior takes advantage of the
mensions and of the light to create
ramatic spaces.
Within a very rigid plan, irregularly built,
he Housing in the Olympic Village
n Barcelona, by Elias Torres and José
ntonio Martínez Lapeña, 1992) attempts
o organize by deforming the original
hape. A more livable and coherent
roject conforms to the site by opening
o the sea panorama and liberating a
arger public inner space. The moving
hutters uncorset the façade and suggest
kind of instability, more convenient
o the spirit of the whole area.
ited in a wonderful historical city,

with one of the most representative
Universities in Spain, the Salamanca
Convention Center (by Juan Navarro
Baldeweg, 1986-1992) understands its
context and does not try to compete with
it. Instead, it formulates a metaphor, and
organizes a sort of internal city. One
architecture appears inside of another.
On the inside, an imposing false vault
presides over the main hall. Here, Navarro
Baldeweg acknowledges his fascination
with gravity as a natural phenomenon,
and shows quite openly the reality of
the faux vault.
The Electric Network Pavilion in EXPO'92
(by Mariano Bayón, 1992) is sited next to
the Fair, but just outside its precinct. That
Pavilion is also one of the few buildings
from the complex which still remains.
The programme is accommodated in
three elements or buildings: offices,
installations and another small pavilion,
all three parts on one combined
basement and isolated from the outside
by a thin translucent marble wall, which
is the thermal barrier. That façade allows
a clear light to reach inside the building
in the daytime. During the night, the
building is converted into a big billboard.

In the interior courtyard, there is a pond
and a fountain, which symbolize the
basic element of light and serve to cool
the atmosphere.
In 1986-1990, Jorge Garcés and E. Sória
were able to renovate the Navarra
Museum in Pamplona, an existing
museum located in a 16th century
hospital. On the façade, the original
ornament was placed against a plain
stone wall to obtain a more monumental
effect. On the interior the intervention
aimed at organizing the space with clear,
strict elements, powerful enough to hold
their own against the original. In the oval
lobby, a straight glass wall allows light to
enter and permits a view to the exterior
wall of the church.

The houses appear as a housing experience of an almost superreal presence.

The housing development in Tharsis by Cruz and Ortiz is a modern dwelling estate with a high standard of quality.

Antonio Cruz and Antonio Ortiz. Housing development in Tharsis, Huelva, 1992

The Public Library of Aragon in Zaragoza (by López Cotelo-Puente, 1984-1989) occupies two lots with different and contradictory zoning requirements. Although built to conform to both conditions, the building's interior does not reflect the exterior fragmentation. At the end, I would like to mention two controversial housing projects. First a housing project near the Avinguda Diagonal (in Barcelona, by Josep Lluís Mateo, 1989-1993) in the new area of the city. The complex's form responds to two conditions: the regulations of the area which organize the lot in bars, and a multipurpose programme of apartments, apartmenthotel, offices, shopping and parking. The five floors of souterrain stipulate the extremely rigorous organization of the floors above. The internally diverse bars are clad with a uniform stone skin.

One of the most controversial housing projects in Spain in the last years, the fundamental "snake" shape of the Housing on the M-30 motorway (in Madrid, by F. J. Sáenz de Oíza, 1986-1991) was determined by the main town planning agency and was the object of a competition. Sáenz de Oíza was awarded the first prize. His project created a sort of castle situated on the motorway - in the conceptual as in the formal sense. A brick wall closes the internal complex of residential spaces from the outside. The typology of flats was carefully developed.

I could discuss some 50 buildings more without any problem. Regardless of the extraordinary events that have shaped those recent years, the complexity of Spanish architecture is, seen on the whole, clearly on the move. It is then necessary to realize that Spain is still in a period of Modernism, which had been truncated in the 30s. What followed later was closer to traditional than inter-national trends. Therefore, the post-

modernist disenchantment and its consequences never occurred in Spain. This may be the reason for the success of Spanish architecture. Its capacity for response is more primitive and authentic, and therefore, more enthusiastic.

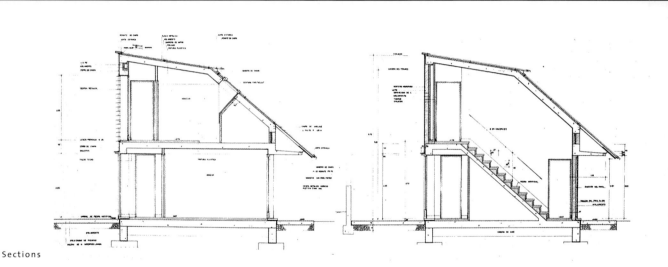

Sections

Observant architects learn from every epoch the history

of art as defined. Thus, architectural history represents

to architects the entire usable history of architecture.

Wilfried Wang on learning from history and on the mediating role of the "fathers" and "grandfathers".

19 | "Every Building is Unique." Observations on Portuguese Architecture. Wilfried Wang.

Portugal

Form of State: Republic since 1976 , **Area:** 92,389 km2, **Inhabitants (1992):** 9,858,000, **Capital:** Lisbon

Gross National Product 1992, per capita: $ 7,450, **Gross Domestic Product 1992:** $ 79,547 Mio, **Unemployment (Average, 1993):** 5.1%

Architects have always had an effect beyond the narrow confines of their national borders. In Portugal, the clear influence of Le Corbusier on Fernando Tavora, of Alvar Aalto on Alvaro Siza, or of Mies van der Rohe on Eduardo Souto de Moura exemplifies this point. This influence does, however, also work in the opposite direction: we know to what a great extent Alvaro Siza influences the contemporary work of many young architects in the United States as well as in Europe. In Portuguese architecture the mediating role played not only by the "fathers", but also by the "grandfathers" cannot be underestimated. An example is the influence of Fernando Tavoras on Eduardo Souto de Moura.

In the early 50s, during the planning of the new Matosinhos harbour north of Porto, Fernando Tavora received a commission to rework a former Quinta (plantation), the Quinta de Conçeiao. He was to realize a design for a tennis club with pavilion in the existing complex. Tavora, born in 1923, who for years was the dean of the architecture school in Porto, was the Portuguese representative to the post-war congresses of the CIAM (Congrès Internationaux d'Architecture Moderne), through which he came into contact with Alvar Aalto, Walter Gropius, Le Corbusier and many others. The design of the stairs and fountains, and the renovated entry sequence at Quinta still bring a great influence to bear on young architects. The pavilion successfully synthesizes regional building traditions with sculptural methods of composition. An early project, the market hall in Braga (1980), of Eduard Souto de Mouras (who was a student of Alvaro Siza, himself a student of Tavora), is structured by similar interests and by such concentrated moments as the detailing of the metal doors. With the choice of materials and their use (granite for the base and walls, white plaster, concrete for sections of the roof construction), both buildings are

marked by a return to the more expressive, vernacular details integral to the architecture of the 50s. Using this example, I wish to insinuate that the temporal factor plays only a small role in good architecture. Observant architects learn from every epoch the history of art has defined. Thus, architectural history represents to architects the entire useable history of the genre, as Josef Frank has already stated, and not a particular orthodox unity which approximates specific architectural criteria.

I would end my preliminary comments here, and present now a few positions within architectural thinking in Portugal. Parallel to the reformative and critically realistic approaches, the trend towards conservation and towards playing cynically with motifs also exists. Portugal, like other countries, is subject to all positive and negative manifestations of late-capitalist society. Speculative office buildings often planned by bad designers appear in the cities, and suburban structures rise between the cities just as they do in France, England or the United States. Emigrants returning from Brazil, Germany or France use their savings to build their dream houses, in which their idealized self-image is reflected in a melange of the latest issues of the magazines "Schöner Wohnen", "Casa-bella" and "Maison et Jardin". This kind of housing also carries the nickname "Casa Maison". In addition to the returning funds brought by the former emigrants there are the investments made by the European Community. Thanks to these funds, huge infrastructural projects have been realized: highways, airports, hospitals, new universities and more. The architects had many commissions until a short time ago; at the moment, a recession has arisen similar to that in neighbouring Spain and elsewhere. In comparison to the well-sated northern European countries, however, there will be much to build and to design in

Portugal for time to come. Having outlined this background, I would now like to represent significant positions of Portuguese architecture. It is above all significant in terms of clarity and quality. That does not mean that there is not even more good architecture in Portugal than mentioned here. That is certainly not the case. It is nonetheless unclear to me what certain projects want to express generally, or what relationship between project and society is intended.

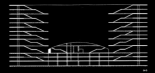

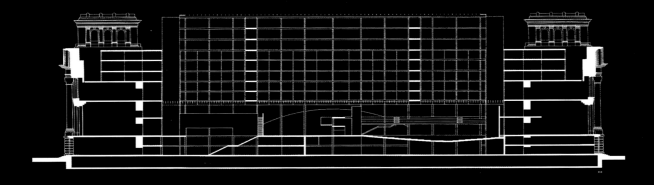

Deutscher Reichstag rebuilding competition, a new construction of two office buildings

A modest but precise framework characterizes the work of Eduardo Souto de Mouras, i. e. an architectural conception which respects the activities and behaviour of its inhabitants as the singular important criterion upon which the building is based. The building itself is only to be understood as a framework which can receive the most differentiated activities, including, to some extent, those which were not predicted. This attitude and architectural language is, in my opinion, clearly affiliated with that of Mies van der Rohe, even if Souto de Moura often designed his early houses within a volumetric typology close to the Portuguese building tradition. Eduardo Souto de Moura, born in 1952 in Porto, completed his studies at the art college in Porto in 1980. Since that time, he has had his own office. Prior to that, he had worked in Siza's office on social housing projects in Porto. The buildings of the post-revolutionary era (April Revolution of 1974) were realized to some extent with the citizens' participation. I would like to present the cultural centre in Porto as an early masterpiece which the architect could finally complete in 1989 after his 1980 competition scheme. The building stands in a garden with a house from the early 20th century; its granite wall is set back and tries, as much as possible, to maintain the feeling of the old garden. A twelve-storey apartment house stands directly next to the cultural centre. In my opinion, the design represents a most intelligent solution.

The building tries, in any case, to make itself noticeable in certain respects. On the interior, one sees a number of interpenetrating spaces. The primary spaces (film theatre and concert hall) can be reached through a large entry foyer. The exhibition spaces in the cellar can be reached via a steel and wood stair. Souto de Moura is actively occupied with details, such as the representation of the constructional layers incorporated into various walls; the window sections; or the roof junctures. It is not surprising that many of the details, if in slightly varied form, reappear in other projects. This characterization of Souto de Moura's architecture should, however, by no means be seen reductively or as the last word. "House 2" in Nevogilde, Porto (1983-1986) reveals his interests in the history of architecture and cultural criticism. The plan may generally follow the principles set by Mies van der Rohe; but the ruin-like stelas near the tennis court, the quasi-fragmentary beam structure of the garden façade, the details of the wall construction, and a decaying ashlar block lend the plan a retrospective, if not melancholy aspect. Souto de Moura's "House 2" is diametrically opposed to those walls of Mies's brick house which stretch into the landscape, those expressions of an abstract embrace of architecture and landscape, of an attempt to synthesize man-made and natural phenomena. At this point, one could say, the counterpoint is reached in Souto de Moura's thinking. No particular tendency

can be recognized in the more recent works. Even if the many multi-storey buildings consciously and necessarily have moved away from the simpler forms, a certain graphic transposition from the work of the Basel architects Herzog & de Meuron (specifically their highbay storage building for the firm Ricola in Laufen, 1984) is recognizable in the latest designs, for example the geological institute for the new university in Aveiro (1989-1994) and the skyscraper design for the Avenida Boavista (1991) in Porto.
It is certain that Souto de Moura has not yet developed a comprehensive understanding of his still-young attitude towards all building types. The divergence between the various building volumes has not led to a conscious differentiation of his language with regard to his own general priorities. The following questions are appropriate in his case: how can architecture develop capaciously for society so that it offers a modest and perhaps elegant frame for that society's various activities? To what extent is this architecture mute, meaning to what extent is it neutral, so that the feelings and associations of beholder and user are not predetermined? Or to what extent is this architecture articulate, in part euphorically looking towards the future, in part gazing melancholically backwards; or may it be sometimes one thing, sometimes the other?

Barbara Hoidn, José Paulo dos Santos. Deutscher Reichstag
rebuilding competition, Berlin

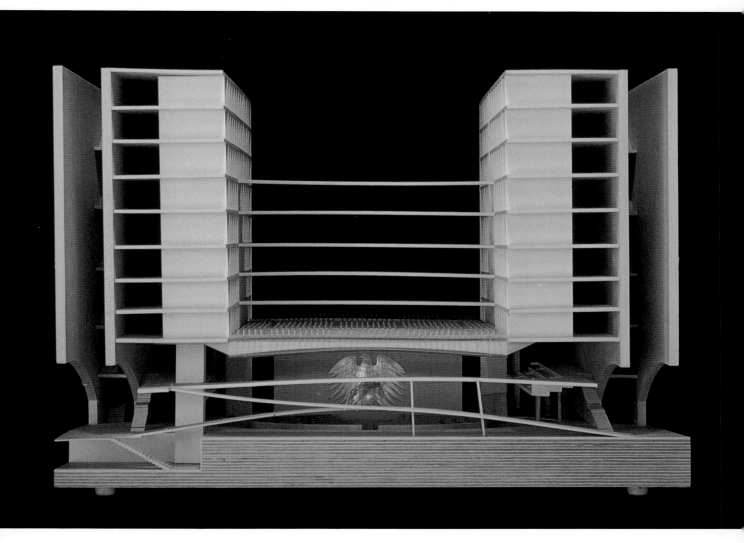

The designs of Hoidn and Santos prove an

interest in a rational and elegant architecture.

Constructions without technophile playfulness.

Barbara Hoidn, José Paulo dos Santos.
Axonometry of the adaption of
the Deutscher Reichstag

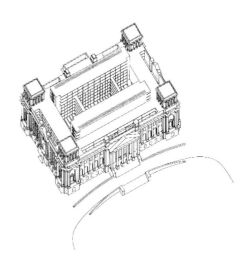

There is certainly good architecture in Portugal.

Alvaro Siza is without doubt the most important Portuguese architect, but there are more to discover.

Barbara Hoidn, José Paulo dos Santos.
Day-nursery in Karow, Berlin

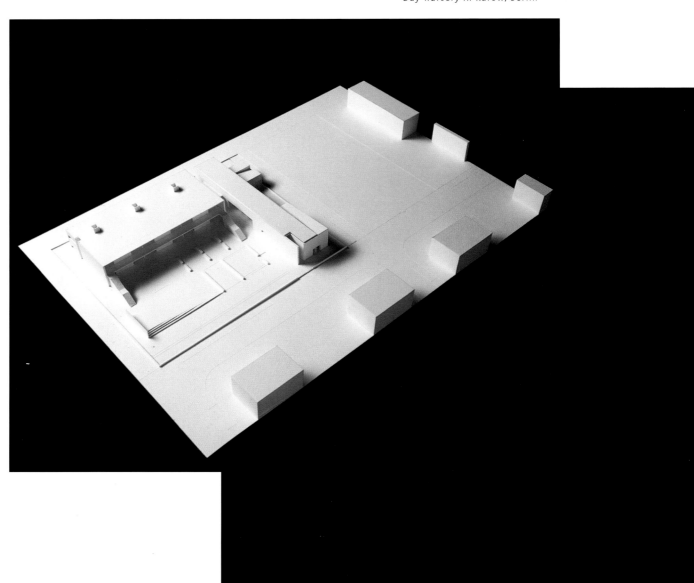

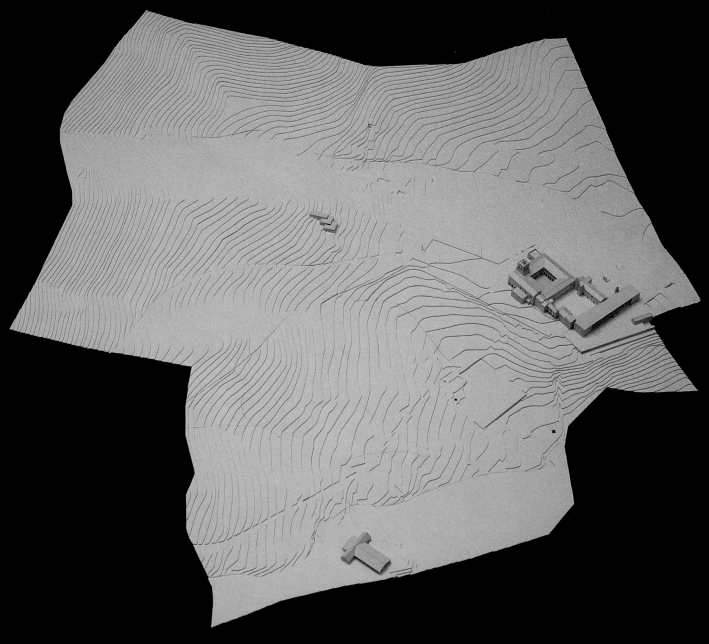

Modell of the day-nursery in Karow, Berlin

At first glance, it seems that there are many architects in Portugal who are bound to the posture of their colleagues or former teachers. This is in some sense true of the work of João Alvaro Rocha. Rocha was born in 1959 in Viana do Castelo and studied architecture until 1982 at the art college in Porto. He thereafter began to work with the office Gigante/Melo. Amongst his early works are facilities for the postal service, single family homes and residential buildings. Rocha's architecture adheres strictly to Modernism, meaning that it adheres strictly to that version of Modernism perpetuated at the school in Porto. One cannot deny the academicism which increasingly inheres to the schools. Fidelity to the principles of Modernism, to its social and cultural programme, are clearly evident. Rocha's work is such that it carefully moves amongst such great figures as Mies van der Rohe, Alvar Aalto, Le Corbusier and contemporary teachers.

His essential prerequisite is most legible in the House Mesão Frio near Valpedre in Penafiel (1987-1990). Parallels to Souto de Moura are obvious: the diagonal wall in House Mesão Frio recalls the Braga market building's longitudinal wall. Both share a longitudinal directionality. For me, however, the constructional details are of particular significance here because they offer additional information about his characteristic self-sufficiency. He assumes that the individual constructional members should be precisely defined, but that their connection should occur through overlap, layering and displacement so that other supportive constituent members become visible. The walls are not smooth but rather orthogonally mixed. One could imagine perceiving an air of rusticism here. The image projected by this architecture is closely akin to the constructivist and abstract works of late-Modern painting, especially that of the North American West Coast, Diebenkorn

and others. I intend with that comment to indicate that the components show themselves recognizably in this kind of architecture but in its overall image, a blending to the point of unrecognizability occurs. This tendency to constitutive and constructional abstraction in architecture has a long tradition which has had more success in small-scale projects than, for example, in housing in the 60s. Nonetheless, this train of thought is in my opinion relevant as long as it is fundamentally grounded in construction. Should the formal language depart from the actual materials and building methods, then the result is that decadent late-Baroque early-Rococo version of decorative Modernism often seen these days in magazines.

Autonomous, dynamic architecture: João Carrilho de Graça.

Northfaçade

Another architect I have selected is João Luis Carrilho de Graça. He was born in 1952 in Portalegre and was graduated from the art college in Lisbon in 1977. Since then, he has had his own office. The early works all describe a geometrical autonomous anchoring and shifting relative to the context. Axial relations, corrective shifts of the building volumes, spatial doublings by means of ancillary frames or mirrors reinstate the authority of architecture as a self-sufficient, autonomous form of art. Squares, cubes and circles re-emphasize this ambition. I have expressed my critical views on his approaches to Carrilho de Graça's personally. For me, his obvious formal talent is wasted on such games. In his most recent building, Carrilho de Graça designed a spatial form which differs in my opinion from his earlier introverted buildings. The College for Social Communication in Benfica, Lisbon (1988-1993), stands on a bluff amidst the city's chaos and defines an open courtyard on two sides. The screen-like surfaces of classroom and office wings, which stand on columns and spur walls, protect only part of the courtyard. Thus, the court reminds the students of the whole city's presence. The choice of materials is more

important than ever: Carrilho de Graça in fact is moving away from the superficial elegance apparent in, for example, the bank in Anadia (1983). The courtyard is paved with irregular polygonal rusty and beige sandstone tiles. The classroom wing is painted ox-blood. The north façade is clad with unpolished white marble slabs which are visibly, but not showily detailed. It remains to be asked, however, in what direction his architecture will develop if one turns a blind eye to the self-referential autonomous moves. The interest in allowing the users to access the experience of the place, the institution and the context would be such a direction. In any case, it does not require formal games but rather a focused reduction and respect of the forms and spaces relative to the users' developing capacities for perception. Perhaps this explains the strong parallels between Carrilho de Graça's work and that of Alvaro Siza. It remains open whether Carrilho de Graça's position, which is incidentally the only one in my compendium not associated with the school at Porto, will be rethought by him as intellectual formalism.
On the occasion of the International Building Exposition in Berlin between

1984 and 1987, a corner residential building, followed by a kindergarten, a seniors' club and a redesign of the block interior, was completed near Schlesisches Tor in Berlin, Kreuzberg (1989-1991). They all are part of a design which Alvaro Siza could realize with his Berlin contact architect Peter Brinkert following an invitational competition in 1980. The corner building was part of a programme to encourage apartment construction. Its design history ended rather sadly after Siza had apparently unrealistically decided to build apartments like those of the turn-of-the-century buildings in the area. Siza found this typology to be agreeable and valued its flexible usage.

Interior view

João Luis Carrilho da Graça. College for Social Communication in Benfica, 1988-93

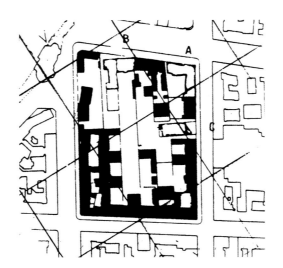

Site plan of the block in
Berlin-Kreuzberg

Architects invent nothing. They work continuously with models which

they transform based upon the problems with which they are confronted.

Alvaro Siza on the duty and methods of architecture.

Alvaro Siza. Kindergarten, Berlin-Kreuzberg

Siza's method of making notes in his

sketch book is a matter of course.

Such selected ideas will be implemented later, perhaps somewhere else.

His original intention was in fact to retain the still-extant base whose function (shops) and structure (solid brick walls) were to be maintained. This conception was not accepted by the client who demanded a more dense building structure for economic reasons; the client realized his demands. In a similar vein, the design had conceived of a façade which fused Mendelsohnian strip windows with the window type typical of traditional tenements. Following the revisions, only small windows remained. The reference to local details is comprehensible in the original design; in the realized building, that reference is only vestigially recognizable. These architectural elements nonetheless contain the fundamental design principles employed by Siza, who always tries to establish a dialogue of give-and-take with the existing situation.

The structure of the realized block interior is exemplary in this respect, unlike many structures developed earlier. It is unfortunately often so in Kreuzberg that block interiors have been pruned, so to speak, and with them their various possible uses. Rather than a careful restructuring of the rather small courtyards, often fragmented by wartime destruction and postwar renovation, and thereby a retention of this manifold, differentiated structure, the radical demolition and hygenization of many block interiors up to the buildings forming the street front was carried out. These particular corners of city life were thus erased. Much of the Kreuzberg admixture was lost. Siza's design for the block at Schlesisches Tor, however, assumed that the new common facilities such as tennis court, playground, and the inhabitants' existing small courts and paths through the block would be made generally accessible because they underpin social integration, if they do not constitute it.

Such a design is based upon an exact observation of existing conditions and usage. Siza's method of making notes in his sketch book is a matter of course. Ideas which will perhaps be implemented later, perhaps somewhere else entirely and unconsciously, are constantly registered. If one beholds the products of Siza's work, one must admit that the buildings do no necessarily have the strength of expression accruing to other IBA projects. Nonetheless, one should not make hasty assumptions and dismiss the three buildings and block interior as conservative. In fact, compared with that which has unfortunately occurred, and continues to occur, in other blocks, one must describe this project's approach as critical realism. As an architect, Siza knows well to what extent a critical attitude towards necessary change can be realized, and at what point it has to aim at the maintenance of a well-tested structure.

Finally, two further projects for Berlin by Team Barbara Hoidn and José Paulo dos Santos. For the former Deutscher Reichstag rebuilding competition Hoidn and Santos proposed a clear solution with a modest exterior. The interior, which was reconstructed in the 60s, should be removed to give away for two multi-storied office buildings. Hoidn and Santos are now designing a day-nursery for Karow, a newly built settlement at the periphery of Berlin. Both these designs prove an interest in a rational and elegant architecture making use of the best methods of production but without the technophile playfulness which can be found in some recent examples of British architecture.

The example of Berlin has demonstrated the urbanistic level of activity within Alvaro Siza's architectural thought. In past years, his projects have grown in size and expression so that one might say, in a mid-point evaluation, that his approach centers on the gradual transformation of society using the traditional means of architecture. Siza reads the context, he reflects it in drawing, and permits the unexpected to become quotidian in the course of repeated viewing.

Alvaro Joaquim de Melo Siza Vieira was born in 1933 in Matosinhos, studied at the art college in Porto with Fernando Tavora amongst others, and opened his own office in 1954.

I would like briefly to show one of his many various projects which, in my opinion, is his strongest work: the new architecture building in Porto (1987-1993). It seems to me like a settlement above the city of Porto, like an acropolis, although not entirely isolated and certainly not introverted. On the contrary, the evocation of the former villas by the studio building to the south, which is protected from the highway on-ramp by common rooms to the north (faculty offices, exhibition hall, library, auditorium), provides the students with a didactically-charged view towards the surrounding area, the field on which they are to labour. These surroundings are everything but complete, expectant or amicable. Elements from topography and from the history of architecture combine in this project. We see here a stair typology akin to that of Balthasar Neumann, a library typology like the Laurentiana's, ramps like those in the Villa Savoye, Villas like those of Frank and Loos, a chimney like those in Rossi's work; but all these elements combined in a courtyard complex which entirely conforms to Siza's approach. Siza has the rare ability to create a simultaneously consolidating and independent architecture from its immediate context. That architecture tends towards formal neutrality and absolute content-related recognizability as soon as its topographic or architectural bond has been identified. In conclusion, one might ask how Portuguese architecture withstands international comparison. I indicated initially the formal and intellectual forces which are based upon mutual exchanges of influences. The observations above have demonstrated the essential differences and parallels amongst the architects discussed. These are intellectual differences which are based upon respective, fundamentally different understandings of the relationship between architecture and society. Souto de Moura's work sees architecture as precise background, as capacious framework in which many activities are possible; or as a structure worthy of recollection which traces a direct lineage to an architecture, orientated towards form. João Alvaro Rocha's buildings lie within the great tradition of painterly abstraction which aims to move away from form and towards content. Architecture thereby becomes almost a self-bearing backdrop. João Carrilho de Graça's position assumes architecture's independence. This architecture reflects fragmentary, tension-filled social relationships. Alvaro Siza's architecture is based in many levels simultaneously. It embraces the tragic and guides the observer to intellectual reflection, it transforms social values and points in quietude towards the future.

One may nonetheless not forget: no building is entirely independent, but every building is unique.

Alvaro Siza's approach centres on the gradual transformation

of society using the traditional means of architecture.

The subtle, topographic-architectural transformation of society: Alvaro Siza's buildings and projects.

Entrance to the architecture school

This crisis has hit architects in full swing. They
have rarely been as busy as in recent times, or,
more accurately described, as active in leaving
the signs of their inventiveness here and there.

François Chaslin on the French construction boom, which was not confined to Paris.

France

Form of State: Republic since 1875, **Area:** 543,965 km2, **Inhabitants (1992):** 57,372,000 **Capital:** Paris
Gross National Product 1992, per capita: $ 22,260, **Gross Domestic Product 1992:** $ 1,319,883 Mio, **Unemployment (Average, 1993):** 11.6%

The architectural climate in France is strange. Beautiful fruits are ripening everywhere amid steadily growing anxiety. In architecture, there is a crisis in which architects had hardly believed, even though their colleagues in the United States or Great Britain had seen it coming for some years now. It arrived belatedly in France, as a number of regulating factors allowed the rendezvous to be postponed, and the suddenness of economic phenomena to be retarded. In France, many believe that when the construction industry is okay, everything is okay. But construction is down and out. Less cement is being sold, and not because of an excess of steel and glass architecture. This crisis has hit the architects in full swing. They have rarely been as busy as in recent times, or, more precisely described, as active in leaving the signs of their inventiveness here and there: aircraft wing-shapes, sloping roofs, steel spurs, oblique glass roofs, coloured blocks and all the slightly gaudy trims that adorn their constructions. There is no doubt a crisis in architecture: a crisis in commissions, a crisis in employment, and no doubt a moral crisis, soon to come. Just where is architectural discussion today, are we standing on the verge of what might be a collapse? The quarrel is still continuing between the "real Moderns" and the "Authentics", now that the anti-Modern trends, Post-Modernism, the Historicism, and that scrupulous analysis of the city known

in our jargon as the "typo-morphos" have faded. On one hand we have the orthodox modernists, the "authentics", who are readily accused of academicism and archaism by their adversaries. They are plentiful among the young generation; they are the people who carry on the pre-war research of Le Corbusier and his contemporaries. They maintain that architecture should begin with itself, and that its central aim is the elaboration of spaces. They vote for white geometry, often in concrete, and are obsessed with natural light. They are for carefully laid-out purist sculptural forms. They are for the very controlled manner that brought us some handsome buildings last year: the headquarters of Canal Plus by the New York architect Richard Meier, near the Mirabeau bridge; not far from there a complex of artists' studios by the virtuoso Michel Kagan; and last but not least the splendid First World War museum at Péronne, designed by Henri Ciriani. Opposing this tendency is a mixed bag of unorthodox moderns, the "real" moderns. They are often to be found in Jean Nouvel's sphere of influence. They want to escape from the limits of an architecture concentrated on its own logic and work to subvert the rules, to bring into being registers of emotion inspired by recent shifts in contemporary sensitivity (op art, land art, minimal or conceptual art, for instance, but also arte povera, cinema and literature). They want the work to have "meaning" above all

(which, oddly, they sometimes call "concept"), have little faith in the true and the beautiful, are constantly looking for something new. They espouse the many dimensions of the present, claim to be free from nostalgia and, in a few cases, seem to cultivate paradox. The superb masterpiece of this genre is the curious private house which the Dutch architect Rem Koolhaas built last year at Saint-Cloud.

Henri Ciriani. First World War museum
in Péronne - photo: Archipress

They vote for white geometry, often in concrete,
and are obsessed with natural light. They are for
carefully laid-out purist sculptural forms.

The orthodox Modernism has in France still a lot of admirers.

Museum in Péronne
photo: Archipress

among the "authentics" there is a desire
for permanency and materiality, a
concern for space and for its fluidity
and physical manifestations; these
interests sometimes go hand in hand
with an aspiration to heightened
complexity, even to a sort of baroquism
as in the works of Henri Gaudin: the
Charlety stadium building in Paris; the
city hall at Saint-Denis, opposite the
basilica; and the new university at
Amiens. This camp is also characterized
by an attention to urban form, very
noticeable since ten or fifteen years in
the work of Christian de Portzamparc,
who finished the sculptural Cité de la
Musique at La Villette last autumn, and
the new lay-out of the Musée Bourdelle.
Gaudin has recently used sophisticated
glass roofs reminiscent of the fine
lightweight technical materiality
generated by Anglo-Saxon high-tech,
a current whose influence is present in
Renzo Piano's apartments in the rue de
Meaux, or in the funicular railway station
at Montmartre, designed by François
Deslaugiers. The tendency becomes more
ethereal and charged with a poetic aura
in the elegant glasshouses that Patrick
Berger has just completed in the Citroën
Park. Other architects aspire openly
to immateriality. "Les Immatériaux",
a seminal exhibition at the Pompidou

Centre a few years ago seems to have
introduced this virus. They cultivate a
taste for the virtual, are often familiar
with the writings of Baudrillard and
Virilio, and favour a transparency that
has produced a few beautiful works
but which often goes no further than
the products of the glass-makers Saint-
Gobain. This "transparentist" manner
should reach full realization in the works
of Dominique Perrault and Francis Soler,
the architects for President Mitterrand's
last two big projects in Paris, the
Bibliothèque national de France and
the International Conference Centre on
Quai Branly. Both are adepts of simple
gestures, of the "founding" act, and
(except for some rather naïve ideas they
have about the democratic character of
this transparency) prefer to "work with
emptiness" so as to lay down strong
objects that generate tension, as Viguier-
Jodry and Seigneur (minimalists too,
but in a different genre) tried to do with
considerable distinction for the French
pavilion at the Seville expo.
Everything would be fine in this contrast-
filled landscape. The confrontation of
trends would be a source of real pleasure
if only architects were not beginning to
feel that city planning has escaped their
control, and that, while they have been
busy exploring one path or another,

concerned ma
supplying soci
one of their tr
away from the
a time when t
integrating, ar
periphery alon
has fallen prey
merchandizers
establishmen
chaos. Entire r
to the ordinar
metropolises.
over-exploited
wrecked, follo

Francis Soler. International Conference Centre, Quai Branly, Paris

s of whether
nese urban
on, many
e state of things,
l", should inform
our future, they
it, we should
nowledge it and
s are doing just
at Lille).
, to be a part of
ents and special
e which give it all
ke it look a little
see the seeds of
nid this chaos, a
iterature, comic
ady dreamed of,
beginnings are
g or this or that
retext that the
" Los Angeles,
caneous disorder,
ity, they want to
ce of chaos into
t. Uncertainty
itional technique
e temporary and
oundations of the
has "exploded",
us cluster" so we
chaos in order
Nouvel said

recently. But most architects are in fact
disenchanted. They no longer believe in
the social role of their profession.
It is the paradox of our times that
everything should seem so playful, that
new buildings seem to be everywhere,
sometimes too many of them, too
diverse, too showy, constituting in the
eyes of certain observers an irritating
clutter of bric-à-brac - all this while more
vital issues are gone with the wind.
In city planning, people feel that nothing
really proceeds from the plan any more.
The city is subject to operations that are
short-term, spectacular, and charged
with media appeal. Politically, it is more
profitable to dynamite blocks and towers
built in the 50s than to develop an
abstract project that will take time to
implement, will be hard to finance, and
which no one can guarantee will alleviate
social angst. In September 1992, the
spectacle began again: four twenty-storey
blocks at Val-Fourré in Mantes-la-Jolie,
four hundred and fifty apartments, were
reduced to dust and rubble, then another
two hundred and eighty, fifteen floors, a
hundred and fifty meters long, at Dijon-
Epirey. Spectacular demolitions are the
object of a media interest which has now
partly replaced the inaugurations and
opening parties of a few years ago.
The social development of urban quarters

and the economic growth of regions
enlist the help of the marketing
consultants, the political advisors, the
inventors of commercial and image-
promotion strategies, the purveyors o
ready-to-use urban ideas, the initiato
technopoles, people who are constan
re-making, or rather mis-making the
and who, using the "rubber stamp" o
a few international star architects,
subject it to experiment in the hope
of immediate results. Empiricism is
widespread, and the exclusive concer
is for the short term.

1 *Nouvel.* Hôtel des Thermes, Dax 1990-92 - photo: Archipress

Jean Nouvel. "La Tour sans Fins pour la Défense", Project 1989

For me, Modernism is not a historical notion relative to the Modern Movement, but it is something that has vitality. Modernism, the criteria of Modernism are further developing.

Jean Nouvel on Modernism.

Jean Nouvel. Congress Centre, Tour 1989-93

Spectacular demolitions of housing developments in France, 1992

Uncertainty becomes a compositional technique in city planning, and the temporary and disruptive become the foundations of the new aesthetics.

Chaos - the city planning starting point of the city and its planning.

Lack of planning is no doubt the great shortcoming of the last decade, even if the idea of the "urban project" remains supreme, at least in discourse. It is, however, a relatively insincere notion, constantly voiced like a ritual chant in hollow official language. It has grown old prematurely through overuse. What can be the role of architecture, which has so long claimed a social and political dimension, when the local authorities are gripped by a sense of urgency, of impending danger, and are ready to drop everything in favour of a swift improvement in the employment figures and the economic development of their region? What can city planning do, this paradoxically idealistic techno-cratic discipline, which has always been focused on the long term? What can it do when policies are governed by electoral objectives, when civic commitment falters, and when solidarity can no longer

stop the rise of discrimination and the constitution of social and ethnic ghettos? What is the architectural project and what is the urban project when society at large has no project to speak of? When it has nothing to look forward to but a clouded horizon, when all it hears are rumours of war, unemployment, social suffering or disease? What is a style and what is its use? What is an architectural doctrine when society has no optimism at all and is devoid of any other ideology than that forged day after day by worry? The times of worry have come to the architects now, too. They know that the employment crisis is at their door, but also that they do not have the intellectual means to answer the questions posed by their century. They are starting to feel that they can not remain complacent in the role of artists or entertainers to which they have let themselves be banished. It is no longer enough for them to be

dynamic, stylish, inventive and para-doxical; one day or another, they are going to have to start dealing seriously with the problems that torment society. But to do so, as it was the case twenty-five years ago, at the end of the 60s, perhaps we shall have to live through a crisis first. Well, here it is.

Maybe it is the painter in me who wants to overcome Formalism and Functionalism and pose the question of form in a new way.

Christian de Portzamparc on the manifestation of form.

Christian de Portzamparc. Cité musical de La Vilette, Paris 1984-90 - photo: Archipress

Henri and Bruno Gaudin. Charlety Stadion, Paris - photo: Archipress

Dominique Perrault. Bibliothèque nationale de France, Paris - photo: Archipress

Patrick Berger. Park Citroën, Paris - photo: Archipress

What is the architectural project and

what is the urban project when society

at large has no project to speak of?

The crisis of the architecture and the city is a crisis of society.

Viguier-Jodry and Seigneur. French Pavilion, EXPO Sevilla 1992

Norman Foster and Richard Rogers have established

a strong international reputation with their own

brand of highly pragmatic architecture.

Pragmatism free of theory? Is this the approach on architecture at the end of the 20th century in Great Britain?

21 | Architectur between Pragmatism and High-tech. Richard Burdett.

Great Britain

Form of State: Parliamentary Monarchy of Commonwealth since 1921, **Area:** 242,429 km2, **Inhabitants (1992):** 57,701,000, **Capital:** London
Gross National Product 1992, per capita: $ 17,790, **Gross Doemstic Product 1992:** $ 903,126 Mio, **Unemployment (Average, 1993):** 9.8%

Architecture has experienced a chequered but steady history in Britain. The bold urban interventions of the Georgian period, the flamboyant red brick civic buildings of the age of Queen Victoria, the heroic social institutions of the post-1945 Welfare State, have reflected the character and spirit of their times. Thatcherism, the brief but intense period of rampant capitalism that spanned the 1980s under the reign of Prime Minister Margaret Thatcher, will be remembered by a clutch of large, undistinguished speculative office blocks clad in 50mm marble, that sit uncomfortably in Britain's cities, many of them still empty. Like their counterparts in Eastern Europe - expressionless gigantic statues of Stalin, Beria and Lenin - they are silent, ghostly representations of a regime that has taken an ideology to its extreme.

It would not be exaggeration to state that over the last decade architecture in Britain has been under attack as a cultural and professional discipline. The paradox is that outside Britain, British architecture is on a high, especially high-tech note. Sir Norman Foster, Sir Richard Rogers and the other architectural knights-in-waiting have established a strong international reputation in Hong Kong, Tokyo or Berlin with their own brand of highly pragmatic architecture, apparently free of theory, cultural conventions and formal restrictions. But it is this very absence of theory, the pursuit of architecture as a technical service rather than a cultural activity, that has contributed to the marginalization of architecture and the design professions at home. While architecture in continental Europe seeks to consolidate its position within the wider cultural debate, architecture in Britain is still struggling to become part of the cultural debate. The naming of the recently created government department of culture as the "Department of National Heritage" succinctly characterizes British insularity and obsession with its own past. The entire design industry has been suffered from the social and political fallout of the Thatcher years, rendering the production of significant new architecture a difficult and isolated task. Opportunities for younger architects are limited, both by the economic recession but perhaps more fundamentally by a

lack of a sophisticated visual culture and the absence of government patronage. Design competitions, the only mechanism that facilitates the introduction of new ideas and new blood to the architectural debate, are foreign to British culture: in 1991 there were 2000 competitions for public buildings in France, 600 in Germany and only 12 in Britain. One of the overriding principles of monetarism is that the free market should dictate supply and demand at all levels of society. In Britain architecture has not been spared from this process of rationalization. Anyone offering a "good deal", anyone who can undercut the services offered by another individual or company, should - so the argument goes - benefit from access to the open market allowing the consumer greater choice, freeing him from the monopolistic closed-shop of the professions. Like all "markets", the design industry should be unimpeded by restrictive practices and regulations. Architects - like decorators, minicab drivers or second-hand car salesmen - do not need to be protected by professional status, they should sell their "products" at competitive rates. The impact of this philosophy on the architectural profession has been dramatic. The status of the architect has gone into a nose-dive, resulting from a lack of self-confidence (within the profession) and lack of faith in the provision of services (from outside the profession). During the 1980s the more commercial nature of development projects has seen the appearance of new types of design professionals - project and construction managers, quantity surveyors, estate agents - who have gradually eroded the traditional hegemony of the architect in the building industry. As in many other countries on the Continent, the Royal Institute of British Architects (RIBA) determined fee scales according to scope of services. This was considered to be restrictive and contrary to the spirit of open competition, and did not recognize the increasingly significant role played by other members of the design team. Mandatory fees were abolished at the end of the 1980s. Architects have demeaned themselves in public by competing for low fee scales - or, even zero fees in a recent notorious case -

undermining the potential for good design. The government has exacerbated this process by demanding that all public buildings should be procured through Competitive Fee Tendering, rewarding short-termism and economic efficiency over design quality. In 1993 a government-led initiative to de-register the entire profession was narrowly avoided as a result of uncharacteristically efficient lobbying by the RIBA. It is no surprise then that in this climate younger architects have had few opportunities to make their mark while many larger commercial practices, tempted by the potential for making a "fast buck" on the Stock Market, have seen their fortunes spiral in high-risk operations worthy of the directors of Barings Bank. Whilst the authority of other, more powerful professions - such as the law and medicine - has never been questioned, the surge of anti-profession-alism has spread across British society. The financial markets of the City of London, the engine of the British economy, were deregulated during the "Big Bang" of 1986 allowing foreign banks, investors and institutions to compete freely with the traditional old-boy network of the British establishment. The physical impact of this move is here for all to see. In London alone more than 5 million square metres of new offices (most of them built speculatively to optimize the soaring rents for office accommodation) were erected at the same time as public housing came to a virtual standstill in a city that now has more than 80,000 homeless people living on the streets or in temporary hostels.

A living testament to the "yuppie" culture is the Docklands area of London. The thriving hub of Britain's mercantile trade for centuries, Docklands stretches for fifteen kilometres along the River Thames to the east of the city centre. With the demise of the shipping industry the area became a no-go zone of urban and industrial decay in the 1970s. Its extensive water frontage and acres of open land provided a unique opportunity for redevelopment and regeneration of the inner city. Rather than creating a framework for growth and participation, the government formed a quasi-private consortium, the London Docklands Development Corporation (LDDC), to encourage private investment in the area. The result is a fragmented collection of idiosyncratic enclaves - some housing, some offices, some industrial buildings - that fail to create any sense of urban order or spatial coherence. At its centre stands the shining marble and steel Canary Wharf development, ten large office blocks set in a turn-of-the-century mid-American setting with elaborate

fountains and expensive park benches stranded in the middle of nowhere. Built in under two years at the end of the 1980s Canary Wharf competes with Eurodisney in Paris as a financial and architectural white elephant. In 1993 the mighty Olympia & York, developers of Canary Wharf, went bankrupt leaving an incomplete and still partly unoccupied monument to laissez-faire culture. Five years after the completion of Canary Wharf, the government has recognized the need to provide public transport infrastructure to this highly inaccessible zone and is now building an extension to the London Underground system that will connect Docklands to central London by 1997. Taking competition to its natural limits, the City of London - the richest, oldest and most traditional core of London known as the Square Mile - prepared to take up the potential challenge posed by the Docklands. In the space of ten years, from 1985 to 1995, more than a third of the Square Mile was rebuilt or refurbished. More building activity occured than at any

other time in the last 150 years.
In an effort to consolidate its position as the leading international financial centre with splendid state-of-the-art offices for the great multinational corporations of the world, the planning rules and regulations were relaxed allowing the construction of vast new groundscrapers and wholescale redevelopments that have changed the face of London. Air-rights developments over railway tracks in precious locations throughout the city were built at Cannon Street, Charing Cross, Victoria and Liverpool Street stations, creating a new typology of office environment.

Canary Wharf, London Docklands

London Docklands

Whilst most of these projects are of poor design, the Broadgate development on the fringes of the City of London stands out as for the quality of its public spaces and buildings (by Arup Associates and SOM, 1985-89) that integrate successfully with the life and texture of the city. Unsurprisingly the building explosion of the 1980s coincided with a political event of momentous implications for London: the abolition of the Greater London Council (GLC) which, for nearly a century, had been responsible for the coordination of planning, infrastructure, public transport, housing and the environmental policy for the capital. Today metropolitan London, the world's fifteenth largest city with a radius of 150 kilometres and a population of over 10 million people, has no overall planning or strategic authority. Environmental, architectural, economic and employment strategies are left in the hands of the individual local authorities (the City of Westminster, the Royal Borough of Kensington and Chelsea, the London Borough of Camden, the Corporation of London, etc.) which, by definition, have local priorities. As a result, all matters of global impact (zoning, land-use, transport, development, etc.) have been left to the market or to newly formed bureaucracies directly appointed and controlled by central government (such as the LDDC).

The failure of the architect, rather than the failures of Modern Architecture, has been fanned by the very public and finely orchestrated attack on the profession by the Prince of Wales. The Prince - who now heads his very own Institute of Architecture in London that teaches students the "real art of design" through life drawings, classical studies and the symbolic meaning of Islamic architecture - has polarized the debate on architecture as a "battle of the styles". It is difficult to forget the surreal scene of a highly popular television programme (appropriately entitled "My Vision for Britain") where Prince Charles points to the buildings he likes and dislikes along the River Thames in London, acting as a self-appointed arbiter of public taste. The profession, reflecting the insecurities of society at large, has responded schizophrenically, fuelling the superficiality of the debate. The "modernists" have entrenched themselves behind the banner of high-tech, while a new breed of neo-neo-classicists ("young fogeys", country gentlemen who wear tweeds and drink tea in stately homes) has emerged as the standard bearer of popular taste. The polarity of this debate can be easily caricatured. On the one hand Richard Rogers was invited to give the prestigious "high-culture" Reith Lectures for the BBC, on the other hand the Prince of Wales has

launched "Perspectives" magazine which proudly markets itself as the leading organ for public debate on architecture in Britain. Norman Foster's Stansted Airport, Richard Rogers' Channel 4 Television Headquarters and Nicholas Grimshaw's International Passenger Terminal at Waterloo Station have been completed at the same time as Leon Krier's neo-vernacular model village of Poundbury in the Duchy of Cornwall (owned by the Prince of Wales). The Royal Family confirmed their distaste for modern architecture by embracing vulgar historicist designs for the re-building of parts of Windsor Castle (the Queen's official residence) ravaged by fire a few years ago. Neo-classical proposals - more reminiscent of Disney-land than a real city - have been approved for historically sensitive sites adjacent to monuments of national heritage, such as St Paul's Cathedral and the Tower of London.

The state of permanent pluralism still charaterizes Brithish architecture today.

No certainities, no dogma in the highly pragmatic cultural environment.

The failure of the architect, rather than the

failure of Modern Architecture, has been fanned

by the very public and finely orchestrated attack

on the profession by the Prince of Wales.

The debate on architecture has polarized as a battle of the styles.

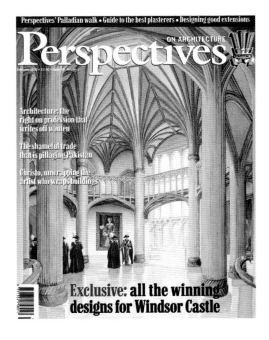

A pool of approved architects - led by the redoubtable Quinlan Terry - are cynically called in by "reborn" developers to recreate a B-Movie version of history that may be more acceptable to planners and communities sensitive to royal moods and aspirations. A further weakness in the constitution of British architecture is the inexplicable divorce between practice and education, underscoring a subconscious desire for the absence of theory rather than the absence of talent. In fact, for the last thirty years some of the most brilliant scholars and critics of modern architecture have been trained in Britain. Yet they never received appropriate recognition in their mother country. Reyner Banham, Kenneth Frampton, Alan Colquhoun, Robert Maxwell, Ed Jones, Tony Vidler and Colin Rowe (the surprisingly belated recipient of the 1995 Royal Gold Medal, nearly 50 years after publication of "The Mathematics of the Ideal Villa") have been part of a celebrated "brain drain" from Britain to the USA, leaving behind a culture starved of critical debate. Not one of these significant characters was rewarded with an academic appointment in Britain commensurate to their intellectual standing.

Public comment on architecture in the national press and media has been left in the hands of, at best, articulate journalists and, at worst, populist hacks in search of royal patronage. While the Architectural Association (especially under the late Alvin Boyarsky) stood out as a centre of academic excellence, it has always occupied an awkward position as pro-moter of the international avant-garde rather serving the pragmatic needs of British practice. Exceptions that prove the rule are the architect of the controversial British Library in London, Professor Colin St John Wilson, who inherited the Department of Architecture at the University of Cambridge from the influential Leslie Martin, and the old-time Archigram radical Peter Cook, whose recent appointment as head of the Bartlett School of Architecture has coincided with a realization of a number of modest projects with his partner Christine Hawley. The division between professional teachers (with little or no interest in practice) and practitioners (with little or no interest in education and theory) is well established in Britain: a pattern that could have been broken by Richard Rogers, who in the mid 1980s considered taking the post now occupied

by Peter Cook, but was unable to reconcile the requirements of his practice with a full-time commitment to education. Yet the mood, if not the tide, may at last be changing.
The arrival of the National Lottery, a weekly gambling bonanza that generates about £500 million a year for new arts buildings, has rekindled an interest in non-commercial buildings, providing an opportunity for buildings that - in the words of the government - demonstrate "design excellence".

PATERNOSTER SQUARE

Architecture is back, so it seems, through the back door. The appointment of Herzog & De Meuron for the new Tate Gallery of Modern Art in London and Zaha Hadid for Cardiff Bay Opera House reflect a softening of the entrenched debate that may at last transcend the superficial battle of the styles that has characterized British architecture for the last fifteen years.

This over-complex web of events and circumstances is necessary to explain the context of architectural production in Britain today. It paints a gloomy yet realistic picture that militates against the creation of critical architecture. If importance were to be measured by the impact of a building on a city and the perception of architecture by the general public, then only those "products" of the above process should be singled out. On these criteria the most "important" buildings in Britain completed in the last five years would have to include Cesar Pelli's 50-floor Canary Wharf Tower, Terry Farrell's energetic Embankment Place and Vauxhall Cross buildings (housing the "secretive" headquarters of the British Intelligence service where latter-day James Bonds receive their instructions) or any one of a crop of horrific neo-something office buildings that have been tortuously designed to "relate to context, grain and scale of the urban surroundings", a phrase that has become the cynical password to justify the willful exploitation of architectural form and expression. Just as Giuseppe Terragni, Walter Gropius or Alvaro Siza contributed

to the advancement of modern architecture within politically complex circumstances, a number of individual buildings have been realized in recent years in Britain that stand out for their clarity of thought and execution, running contrary to the prevailing culture. The five buildings by architects as disparate as Richard Rogers, Tony Fretton, Richard MacCormac, Michael Hopkins and Ian Ritchie are not intended to show the emergence of a consistent "school" of contemporary architecture, nor a shared philosophy of design. They represent a synthesis of the issues that shape the architectural debate. Richard Rogers' search for a more humane architecture that reconciles scale, context and form alongside innovation, performance and change; Michael Hopkins' exploration of compositional and environmental potential of "heavy" materials and traditional methods of construction; Ian Ritchie's ability to harness innovation in construction technology to provide a sense of permanence and authority to even the most light-weight shed; Richard MacCormac's studied re-interpretation of the Arts and Crafts movement with its attention to craft, detail and nature; and Tony Fretton's solitary journey to re-discover the liberating formal properties of architectural purism. These are the salient themes that drive contemporary architecture in Britain today. While each project reflects the particular set of beliefs and concerns of the individual architect, they share a certain tentativeness and modesty which renders

them appealing. They are not built edifices to ideology but suggestions of a possible line of enquiry. In their different ways they reveal a common sense of insecurity. These buildings could only have been produced in a highly pragmatic cultural environment where there are no certainties, no dogmas that can be embraced or criticized, no theory to explain the wide variety of architectural approach and languages. The state of permanent pluralism still characterizes British architecture now as it did at the time of Pugin, Ruskin and the neo-classical revival a century or two ago.

The Channel 4 Headquarters Building marks a clear shift in the design

sensitivities of the high-tech school, a softer, contextual solution that

has classical overtones in its planning and organization.

A design, which also reflects the partice of urban projects.

Richard Rogers. Channel 4 Headquarters Building, London 1994 -photo: Morley von Sternberg

Richard Rogers Partnership, Channel 4 Headquarters Building, London, 1994: Located at the heart of London within sight of the Houses of Parliament and Westminster Abbey, the building is a set-piece of urban theatre within a tight inner city site. It marks a clear shift in the design sensitivities of the high-tech school, a softer, contextual solution that has classical overtones in its planning and organization. In tectonic and aesthetic terms the design is in direct lineage to the Lloyd's Building, but its response to the site reflects the increasing formality of the practice's urban projects (such as the Baroque layouts for Berlin Potsdamerplatz and Shanghai masterplan).

The main entrance to the building is placed on a diagonal, creating an organic knuckle between two orthogonal limbs. A glass and steel canopy over a light-weight bridge penetrates the inclined glass atrium supported by steel cables from red cranes. From the bridge one can see straight through the lobby to the garden or look down through a glazed umbilicus into the bowels of the building. The entrance is flanked by a tall vertical shaft animated by glazed lifts that expose the life of the building to the outside world. Horizontal movement similarly occurs near the external face of the building and on linking glass and steel bridges. The curved linking element on the courtyard elevation contains offices with a south-facing terrace. At entrance level, the double-height curved staff restaurant area, the main public focus of the building, extends to an outdoor seating area overlooking the garden. The linear blocks, clad in horizontal bands of glass and steel integrated panels, contain conventional office spaces while a television studio and viewing theatre are located at basement level. The vertical shaft is topped by a telecommunications mast, steel flues and technical plant (neatly wrapped in steel boxes) while all main structural elements are painted the same dark red of the San Francisco Golden Gate Bridge.

In tectonic and aesthetic terms the design is in direct lineage to the Llody's Building.

The use of glass and steel characterize the unique style of Rochard Rogers.

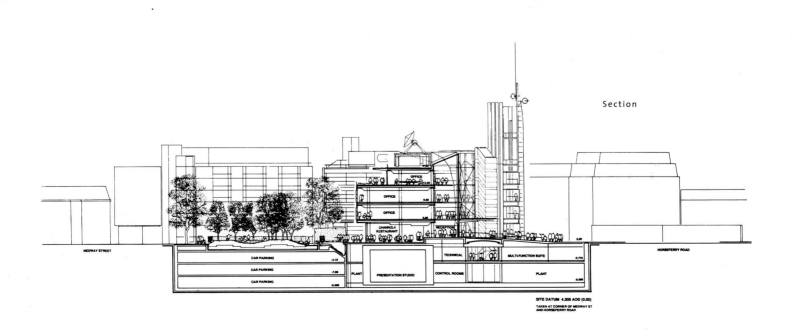

Section

Michael Hopkins & Partners, Office and retail building, Shad Thames, London, 1990-91: The office and retail building represents a more contextual departure for architects normally associated with expressive high-tech forms (such as the tent structures and steel pavilions of Lord's Mound Stand in London or the Schlumberger Building in Cambridge). Located south of the River Thames in an area surrounded by a dense pattern of 19th century brick spice and tea warehouses, its formal solution emphasizes the verticality of its neighbours by exposing the concrete structure at roof level. The building is set back from the street creating a wedge-like space, forming an entry to the ground floor shop. The building is an orthogonal box which stretches from the street to the canal, taking advantage of the idiosyncrasies and the irregular geometry of the site to place all vertical circulation and service areas in the leftover spaces, leaving a pure geometrical volume for the main internal spaces. The design process is additive: components are grafted on the primary structure, the façades are clipped on, and the individual design elements relate to the structure of the whole in a clear and rational manner. The design is an essay is restraint. Yet, its lead skin gives the building a strong evocative energy. The detailing and materiality of the surfaces give a sense of texture and roughness that provides grain and scale, as well as relating to the rough, industrial texture of the surroundings. The well-known repertoire of high-tech strategies - the placement of all services on the exterior, fully flexible space, maximum efficiency of layout, etc. - have been reinterpreted in a more formal and relaxed vocabulary creating a calm and uncomplicated sense of space within. The successful marriage of high-tech design with more conventional building techniques accounts for the exceptionally fine quality of the concrete columns (a material that does not normally weather well in Britain), achieved by adapting Tado Ando's labour-intensive technique of sanding all surfaces by hand.

Ground floor shop - photo: Martin Charles

The design is an essay in restraint. The lead skin

gives the building a stronge evocative energy.

The building is a careful compromise between the well-known repertoire
of high-tech and the conventional technics of building.

Michael Hopkins. Office and Retail Building,
Shad Thames, London 1990-91 - photo: Martin Charles

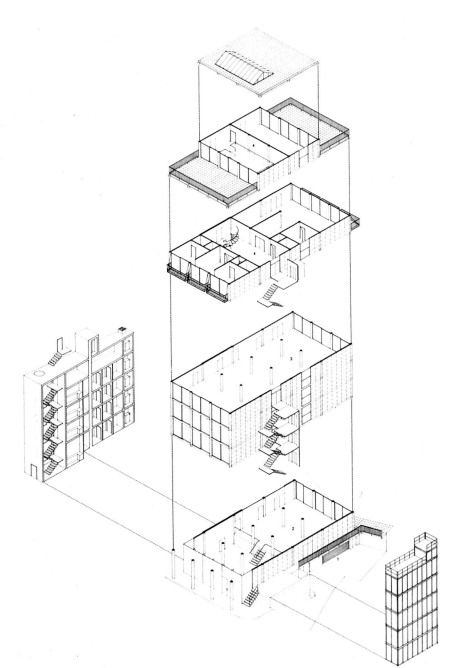

Axonometry

The contextual integration of old and new is achieved through careful detailing

and choice of materials, following faithfully in the Arts and Crafts tradition.

The Chapel in Cambridge marks the marriage between mainstream modernism and the powerful english Arts and Craft tradition.

Interior view

Richard MacCormac. Chapel of the Fitzwilliam College, Cambridge 1992

MacCormac, Chapel, Fitzwilliam College, Cambridge, 1992: The Fitzwilliam Chapel building is a small but significant building that marks the marriage between mainstream modernism and the powerful Arts and Crafts tradition in Britain. Strongly influenced by William Morris and John Ruskin, Richard MacCormac has worked extensively in Cambridge and Oxford colleges, the ultimate repository of British conservatism and high culture. Established in 1966, Fitzwilliam College is a relative newcomer to the fold with buildings by Denys Lasdun forming the backdrop for the new chapel. The chapel is located at the head of Lasdun's student block establishing a dialogue with the existing structures and the splendid 19th century gardens. A large, beautiful plane tree sits on axis with the chapel, creating a processional linear link between the garden, the new and existing buildings. MacCormac refers to the imagery of the ship as an inspiration for his design,

playing on the literary analogy between navis (the central space of the church) and navis, Latin for ship. The religious connotations of the vessel as a vehicle of transportation from the real world to the spiritual world completes the analogy. The structure and construction techniques of Viking ships account for the shape of the building, with the belly of the boat defining the upper volume of the chapel and a lower level crypt space. The spatial effect is one of increasing depth as one moves into the building. The contextual integration of old and new is achieved through careful detailing and choice of materials, following faithfully in the Arts and Crafts tradition. The new brick is of a lighter colour, but the marriage is achieved by the use of a dark mortar which forms a continuous colour plane across the surfaces of both buildings. The transient nature of the linking block is articulated in a light-weight structure in glass and timber that announces the presence of a new world.

The curved stairs lead to the main chapel with glazed areas overlooking the garden as one moves to the heart of the shrine. In the chapel the sacred space is defined by a rectangular baldacchino that frames axial views of the tree and garden beyond.

Ian Ritchie. B8 Building, Stocley Park, Heathrow 1990

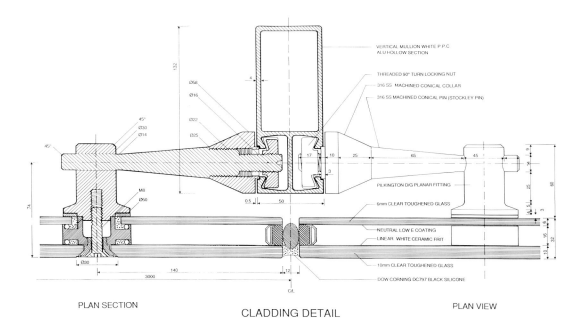

PLAN SECTION

CLADDING DETAIL

PLAN VIEW

VERTICAL MULLION WHITE P.P.C
ALU HOLLOW SECTION

THREADED 90° TURN LOCKING NUT

316 SS MACHINED CONICAL COLLAR

316 SS MACHINED CONICAL PIN (STOCKLEY PIN)

PILKINGTON D/G PLANAR FITTING

6mm CLEAR TOUGHENED GLASS

NEUTRAL LOW E COATING

LINEAR WHITE CERAMIC FRIT

10mm CLEAR TOUGHENED GLASS

DOW CORNING DC797 BLACK SILICONE

Ian Ritchie Architects, B8 Building, Stockley Park, Heathrow, 1990: The speculative, low cost office building is set in a state-of-the-art business park and golf club on the site of a former rubbish dump near Heathrow Airport outside London. The rectangular building is a dumb box, built quickly and cheaply to stringent budgetary constraints. Arranged around a central atrium, the design is broken down into its essential elements: structure, glazing and the roof volume (containing air-conditioning and services). The south, east, and west façades are defined by a distinctive curved sun shading device supported on slender steel columns that stand proud of the main structure, giving the building a strong sense of grounding and permanence. Specially designed structural glass avoids the need for obstructive (and expensive) mullions, providing totally uninterrupted views of the surrounding countryside. The large glass panes are supported at four points by aluminium brackets and fins, further minimizing visual intrusion. Fritted glass reduces the impact of glare and heat gain, creating a completely translucent interior that is highly efficient in terms of environmental performance. By reducing technological expression to minimum (the wall, the frame, the brise-soleil) the building achieves a classical simplicity that transcends the cacophony of high-tech language, establishing a new model for the tradition of British Modernism.

By reducing technological expression to minimum

the building achieves a classical simplicity.

The B8 Building by Ian Ritchie as an example of a modern architectural language.

View from the street
photo: Lorenzo Elbaz

Tony Fretton. Lisson Art Gallery, London 1991-93 - photo: Lorenzo Elbaz

The Lisson Art Gallery by Tony Fretton (1991-1993), one of the radical yet established venues of London's art scene, is situated on the periphery of central London: a highly fragmented urban district based on a rudimentary street pattern lined by buildings of different scale, texture and use including a vibrant street market, a few elegant Georgian stuccoed houses and 1960s residential point blocks. Amongst this mixed background, the clean, serene, well-proportioned façade of the Lisson Gallery makes its presence felt on the street. While it maintains the building line of its Victorian neighbours, a series of planar voids and solids establishes a more dynamic dialogue with the street itself. In order to rationalize the floor levels of two separate buildings (the new Lisson Gallery is an extension to a previous building designed by Tony Fretton on an adjacent site) the basement of the new lower gallery has been dropped creating an unexpected relationship between the street and display area, a role reversal between the "lofty" gallery and its urban surroundings. From the street one can look down and into the gallery, which emphasizes the social programme of the gallery and the intrinsic political nature of artistic production and observation. The character of the interior is determined by a few simple gestures that transform the quality of an otherwise mundane space. Daylight and artificial light are bounced off wall surfaces into the galleries and connecting rooms, creating a hierarchy of spatial environments. The details are resolved with a certain coarseness and simplicity - this is not highly crafted jewellery - that reflects the roughness of the surroundings and the tough requirements of the art displayed. The design is a rare example of architectural purism, extending and reinterpreting the language of Le Corbusier and Eileen Gray - planes, surfaces and light - to suit the British context. Like a comfortable, worn shoe, the design fits the gallery and the neighbourhood well.

The design is a rare example of architectural purism, extending and reinterpreting the language of Le Corbusier and Eileen Gray.

A reinterpartion of the classical Modernism, the Lisson Art Gallery by Tony Fretton.

With Ireland's economical miracle

in the early 1960s emerged a talented

generation of young architects.

But the change of Ireland in the 60s was short-lived.

22 | COMING OF AGE. CONTEMPORARY ARCHITECTURE IN IRELAND. SHANE O'TOOLE.

Ireland

Form of State: Republic since 1937, **Area:** 70,283 km2, **Inhabitants (1992):** 3,547,000, **Capital:** Dublin
Gross National Product 1992 per capita: $ 12,210, **Gross Domestic Product 1992:** $ 43,294 Mio, **Unemployment (Average, 1993):** 16.9 %

t has been twenty one long years: about time for a coming of age. Back in 1973, the year I left school, Ireland voted "yes" and joined the EEC - the European Economic Community, as it then was. Joining the Common Market would be all about bringing untold new benefits to our economy, or so we thought. It was and it did, but we can now see that the issues involved were much bigger than all of that. The real benefits have turned out to be cultural in nature. Right across the board. Our participation in the EU has, it seems to me, increasingly caused even the powerful and narrow concerns of Irish economic self-interest to be transcended generally, so as to prompt a liberating reassessment of identity. Ireland's "economic miracle", such as it was, occurred in the early 1960s and with it emerged a talented generation of young architects. (Foremost among those who dominated the 60s were the Mies-inspired pair, Ronald Tallon and Robin Walker, the younger partners of Michael Scott, the father of modern architecture in Ireland. Their practice, Scott Tallon Walker Architects, was awarded the RIBA Gold Medal for Architecture in 1975.) It was almost inevitable, given the strength of familial and linguistic bonds - especially following hard on the heels of that most American of decades, the 1950s that that generation should, as it set about transforming the face of Ireland, look, enthralled, to the United States for its inspiration. The whirlwind of change was comparatively short-lived. By 1973, storm clouds were gathering on several fronts. Architects, apparently rudderless in the wake of the demise of the great Masters, found themselves increasingly criticized by, and alienated from, the communities they served. And, over the horizon, loomed the first oil crisis, about to shake to their foundations the certitudes of western society. There is a well-known drawing from that very same year which hangs in the hall of the Royal Institute of the Architects of Ireland. In it, the small, abstract, cubic forms of the building - a national management institution - are, somewhat surprisingly, threatened by an enormous, brooding, thunderous sky. One senses a doom-laden atmosphere hanging over

the field of architecture itself. Whereas it was noticed quite early that contemporary architecture, with its American imperatives, was sacrificing a sense of place and bequeathing in its stead a lieu vague, the critic, Fintan O'Toole, has remarked that well into the 1980s, Dublin retained the aspect of a mirage(1). Its cultural invisibility meant that it could literally disappear, that buildings which had stood for centuries would be demolished in the night, leaving its citizens rubbing their eyes and trying to remember, until they got used to empty spaces, what had been there before, what the city really looked like. The tradition of living in the city had also been interrupted. Frank McDonald, the campaigning Irish Times journalist, has pointed out that "in 1926, when it was a compact sort of place, nearly two-thirds of Dubliners lived in what we now call the inner city - the 1,500 hectares or so locked in between the Grand Canal, the Royal Canal and the North Circular Road. Now it is fewer than one in twelve. Indeed, over the past 25 years, the population of the city's historic core has been cut in half - from 160,000 to just 80,000. The heart of Dublin has been almost stripped bare of the population that once sustained it"(2). Uncontrolled suburban expansion was permitted to bury the surrounding countryside under concrete during a time of relatively modest population increase. Villages lost their individual identities and were swallowed up in the sprawl. The bloated, mono-functional, low-density city was unable to support the extension of an adequate public transport system. Dublin became a car-dominated, sub-urban conurbation, a classic American "doughnut". The generation which came to maturity as Ireland joined its European partners in 1973 were in a position to see things differently. They saw Dublin as their city, not as the relic of an alien culture. Eyes turned with enthusiasm towards mainland Europe. America was no longer the automatic role model. Young Irish architects worked in large numbers in London, Paris, Berlin and, later, Barcelona, before returning home with new ideas. There was much talk of Dublin's future being as "a European city".

Central to those discussions were many of the architects who would later form the urban design consortium known as Group 91 and who have, from time to time since 1980, collaborated on self-generated urban design projects, mostly for their native city. Their exhibitions and publications - on the "house" as the natural increment of development in Dublin, on the quays and docklands, on the role of monuments in the city - have contributed significantly to, and often led, public opinion. Under the banner of the City Architecture Studio, the redevelopment of Dublin's docklands was foreseen years before officialdom recognized its potential. As Group 91 - formed during Dublin's year (1991) as European City of Culture - they won the competition to prepare the architectural framework plan for Temple Bar, Dublin's cultural quarter, due for completion in 1997 (3). Very little was built in Ireland in the 1980s, but there was plenty opportunity to dream of what might be. As Edward Jones has noted, the Irish theoretical projects of the 80s sought, on the one hand, to re-establish continuity with the tradition of country building and, on the other, to make a passionate case for the reconstruction of the city within its own traditions (4).

The Irish Pavilion, Leeuwarden (The Netherlands), 1990, and Irish Museum of Modern Art, 1991, O'Donnell and Tuomey Architects.

Peter Wilson has described this long-demolished and by now mythical project as "an object which makes the heart beat faster - a very, very fine piece of architecture"(5). Commissioned for an international exhibition of art and architecture, and intended to make for Brian Maguire's prison paintings and love drawings a home, the Irish Pavilion encapsulated many of the 1980s' architectural concerns, including identity (the "Irishness" of Irish architecture), working with (rural) associations which are open to interpretation, and, above all, the psychological relationship between art and architecture. John Tuomey has described how the design of the building is a direct response to the content of Maguire's paintings: "There are a few, key paintings, like Liffey Suicides. Brian told us that whenever they drag the river for a body, they would often find more than one. He made this painting looking up, from the viewpoint of these white bodies floating on the river, towards a crowd of people on top of the bridge looking down. There was an idea from the beginning that the viewer should be below, should be underneath, when looking at that painting, and ideally, there would be people above. That came before architectural design. It was an idea. Then there was The Hanged Man, which is a completely devastating painting, which we felt had to be seen on its own. You're looking in the door of a cell, there's a

hanged man and there's a window, which is punched very deeply into the cell wall. So the idea of just taking that painting and punching it into the wall, punching it through the wall, and standing in a restricted place like in a cell, but also standing in a way where you're very conscious of precarious balance, was very strong. That was a second idea. There was another one, the portrait of the prisoner, Peter, who is standing in his cell. He has become in some way freed, by becoming an artist in his mind, and the door in the painting is open behind him. We wanted to emphasize that aspect. So, when you go into the cell to see the love drawings and you turn around to come back, the doors are open and there is a literal connection. Our biggest fear of all of that - I don't know if this was Brian's biggest fear - but our biggest fear was that by trying too closely to fit the architecture to the painting, that we would somehow make a kind of a mise en scène or shop-window effect of depicting the paintings too literally in real architectural stuff, which would trivialize or diminish the intensity of the paintings. Our intention was to intensify, or to at least con-centrate, the experience. In our view, that was the artistic risk that the thing involved. I remember doing the first drawings for it, based loosely on those ideas and on all the other things I had in my mind, like Ireland being an island, and our own architectural interests. When Brian came in and I showed him the very first sketches, he pointed out to me that there was no wall in it to hang pictures on. It was all doors and openings and

columns and windows. I mean, there were, like, fourteen doors in it and the whole front of it was open, with a big truss. It was open and it was a gateway, which was a direct memory on my part of the ferry terminal at Staten Island, which is like death or sex or something. You're on the front of the boat and, as you go into the darkness, complete darkness, the big canopy comes out over you, the brick walls on either side. The boat seems to have a heartbeat, a kind of slapping throb and somehow - I don't know why - but Brian's paintings reminded me of that kind of experience. So the form of the pavilion is actually a pretty direct response to that memory. It was pretty good, atmospherically, but there was nowhere to put pictures. Version two was really the same, but with walls. We set a rule. The first rule - I don't know if you knew about this rule, Brian – but the rule was, wherever you are, you are opposite a painting.

Drawing of the Irish Pavilion

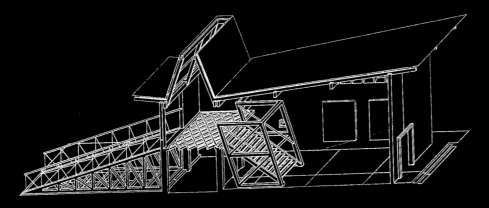

The Irish Pavilion encapsulated many
of the 1980s' architectural concerns.

The search on an Irish identity, on the Irishness of architecture.

Model of the Irish Pavilion

O'Donnell and Tuomey Architects. Irish Pavilion, 1991

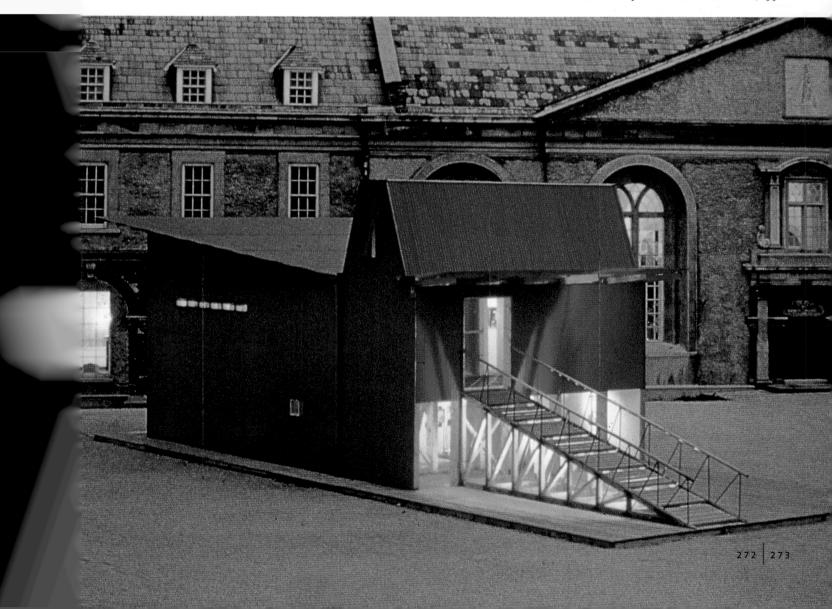

De Blacam and Meagher Architects. Chapel of Reconciliation, Knock Co. Mayo 1988-1990

Elevations

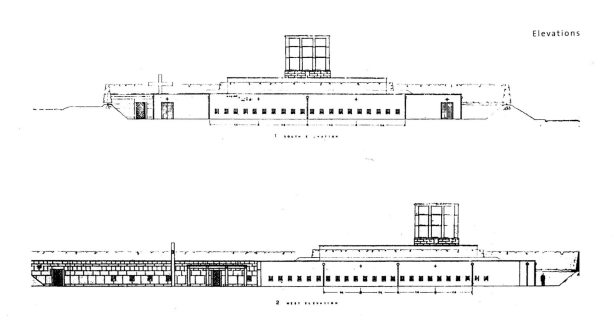

1 SOUTH ELEVATION

2 WEST ELEVATION

Our first instinct was, you come in a door and you are looking at a window, like you do in a house. You want to line things up across. But we changed that, if you like, architectural space idea, to the body and the picture. The outcome is that wherever you stand, wherever you enter, wherever you leave or wherever you come back, you are either specifically located in relation to an architectural event which, by analogy, works with a painting, or else you're facing directly at a painting. By doing that, we lost half the doorways and got in all the pictures"(6).

Chapel of Reconciliation in Knock, Co. Mayo, 1988-1990, de Blacam and Meagher Architects. In the architect's own words, the idea of this competition-winning chapel - intended to accommodate the rite of confession for large numbers of penitent pilgrims to the shrine at Knock - is to reform the landscape in which it is set and to make a sacred place. The landscape is bounded to the south by a ring of fourteen white crosses on a hill, known as "Calvary", and to the north by

the "Apparition Chapel". The new chapel occupies a gentle fold in the land, which absorbs the height of the building, permitting the creation of a landscape which links shrine and "Calvary". Externally, the chapel, with its grass-covered roofs, is represented by figurative symbols in the landscape - the carbonized cross (Passion), the oak entrance portico (reconciliation) and the glass lantern (Eucharist). The interior is dark at the perimeter, where small windows light each of the confessionals, but increasingly brilliant as one approaches the sanctuary. The presence of the symbolic is particularly evident in the geometrical elements employed: the square for the ground plan, the circle for the arrangement of the congregation, and an apparently invisible triangle, present nevertheless in the very pyramidal conception of the building. John Olley has remarked on a certain resonance with the work of Lewerentz. The lantern and its position on the body of the church point to an adaptation of

Lewerentz's 1931 chapel at Enkoping. Inside, the seating in the chapel nods to the informal layout in St Pater's, Klippan, as its rigid concentric semicircles with radial aisles ease to a scatter of variable arcs. Also from Klippan comes the central structural element, the stout column and short cross-beam - a logical "T"-structure, loaded with symbolic weight, recalling the central symbol of both the New and the Old Testament - the tree of life and the cross.

Entrance

The presence of the symbolic is particulary

evident in the geometrical elements.

Architecture as a reminder of the symbols of the Old and the New Testament.

Tomás de Paor and Emma O'Neill. Visitor Building, Cork 1991-1993

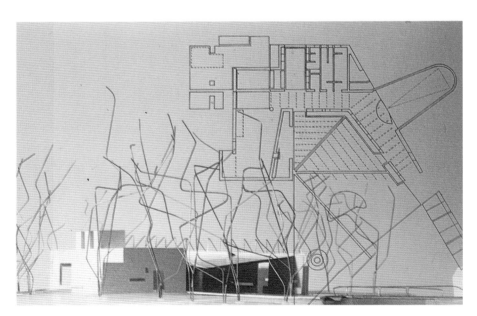

Ground plan and model

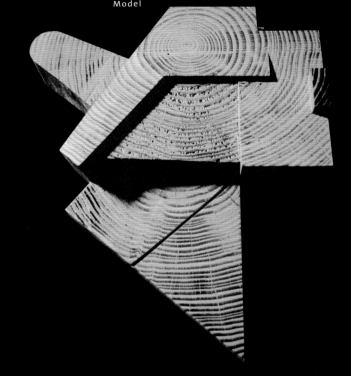

The building is both entrance to,

and exit from, this great landscape.

Inspired by the Scandinavian tradition: the brickwork of the Visitor Building.

Visitor Building. Royal Gunpowder Mills, Ballincollig, Co. Cork, 1991-1993, Tomás de Paor, Emma O'Neill (DPON Architects). This impressively focused first building, won in national competition by newly qualified architects, glows with an unusual intensity, born of the authors' decision to live on site virtually throughout the period of its construction. Ballincollig Royal Gunpowder Mills operated from 1793 to 1903. The River Lee provided power to drive the 24 mills and transport all materials between each stage of production. The new Visitor Building, although modest in scale, employs a sophisticated architectural promenade as a device through which the large site, with its extensive network of canals, paths and ruins, may be regulated. The new site strategy was generated by the overlay of the two existing waterway/building patterns: the first, of buildings placed perpendicular to the straight line of the mill race; the second, of buildings sited relative to the meander of the Lee and main canal. The building is both entrance to, and exit from, this great landscape and, like Janus, the god of gateways, presents two different faces. Entry is through an existing screen of stunted beeches and beneath a steel-and-timber canopy. A brick-clad block houses the main exhibition space and foyer to the park. A clerestory-lit linear exhibition leads past a douglas-fir-clad AV room, to an asymmetrical, lightweight bridge (not yet installed) leading to the park. Exit from the park is across an old stone bridge, by an alder and through a glass-fronted tea-room. The floor of the tea-room extends to the edge of the canal, forming a terrace. The dense, Scandinavian-inspired brickwork at Ballincollig, with its exceptionally thick mortar joints, is visually superb. There is nothing like it anywhere else in Ireland. Peter Cook has remarked of this project - referring en passant to the better-known Irish work of recent years - that he had found some evidence to suggest that another generation, with quite a different sensibility and quite different formalism, might be waiting in the wings (7).

A spare and rigorous creation of spaces and raw materials: the library in Cork.

Section of the library

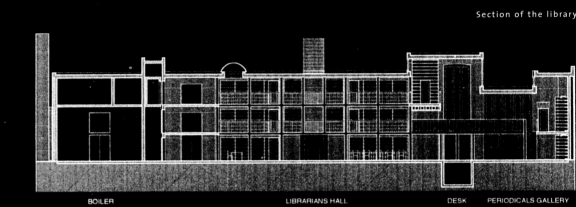

BOILER   LIBRARIANS HALL   DESK   PERIODICALS GALLERY

The Library of the Regional Technical
College, Cork, 1992-1994, by de Blacam
and Meagher Architects and Boyd Barrett
Murphy O'Connor Architects.
De Blacam and Meagher are renowned
for the "integrity" of their approach to
architecture over many years, for their
spare and rigorous creation of spaces
using only the simplest of means -
structure, light and "raw" materials.
The library is the first phase of a new
building which, in its completed form,
will make a new entrance to the college.
The curved, south-facing wall marks the
edge of New Square. When complete,
the library will house 70,000 volumes
and provide 500 study spaces.
The reading room, accessed directly from
the main entrance hall, has a fan-shaped
form and is supervised from the entrance
control desk. Adjacent are long, galleried
rooms, where further study spaces are
provided. Along the convex curve of
the south wall, a casual reading area
is provided at ground floor level.

Throughout the library, the walls are lined
with books. These are accessed on the
upper floors by timber galleries. Books
on the second-floor gallery are on closed
access, and are directly linked with staff
areas. The galleried rooms are lit by floor-
to-ceiling windows on the north façade.
The reading room is lit by a north roof
light which traverses the building, above
the main circulation route. The roof light
increases in height as the room increases
in depth, giving adequate daylight for
reading in all parts of the library.
The curved south wall of books is also
lit by a high-level north light, while at
low level, small windows pierce the wall,
admitting controlled shafts of sunlight
into this most serene of interiors, which
points the way about how public
buildings could be built.
My last project to present is the Irish Film
Centre. Temple Bar in Dublin (1986-1992)
by O'Donnell and Tuomey Architects.
If the Irish Pavilion provides a good
summary of the key areas of interest

for individual buildings in the 1980s,
then the IFC demonstrates the stamina
required for urban design and is, in the
words of Mike Gold, a "sophisticated
essay in spatial and formal collage,
suggestive as well of a vivid and supple
method for dealing with growth and
change in richly textured towns and
cities, one more hopeful than either
more obviously classical or modern
precedents" (8).

Hall

De Blacam and Meagher Architects/Boyd Barrett Murphy O'Connor Architects.
Library of the Regional Technical College, Cork 1992-1994

O'Donnell and Tuomey Architects.
Irish Filmcentre, Dublin 1986-1992

Model of the Irish Filmcentre

Dealing with growth and change

in richly textured cities.

The Irish Film Centre, a hopeful urban project.

This project magically balances substance with veneer

and provides Dublin with a place for promenading.

Seán O'Laoire on the architecture of the Irish Filmcentre.

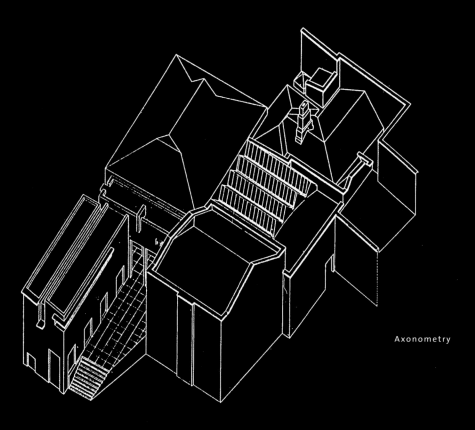

Axonometry

In 1986 the Irish Film Institute bought
the former headquarters of the Quakers,
a remarkable assemblage of old buildings
accumulated gradually since 1692 and
grouped around a covered space which
was once an open yard. It occupies
the centre of a city block and has no
significant street frontage, but narrow
access routes from three streets.
The building accommodates all aspects
of film culture. It includes two cinemas,
a film archive, specialist shops, a
restaurant, a bar and offices for film
bodies. Both of the cinemas are housed
within the walls of existing rooms, as
are the bar and some offices. The foyer
occupies the central space, with a new
glass roof installed at high level. This
space has the quality of an external
courtyard, overlooked by the façades
of different buildings. In general, new
elements are treated as installations,
standing in contrast to the existing
building and combining with it to create
an appropriately lively environment for

the viewing and discussion of film.
Seán O'Laoire has noted that this project
magically balances substance with
veneer and provides Dublin with a
place where citizens' repressed desire
for promenading can be relieved to a
limited extent. It provides a magnificent
contribution to the repository of public
spaces and demonstrates in an archetypal
manner how such assemblies of under-
utilized or redundant buildings and
random spaces can be given coherence
and viability. While clearly the effect of
the whole assembly is larger than any
of the individual bits, the fundamental
device used by the architects, who are
masters of expressive form-making, is to
allow the parts to speak for themselves.
This they have done in a subtle and
interesting manner, introducing the more
ephemeral elements into places such as
the public square, where the Italianate
colours are entirely appropriate to the
feel and metaphorical intention of the
space. Play it again, and again and again...

Postscript: Temple Bar
Located in the centre of Dublin, Temple
Bar is bounded on the north by the Liffey
Quays and to the south by Dame Street,
the city's financial district. It covers an
area of approximately 12 hectares,
stretching from Trinity College and the
18thcentury Parliament complex in the
east to City Hall and Christ Church
Cathedral on its western boundary.

Foyer of the Irish Film Centre in Dublin

Notwithstanding its prominent location in the city, the future of Temple Bar was at risk for more than 20 years, following a decision at the end of the 1960s to establish in the area a central city bus station for Dublin. The diversity of Temple Bar, with its small-scale clothing factories, recording studios, art galleries and theatres, had been threatened.

In the wake of sustained public concern throughout the 1980s, the Government cancelled plans for the Transportation Centre and - through the Office of An Taoiseach (Prime Minister) - established by legislation Temple Bar Properties (TBP), a company charged with over-seeing the sensitive renewal of the entire area as a cultural and residential quarter, as Dublin's "rive gauche". TBP promoted an invited national competition in October 1991 to find an Architectural Framework Plan for Temple Bar. The competition aimed decisively at the design of public space - streets, squares and their sequence and proportions - acknowledging it as a subject of cultural importance to the identity of the city and, hence, a public responsibility. Barcelona-based architect, David Mackay, one of the assessors, remarked: "In the Temple Bar archi-tectural competition, both public institutions and architects have regained their roles in setting the collective framework for the individual users and private enterprises to complete and continue the building and renovation of the city. It promises a creative partnership that stems from both the public and the private sectors - the public sector responsible for the creative aspects of the public space, and the private sector responding in the private space to the cultural quality of the framework." As noted previously, the competition was won by Group 91. Three major elements

of the architectural framework plan - Temple Bar Square, Curved Street and Meeting House Square, which adjoins the Irish Film Centre - as well as the associated buildings which define their edges will be completed during 1995. Realization of the second phase of the Temple Bar Framework Plan - the largely residential area between Parliament Street and Christ Church - is scheduled for completion in 1997, increasing its resident population from approximately 250 to more than 2,000. Temple Bar is to become an engine of cultural tourism in Dublin and a "living city" model of urban regeneration. Finance is coming from three quarters - the EU structural funds, which are being matched by central government, as well as unique mechanisms to encourage and stimulate selective private investment. It seems we have arrived at a key moment for Dublin, one which fills Dubliners with hope for a better future for their city.

Notes:
(1) Fintan O'Toole's essay, Dublin, in: 11 Steden, 11 Landen: Hedendaagse Nooreuropese kunst en architecture/ 11 Cities, 11 Nations: Contemporary Nordic Art and Architecture, edited by Erica Vegter-Kubic, Leeuwarden 1990
(2) Saving the City: How to Halt the Destruction of Dublin, by Frank McDonald, Dublin 1989.
(3) Temple Bar Lives! - A Record of the Architectural Framework Competition, edited by Jobst Graeve, Dublin 1991
(4) A Country Villa and a City Plan, by Edward Jones, in: Figurative Architecture: The Work of Five Dublin Architects, AA exhibition catalogue, London 1986
(5) Quoted in: New Irish Architecture 7: AAI Awards 1992, edited by John O'Regan, Dublin 1992.
(6) Works 8: The Irish Pavilion
(7) New Irish Architecture 8: AAI Awards 1993, edited by John O'Regan, Dublin 1993
(8) New Irish Architecture 3: AAI Awards 1988, edited by John O'Regan, Dublin 1988
O'Donnell and Tuomey: Buildings and Projects, 1981-1988, Dublin 1988
Irish Film Center, including critique by Seàn O'Laoire, in: Irish Architect, Dublin, November/December 1992
Irish Reels, by Cartherine Slessor, in: The Architectural Review, London, January 1993

It seems we have arrived at a key moment for Dublin, one which

fills Dubliners with hope for a better future for their city.

Hope for Dublin in the 90s?

Biographies

ANNETTE BECKER
born in 1959, studied art history, archaeology and philosophy. Since 1990 curator of the German Architecture-Museum in Frankfurt.

RICHARD BURDETT
born in 1956, graduated from the Bartlett School, London. Since 1991 director of the "Architecture Foundation" in London.

MARTA CERVELLÓ
born in 1959, graduated from the School of Architecture of Barcelona (ETSAB). Since 1990 member of the board of the Association of Catalan Architects.

FRANÇOIS CHASLIN
born in 1948, architect and critic for an array of French magazines and newspapers. For years editor-in-chief of the magazine "L' Architecture d'Aujourd'hui" in Paris.

ROGER CONNAH
writer, researcher, film director and designer.
Roger Connah lives in Helsinki.

MARCO DE MICHELIS
born in 1945, teaching architecture history at the School of Architecture in Venice. Since 1993 director of the Architecture-Gallery of the Triennale in Milano.

KIM DIRCKINCK-HOMFELD
born in 1950, graduated from the Royal Danish Academy of Fine Arts in Copenhagen. Editor-in-chief of the magazine "Arkitekten".

MARC DUBOIS
born in 1950, Professor at the School of Architecture Sint Lucas Gent, President of the Stichting Architectuurmuseum (S/AM) Gent.

MATÚŠ DULLA
born in 1950, head of the Department of architectural history at the Slovak Technical University in Bratislava.

Neven Fuchs-Mikac
born in 1947 in Oslo, graduated in Zagreb. Since 1984 assistant professor at the Oslo School of Architecture under Sverre Fehn.

Ákos Moravánszky
born in 1950, graduated from the Technical University in Budapest. Since 1991 professor for the history of architecture at the MIT in Cambridge, USA.

Henrieta Hammer-Moravčíkova
born in 1963, graduated from the Faculty of Architecture STU. Since 1993 head of the Department of Architecture at the Slovak Academy of Science.

Shane O'Toole
born in 1955, President of the Architectural Association of Ireland, Director of the "Group 91 Architects", he taught at the University College in Dublin.

Andrej Hrausky
born in 1951, graduated in Ljubljana. Since 1989 director of the architectural gallery DESSA in Ljubljana and member of the editorial board of "AB" and "Piranesi" magazines.

Yorgos Simeoforidis
born in 1955, architect and critic, taught in Great Britain and USA. Now living in Athens, he runs the architectural review "Tefchos" .

Ulrike Jehle-Schulte Strathaus
earned her PhD in art history at the University of Basle. Since 1984 director of the Architecture Museum in Basle.

Vladimir Šlapeta
born in 1947. Since 1973 director of the Architecture Collection at the Technical Museum in Prague and since 1992 professor at the Prague University.

Otto Kapfinger
born in 1949, architectural critic and journalist. Otto Kapfinger lives in Vienna.

Dietmar Steiner
born in 1951, studied architecture at the Academy of Fine Arts in Vienna. Since 1993 director of the Architektur Zentrum Wien.

Alexander Laslo
born in 1950, architect, architecture critic and author, editor-in-chief of the magazine "Covjek i prostor" in Zagreb.

Wilfried Wang
born in Hamburg, studied architecture in London. Director of the German Architecture-Museum in Frankfurt.

Jöran Lindvall
born in 1939, studied at the Institute of Technology and at the Stockholm University. Since 1985 director of the Swedish Museum of Architecture.

Ana Maria Zahariade
born in 1940, studied at the Institute of Architecture in Bucharest. Assistant at the Architectural Design Chair IAIM since 1990.

Bart Lootsma
born in 1957, graduated in architectural history and theory from Eindhoven University of Technology. Editor of the magazine "de architect".

Editor: Dietmar Steiner, Architektur Zentrum Wien

Copy Editor: Andrea Nussbaum, Wien

Assistant Editor: Lynnette Widder, Berlin

Coordination: Birgit Seissl, Architektur Zentrum Wien

Translation into English: Maria M. Clay, Wien; Axel Haase, Christian Rochow, Lynnette Widder, Robin Benson, Berlin

Graphic Design Concept and Layout: Dominique Roski, Wien

Production Support: Davide Zavatti, Wien

Deutsche Bibliothek Cataloging-in-Publication Data

New building today : European architecture of the 1990s / ed. by Architektur Zentrum Wien.

[Copy ed. Andrea Nussbaum; Lynnette Widder. Transl. into Engl.: Axel Haase ...]. -

Basel ; Boston ; Berlin : Birkhäuser, 1995

Dt. Ausg. u.d.T.: Neues Bauen heute

ISBN 3-7643-5226-4

NE: Nussbaum, Andrea [Red.]: Architektur-Zentrum <Wien>

Library of Congress Cataloging-in Publication Data

A CIP catalogue record for this book is available from the Library of Congress, Washington D.C., USA.

Cover: Truck Garage, Terminal Rølsøy, Oslo

Architect: Jan Olaf Jensen, 1990

Photo: Jiri Havran

Photos 1st Vienna Architecture Congress: Gerhard Koller, Wien

Photos 2nd Vienna Architecture Congress: Stefan Haring, Wien

Photo page IV/V: EUMETSAT, Zentralanstalt für Meteorologie und Geodynamik, Wien

© 1995 Birkhäuser – Verlag für Architektur, P.O. Box 133, CH-4010 Basel, Switzerland

This edition is also available in German.

Print: Printed Matters, Vienna

Lithography: Printed Matters, Vienna

Printed on acid-free paper produced of chlorine-free pulp. TCF∞

Printed in Austria

ISBN 3-7643-5226-4

ISBN 0-8176-5226-4 $724.9n$

987654321

The Architektur Zentrum Wien whishes to thank for their support: